HANNIBAL'S MARCH
IN HISTORY

Hannibal's March in History

BY

DENNIS PROCTOR

CLARENDON PRESS · OXFORD

1971

Oxford University Press, Ely House, London W.1

GLASGOW NEW YORK TORONTO MELBOURNE WELLINGTON
CAPE TOWN SALISBURY IBADAN NAIROBI DAR ES SALAAM LUSAKA ADDIS ABABA
BOMBAY CALCUTTA MADRAS KARACHI LAHORE DACCA
KUALA LUMPUR SINGAPORE HONG KONG TOKYO

PRINTED IN GREAT BRITAIN
BY WILLIAM CLOWES & SONS, LIMITED
LONDON, BECCLES AND COLCHESTER

à

CLAUDE TROMEL

ACKNOWLEDGEMENTS

THREE old friends, and one who I should like to think may become one, have given me invaluable help in the production of this book. Marion Mainwaring read the first draft in manuscript and has contributed unfailing encouragement and good advice ever since. Patrick Wilkinson and Donald Lucas read the typescript and helped me to eradicate many faults, though they cannot be held responsible for those that remain. To the former in particular and his long list of stylistic infelicities, which none but a true friend would have laboured to compile, I owe a special debt of gratitude for trying to make the book more readable. To the generosity of Professor F. W. Walbank in commending the book despite the fact that I have frequently been critical of his own conclusions I owe the fact that it is being published at all, and I am also in his debt for taking the trouble to correct me on a number of points where I had plainly gone wrong. I must also record my gratitude to Claude Tromel (to whom the book owes its origin) and to Jean-Jacques Guérold for their friendship and encouragement. I am only sorry that I have had to deny our village in the Comtat Venaissin a local niche in the history of the march.

Finally, I wish to express my unbounded admiration and gratitude for the forbearance and scholarly care of the staff of the Clarendon Press in editing the copy of an unfledged writer and helping it on its way into print.

London   DENNIS PROCTOR
March 1971

CONTENTS

MAPS

ABBREVIATIONS

1. *Works referred to, after the first occurrence, by author's name alone*

Cluver, *Italia Antiqua*, 1624, Book I, excursus, pp. 365–84.

Colin, J. L. A. *Annibal en Gaule*, 1904.

de Beer, Sir Gavin. *Alps and Elephants*, 1955. (See below, p. 15 n. 11.)

de Luc, J. A. *Histoire du passage des Alpes par Annibal*, 1818.

Devos, G. *D'Espagne en Italie avec Hannibal*, 1966.

De Sanctis, G. *Storia dei Romani*, Vol. 3, Part ii, 1917.

Dunbabin, R. L. *Classical Review*, 1931, pp. 52–7 and 121–5.

Holsten, L. *Annotationes in Italiam Antiquam Cluverii*, 1666.

Hyde, W. W. *Roman Alpine Routes* (Memoirs of the American Philosophical Society, Vol. 2, 1935).

Jullian, C. *Histoire de la Gaule*, Vol. 1, 1908.

Kahrstedt, U. *Geschichte der Karthager*, Vol. 3, 1913.

Marquion, P. *Sur les pas d'Annibal*, 1965.

Perrin, J. B. *Marche d'Annibal des Pyrénées au Pô*, 1883.

Veith, G. *Heerwesen und Kriegsfuehrung*, 1928, in Mueller's *Handbuch*, Abt. 4, Tl. 3, Bd. 2.

Walbank, F. W. *Historical Commentary on Polybius*, Vol. 1, 1957.

Wilkinson, H. Spenser. *Hannibal's March through the Alps*, 1911.

2. *Other abbreviations*

CAH   *Cambridge Ancient History*
CR   *Classical Review*
JRS   *Journal of Roman Studies*
OCD *Oxford Classical Dictionary* (2nd edn., 1970)

INTRODUCTION

I N 218 B.C. Hannibal, the young commander of the Carthaginian forces in southern Spain, opened hostilities against Rome by crossing the Ebro and marching from Spain across Gaul and over the Alps into Italy, there to inflict a series of crushing defeats on Roman armies and to rove at large for fifteen years up and down the peninsula and into Sicily. No less than seven accounts of the operations are said to have been written during his lifetime or very soon afterwards, two of them by Greeks who accompanied him on his march from Spain and two of the others by Romans who fought against him; but Polybius, writing his *History* perhaps seventy years after the event, found fault with three of them for their errors, and when Livy was writing his, about 120 years later, the truth about the march had already become a subject for controversy. The argument about it has gone on ever since for nearly 2,000 years: the books that have been written on the subject since printing began would stock a fair-sized library, and five in English or French have appeared in the last fifteen years, the latest of them in 1969. It may well be asked why anyone should write yet another book on such a well-worn theme.

I certainly had no such intention when I began the studies that have led to this one. I had in mind merely a little casual reading to satisfy a personal curiosity on one or two points about the march that bothered me; but as I read on and got drawn deeper and deeper into the literature, it was borne in on me more and more that there had been far too little straight thinking on the subject, and in the end it has seemed to me that there *is* room for a book which attempts to repair the deficiency. This is a bold, not to say presumptuous, claim when one considers the quality of some of the minds that have not disdained to lend themselves to the discussion, from Scaliger and Casaubon to Gibbon, Napoleon, and Mommsen, yet even these stand in need of correction at some point or other, and the smaller fry more often.

There seems to be something about the march of Hannibal

that is inimical to straightforward, honest thought. Writer after writer fastens on some selected part of the evidence and constructs a theory on the basis of it. Then, if he notices any conflicting evidence at all, he either twists some unnatural sense out of it or, more commonly, passes over it in silence. The result is that the great mass of literature on the subject presents a confused picture of partial solutions fraught with inconsistencies and logical incompatibilities to anyone who tries patiently to assimilate *all* the evidence. Few writers, moreover, have taken much trouble to inform themselves of what others have made of the same problems: conclusions are frequently proclaimed as new, which in fact have been arrived at by others before. There is therefore a genuine need, it seems to me, for applying some plain, hard thought to the totality of the evidence, and at the same time for reviewing, not indeed all the opinions that have ever been expressed about Hannibal's march, for that would be impossible in one lifetime, but the evolution of the main ideas about it through the centuries; and these have been my twin objectives in writing the present book, which is as much a study of the movement of thought on the subject as a study of the march itself.

At the heart of all the modern conceptions of Hannibal's route lies a doubtful reading in the texts of Polybius and Livy. The critical half-way point in the march between the Pyrenees and the plains of the Po was a place called the 'Island' formed by the confluence of the Rhône and another river, and the view which has prevailed for over two centuries is that the other river in question was the Isère. This is the standard version of the account of the march to be found in any textbook or work of reference. But it rests on a conjectural emendation of the name of the river made by the Renaissance geographer, Philip Cluver, and it is not easy for any casual student of the subject to discover that this is not the name in any of the extant MSS. of Polybius or Livy. In the case of Livy the reader of either of the currently available English editions, the Oxford and the Loeb, is indeed well served by their editors: both of them plainly display the fact that Isara (Isère) is not the reading of the MSS. But the current Teubner editions both of Polybius and of Livy, and the Loeb edition of Polybius, print a name signifying the Isère in their texts without giving the slightest indication that it is not to be found in the MSS. It is not surprising, in the circumstances, that the same reading is adopted in every modern school edition of Livy's popular Book xxi, and that generations of schoolboys have been brought up on this version of Hannibal's route.

It has been left to two recent writers, Sir Gavin de Beer and a French engineer, Georges Devos, to bring the facts about the text more fully into the light. Their view is that the words in the MSS. of the two authors stood for quite a different river nearly 100 kilometres away, and they have thus called in question a whole system of ideas about Hannibal's route which has stood virtually unchallenged since Cluver's emendation won general acceptance over 200 years ago. One of the main themes of the present book is to trace the origin of Cluver's emendation and the changing course of ideas about Hannibal's route which have developed from it through the succeeding centuries.

My starting-point, however, was something quite different. It was a public lecture given by Georges Devos himself in the town hall of my village in the Comtat Venaissin, which had been advertised by hand-drawn posters bearing the legend, 'Hannibal est-il passé par ici?' Monsieur Devos lives in a neighbouring village, and his lecture—attended by my wife, but not by me for I was away—had the same Provençal sparkle as the poster. My wife brought away from it a signed copy of his book, *D'Espagne en Italie avec Hannibal*, on which I seized as soon as I returned. It too was written with gay meridional *élan*, and I found it enthralling; but there came over me as I read it that vague, but generally reliable, feeling commonly imputed to the master-mind in a detective story that there was something in the exposition which did not quite 'fit', and I decided that I must find out more about it.

So I began the course of reading which has led in the end to this book, though I little thought then that this was how it would end. I turned first, as everyone with the faintest interest in the subject must, to the texts of Polybius and Livy, but I was still not satisfied. I went on therefore to inquire what others had made of the same problems which worried me. I resorted first to F.W. Walbank's *Historical Commentary on Polybius*, and from this, still unsatisfied, I followed up the copious references which Walbank gave to other writers, and then followed theirs in turn to others, and so on. Thus was I well and truly ensnared, and the present book is the result.

The particular question which first puzzled me was, why did Hannibal wait until the end of May or early June, as Devos implied, before setting out from the south of Spain on his dangerous march when he must have known that he had to cross the Alps before the passes closed in autumn? Devos himself was interested in the route rather than the time-table of the march, and he offered no explanation of the delay. To learn what others had to say about this was my first reason for turning to Walbank, and from him to others.

I found that few of the writers who had specialized in the march of Hannibal had taken much interest in the timetable. For the most part it seemed that only the general historians of the Romans, the Carthaginians, and the Gauls, such as Mommsen, De Sanctis, Kahrstedt, or Jullian, or the contributors to the *Cambridge Ancient History*—concerned, as these historians no doubt were, to relate the timing of the march to the rest of their chronology—had paid any serious attention to this aspect of the march; but they all gave different answers not only from Devos but from each other, and none of the answers seemed wholly satisfactory. I therefore set to work to establish a timetable myself from a study of the texts of Polybius and Livy, and this is the subject of Part I of this book. The problem is not a very important one, and maybe not very interesting, but I have probably spent more time on it than anyone in the world since Seneca first described the march of Hannibal as what we should now call a favourite subject for a Ph.D. thesis, and it seems only sensible that the results of my labours should be made available to any future students of the subject.

In the course of working on the timetable I stumbled on a little ganglion of facts surrounding Hannibal's crossing of the Rhône which it seemed to me had been insufficiently appreciated and which, if carefully untwined, would yield more certainty about the position of the crossing-place than had generally been allowed. From this I was led on to a similar unravelling of the evidence about subsequent stages of the route, and Part II of the present book on the geography of the march is the result of that.

My aim in both parts has been essentially the same—to follow attentively the texts of Polybius and Livy, to draw out the implications of *all* the evidence, and, where contradictions or inconsistencies occur, to look for reasons for a choice between the alternatives. The main justification which I would claim for presenting yet another work on the march of Hannibal is that there *is* some certainty to be derived from a careful study of this kind if all the evidence, not merely an arbitrary selection of it, is brought under assay, and that such a method, pedestrian though it may be, is a better way of moving to a conclusion than the more intuitive, though perhaps more imaginative, swoops of most previous writers. I have eschewed romance, and found it no hardship to do so, since, unlike Sir Gavin de Beer, who describes how he has been under the spell of Hannibal since boyhood and, indeed, has recently written another book about him, I scent an aura like Hitler's around Hannibal rather than any glamour. It is the logic of the narrative that I have been intent to follow, and I have approached the subject of his march purely as an intellectual exercise in truth values, though it cannot be denied that the story has both intrinsic interest and the interest that attaches to any subject which has engaged for centuries the attention of some distinguished minds.

The scope of the book is wider, however, in two respects than a study of the texts of Polybius and Livy alone. On the one hand, I have been concerned to focus their narrative, particularly the part about the crossing of the Alps, against the background of common knowledge of Gaul and the western Alps obtaining at the time in Rome, as seems to me essential to a sound appraisal of their evidence about Hannibal's transit. I have tried to evaluate what the state of this common knowledge was, and I have reviewed the various statements about the Alpine passes left on the record by ancient authors, including those of Polybius himself, which have some surprising logical implications on the question of Hannibal's pass.

On the other hand, I have delved fairly deeply, as I have said, into the literature of the subject from the Renaissance scholars onwards. It is some time, I think, since this has been done quite so thoroughly by any one writer, and the principal merit I would claim for such a procedure is that the modern conceptions of Hannibal's route are based on the ideas of earlier writers to an extent that is often quite unrecognized, and that unless one uncovers some of the assumptions that derive, not from the ancient texts, but from these later accretions to the tradition, one will not arrive at a true understanding of the march itself. I think that the diffused light shed on the ancient texts through this somewhat opaque medium throws the evidence of Polybius and Livy more clearly into relief than a spotlight trained on the ancient texts alone.

By 'the ancient texts' I mean simply Polybius Book III and Livy Book XXI. They are the earliest surviving histories of the march, and in my opinion they are the only ones that need be considered. Apart from an absurd passage of Ammianus Marcellinus about Hannibal's route across the Alps which is a garbled version of Livy's account, a remark of Appian's that the march took six months (whereas Polybius and Livy said five), and one or two minor details in the Byzantine chronicler Zonaras drawn from one of the lost books of Dio Cassius, there is nothing significant in the surviving works of any of the later writers which is not to be found in Polybius or Livy or both; and there is no indication that any of them drew on a substantially different tradition.

As between Polybius and Livy there is, I am afraid, no doubt that one must count Polybius, graceless writer though he was, the more reliable. He was writing probably about seventy years after the event, whereas Livy was writing perhaps 120 years later; he had talked with eyewitnesses of the march and crossed the Alps to see the country for himself; and his mind was altogether more concentrated on facts than Livy's. The literary sources available to both writers were presumably the same, except that Livy had Polybius as well as the earlier accounts (all written in Greek) to draw on, and he had, in addition, Coelius Antipater, who wrote a history of the period in Latin about thirty years after Polybius.

With the mention of sources it is necessary to tread warily. Polybius, as I have mentioned, had no less than seven possible ones, and Livy therefore nine—none of which (except Polybius) have survived. Professional scholars have sometimes shown a natural impatience with amateur students of the subject who treat the words of Polybius and Livy as holy writ without realizing that it may sometimes be necessary to look behind

them to their authorities and to identify the vestiges of different
and perhaps conflicting sources embedded in their texts. I have
worked with a keen sense of this sword of Damocles over my
head, but I have come to the conclusion that there is not much
to be feared from it. In the study of the timetable the problem
hardly arises: the indications of time given by the two historians
are nowhere seriously in conflict. In the geography of the
march too there are whole tracts of it on which their accounts
are substantially in agreement, notably the crossing of the main
range of the Alps and the events surrounding the crossing of the
Rhône, where their *narratives* of what took place are almost
identical, and it is only the author's comments which sometimes cause difficulty.

In the intermediate section of the march, however, the
accounts of the two authors certainly do conflict, to such an
extent that they seem to be describing two completely different
routes; and I may as well state at once my conviction that those
writers who try to reconcile the accounts as they stand as
though there were no discrepancy between them are altogether
misguided. Yet even here there is no reason in my view to
postulate two conflicting traditions. Livy, as de Beer somewhat
unkindly put it, used scissors and paste on his authorities and
sometimes arranged his excerpts in the wrong order, and I am
convinced that this is what happened here. He turned from
one source to another, as has frequently been pointed out, and
muddled up the two accounts in his own narrative. But the
mistakes which resulted are plainly discernible; only a simple
adjustment is required to bring his narrative into line with
that of Polybius; and there is no reason to infer that there was
any conflict between the sources.

Still, one cannot pretend that there are no differences at all
between the accounts of the two authors. There plainly are
places where they have been drawing on different sources,
though usually it is not a question of two conflicting versions,
but of one author omitting or mentioning more briefly something which the other treats more fully. In such cases my guiding principle has been to prefer the more detailed and circumstantial account to the more summary, to assume, when one
author mentions something which the other omits altogether,
that there is no smoke without fire, and to give more weight

to facts which emerge, perhaps quite incidentally, from the narrative than to statements by the author himself—in short, to put more trust in the logic of events than in fallible human comments. I have not by-passed these or any other difficulties: I have tried to bring all of them into the light and to confront them.

There is no new knowledge in this book, only some new thought on old data. About Hannibal's route there are no new conclusions either. It has been an at first disappointing, though later reassuring, experience to find that every single conclusion about the route which I had reached by ratiocination on the texts had been anticipated by someone or other in the past; but I can at least claim to have discovered the fact, which is more than some others have done for their conclusions. Part I on the chronology of the march is perhaps the most thoroughgoing study of that subject that has yet been made, and the conclusions must stand or fall on the argument there presented. In Part II, on the geography, I would say that the conclusions (none of which, taken in isolation, is new) are in descending order of certainty as the march proceeds. I regard the position of the Rhône-crossing (my original jumping-off point) as established beyond any reasonable doubt; and next to it, and hardly less so, the position of the 'Island' which was reached after a 4-day march up the Rhône from the crossing-place. I think myself that the route of the approach march to the Alps which followed the halt at the 'Island' is only a shade less certain, but since only a handful of previous writers have arrived at the same conclusion about this as I have, I hesitate to make quite such a positive claim on its behalf. In the final stage, the crossing of the frontier range of the western Alps, I have shown how the field of choice for Hannibal's pass is narrowed down by a review of the evidence, internal and external; but I have merely indicated my own preference among the candidates—which is, in fact, currently the most popular one.

It is possible that all such speculation may one day be put to rest by the discovery of some new archaeological evidence, perhaps in the excavations for a new road or a new dam or even a new rocket base. However, the detritus of an army on the march cannot have consolidated like that of a town; and even if some unmistakably Spanish or Numidian remains are unearthed, there may still be room for doubt whether they belonged to Hannibal's army or to that of his brother Hasdrubal, who followed him across the Alps eleven years later, or to any of the other parties of troops or messengers who must have passed to and fro between Hannibal and his base during the fifteen years which he spent in Italy and who did not necessarily take the same route. In the meantime this study of the geography of the march is offered as a contribution pushing forward the frontier of certainty somewhat further than before.

I should perhaps declare my own preferences so that the reader may be warned of them. Those writers who have recognized that Livy's text as it stands is incompatible with Polybius' account without seeing how the discrepancies arose and how simply they can be removed have generally held that Polybius' version is the only valid one, and Livy has come in for some rough treatment from some of them. 'Omne coelum omnesque terras hac sua Hannibalici itineris descriptione conturbavit nobis Livius', and 'quanto magis Livii orationem verses, tanto plures maioresque eius circa hunc Hannibalis transitum errores deprehendas', wrote Philip Cluver in 1624; a man 'with a flypaper mind but without much critical faculty', was de Beer's description of him in 1955; and the strictures of Paul Marquion, his latest and perhaps most emphatic critic, are longer and still more severe. Polybius, on the contrary, is praised to the skies by them and others as the model historian. He is certainly the more reliable on questions of fact, and I would agree with these critics that the basic framework of the march is mainly his, but one cannot love him as a writer. He does indeed seem to have been a lovable person in real life, according to Strachan–Davidson's attractive study in *Hellenica*; but, if so, he gives the lie to Buffon's dictum that 'le style est l'homme même', for his literary style is such that, as T. R. Glover pungently remarked, 'he can be readable in any language but his own'. To the richly baroque Livy, on the other hand, I have warmed more and more, mistakes and all, the more I have read him; and I have come to understand why A. E. Housman is said to have regarded him as the greatest of Roman stylists.

A word must be added about the climate in 218 B.C. It is

well known that there have been large secular fluctuations
in the climate over the last two or three thousand years; and
the determination of the peaks and the troughs is a highly
technical matter. I have accepted in their entirety the findings
of Sir Gavin de Beer in his appendix on the subject to the effect
that the climate in 218 B.C. was perhaps a little warmer, but
certainly not colder, than it is now, and I have therefore treated
the seasons of the year throughout on the assumption that they
were much the same then as they are now. This is naturally of
special significance in the discussion of the timetable, for there
is not a single calendar date in Polybius' or Livy's narrative
of the march. One such date, which calls for some discussion,
occurs in the period after the march was over, but all the
indications of the timing of the march itself are in terms of
seasons of the year or astronomical phenomena. I have generally converted these into months in our own calendar as the
clearest way of presenting the timetable to a modern reader,
but I have avoided the spurious accuracy of specifying particular dates in a month.

   For similar reasons I have expressed all measurements of
distance on land in a modern scale, and I have used kilometres
rather than miles in order to facilitate reference to the maps
of the region, which are mostly on a kilometric scale. The ratio
which I have adopted for Polybius' measurements in stades
is that on which all the modern authorities agree, viz. 1 stade=
177·55 metres, or 1 kilometre=approximately 5·6 stades. Livy
gives only one measurement in Roman miles, and I have converted it in the ratio, 1 Roman mile=approximately 1·5
kilometres, or about 8 per cent less than an English mile.

PART I

CHRONOLOGY

I

THE STARTING DATE

THE number of pages that have been printed on the march of Hannibal and his army would probably be sufficient to strew the whole of his route from southern Spain to north Italy, but most of them have been heaped on his passage of the Alps, drawn by the fascination of that age-long problem. Polybius and Livy, our earliest surviving chroniclers of the march, set the fashion, for they both gave detailed narratives of the last 500 kilometres from the crossing of the Rhône to the plains of the Po, while dismissing in a few paragraphs the previous 1,000 kilometres from Cartagena to the banks of the Rhône; and since their time only a few pages seem to have fluttered down, almost at random, over the earlier stages of the march. Most writers on the subject, eager to come to grips with the more interesting part, have skimmed lightly over the preliminaries, choosing merely whichever facts in the ancient narratives seemed to give a foothold for the advance to the next stage and not worrying too much whether they fitted into a consistent pattern with the rest. The result is that many of the pronouncements on the whole march have a somewhat Olympian air, as though dropped from a great height without much regard for the accidents of time and place on the ground, and few of them have shown any concern for exactness about its timing. But much was happening both before the march began and during its early stages which, if carefully attended to, yields more precise information than one would gather from such pronouncements; and the object of the present study of the timetable is to show what can be discerned in a worm's-eye view by following closely the texts of Polybius and Livy before the march began, while it was in progress, and after it ended.

The standard account of the march in almost any textbook or work of reference is that Hannibal set out from Cartagena in

April and arrived on the plains of the Po sometime in the autumn.[1] The latter date is usually left somewhat indeterminate, and there is good reason for being cautious about it; for an end-date in October[2] or November,[3] as is sometimes specified, is not very easy to reconcile, on the basis of a starting-date in April, with Polybius' statement (confirmed by Livy) that the whole march took five months.[4] Appian, it is true, said that it took six months,[5] but he was writing 300 years after Polybius, and no one has found any reason to prefer his figure to the other.

Some writers, recognizing the difficulty, put the departure from Cartagena early in May, and date the arrival on the plains of the Po to the beginning of October, but this raises another difficulty. Polybius and Livy both say that it was close to the setting of the Pleiades when the army was on the frontier pass,[6] after which it had another week to go before it camped on the plains of the Po, and the accepted meaning of 'the setting of the Pleiades', as I shall hope to show later on, was a date in early November. Such a timetable also raises a new question: why did Hannibal wait so long before setting out on his hazardous march, when he must have known that he had to cross the Alps before the passes closed in the autumn? F. W. Walbank, perhaps for this reason, puts the departure from Cartagena about the end of April and the arrival about the end of September;[7] but this does still more violence to the natural meaning of the expression 'the setting of the Pleiades', and Walbank still considers it necessary to account for Hannibal's late start. He adopts the view of B. L. Hallward that it 'was probably designed to allow the spring flooding of the Spanish rivers to subside'.[7] Hallward himself, hedging both the options, says that the departure was 'not earlier than the beginning of May' and that, at the crossing of the pass over the Alps, 'it was now past the first week of September',[8] which, in fact, raises both questions, that of the late start and that of the setting of the

---

[1] e.g. H. H. Scullard, *A History of the Roman World from 753 to 146 B.C.*, 1951, pp. 187–9; *Oxford Classical Dictionary*, 2nd edn., 1970, p. 487; *Collier's Encyclopaedia*, Vol. 11, 1962, p. 634.

[2] e.g. *Encyclopaedia Britannica*, Vol. 11, 1969, pp. 63–6.

[3] e.g. W. E. Heitland, *The Roman Republic*, Vol. 1, 1923, pp. 230–3.

[4] Polybius III. 56. 3 and Livy XXI. 38. 1 and XXVII. 39. 4.

[5] Ἀννιβαϊκή, 52.   [6] Polybius III. 54. 1 and Livy XXI. 35. 6.

[7] *Historical Commentary on Polybius*, Vol. 1, 1957, notes on III. 34. 6 and V. 1. 3.

[8] *Cambridge Ancient History*, Vol. 8, 1930, pp. 36–8.

Pleiades, in a still more acute form. Mommsen had given an even earlier timetable: he put the start from Cartagena early in April and the arrival on the pass (contemptuously dismissing the reference to the setting of the Pleiades) at the beginning of September.[9] G. de Sanctis, who treated the setting of the Pleiades in equally summary fashion, gave much the same timetable as Mommsen's, only 10 days to a fortnight later.[10]

Among recent writers, Sir Gavin de Beer,[11] Paul Marquion,[12] and G. Devos[13] have all accepted the straightforward meaning of 'the setting of the Pleiades' as late October or early November and have therefore put the end of the march sometime in November; and since they have also accepted Polybius' statement that the march lasted about five months, they have put the start of it at the end of May or early June. All three of them, being more concerned with the route than the timing of the march, refrain from examining in detail the events which took place before it began. Only Marquion among them seems conscious of any difficulty about the lateness of the start; but he proffers a more cogent reason for it than anyone else has suggested—that Hannibal had to wait for supplies from the new harvest to ensure the victualling of his army on the march.

What, then, do Livy and Polybius themselves say about the starting date? They give, between them, a full account of the events which took place before Hannibal was ready to set out. This points, as we shall see, to a late rather than an early date of departure; but neither of them gives any precise indication of the date itself. Livy says nothing at all on the subject. Polybius makes two references to the time of year which we shall now examine.

First, while still describing the course of events before the

[9] W. P. Dickson's translation of *The History of Rome*, Vol. 2, 1913, p. 263.

[10] *Storia dei Romani*, Vol. 3, II. 1917, p. 79.

[11] *Alps and Elephants*, 1955, pp. 70 and 103. The author no doubt regards this book as superseded by the 'revised and enlarged edition of the original work', published in 1967 under the title *Hannibal's March*, which in turn has been largely rewritten (though without any further changes of substance) in his book *Hannibal*, published in 1969. Where there are any significant differences between the earlier and the later books, I have mentioned them, with appropriate references, in the text; but since the thesis (and most of the wording) is substantially the same in both books, this and all subsequent references to de Beer are to his first book on the subject, *Alps and Elephants*, unless otherwise stated.

[12] *Sur les pas d'Hannibal*, 1965, p. 63.

[13] *D'Espagne en Italie avec Hannibal*, 1966, p. 123.

start, he says that Hannibal collected his troops from winter quarters in Cartagena and unfolded to them his plan of invading Italy; and that he did this ὑπὸ τὴν ἐαρινὴν ὥραν, which the Loeb translator, W. R. Paton, renders 'in the early spring'. On the troops' enthusiastically assenting to the project, Hannibal fixed a day on which to start and dismissed the parade.[14] Now the primary meaning of ὑπό with the accusative in a temporal sense, according to Liddell and Scott, was 'just after', not 'just before', and though, as such expressions tend to do, it lost its original precision and came to mean no more than 'round about', there does not seem to be any justification for holding that the process went so far to the other extreme as to signify here an early rather than a late phase of the spring. When Polybius did mean the former, he used a different expression, 'when spring was coming in'—ἐνισταμένης τῆς ἐαρινῆς ὥρας—[15] which, however, the Loeb translator still renders by the same words, 'in the early spring', thus himself casting a doubt on his translation of the previous expression.

Probably Polybius himself had only a hazy notion of the date and meant no more than 'in the spring'; but nearly all the commentators—those of them, that is, who have attended to the matter at all—seem to have made the same assumption about the meaning of the phrase as the Loeb translator, partly perhaps because Livy says that Hannibal had released his Iberian troops to their homes on parole to return in the early spring— primo vere.[16] But it does not follow from this that he unfolded to them his plan of invading Italy as soon as they reported back. On the contrary, there must have been a period of retraining and preparation, which Kahrstedt puts at about two months,[17] before the march could start; and—apart from the fact that, as we shall see, Hannibal had not yet taken the final decision himself—he would not have fixed a day on which to start (as Polybius explicitly says he did) as far ahead as that.

But the main reason why people have jumped to the conclusion that the address to the troops (and therefore the start of the march) must have been at the beginning rather than the end of spring, and the reason why there is a similar predilection for early rather than late dates in everything connected with

[14] Polybius III. 34. 6–9.   [15] III. 77. 1.   [16] XXI. 21. 6.
[17] *Geschichte der Karthager*, Vol. 3, 1913, p. 370.

Hannibal's march, is the instinctive assumption which seems to underlie nearly all the modern accounts that, with a long and dangerous journey before him, he *must* have started as soon as the weather was good enough, which, to an English reader, suggests the end of March or early April. But enough was to happen, as we shall see, to show that it was a good deal later, and to explain the reason for it, without imputing a motive such as waiting for the spring flooding of the Spanish rivers to subside, which would have been a feeble reason for delay compared with the far greater dangers of crossing the Alps late in autumn.

There is, moreover, a general tendency among commentators in northern countries to foreshorten the passage of the seasons as conceived by ancient Mediterranean writers. The common expression, for instance, that a commander 'moved into winter quarters', which, to an English reader, conjures up a picture of troops snugly installed in billets by Guy Fawkes Day, signified, as we shall see in both of the successive winters with which we shall be concerned, a date around the New Year; for the open weather during which the troops could keep the field continues later in Mediterranean countries than it does in the north, and 'winter' for Roman campaigners meant 'Generals Janvier and Février'. It is true that the setting of the Pleiades in early November was the official beginning of winter.[18] But for the farmer this marked the opening of the main agricultural operations of the year, which he aimed to complete before the weather closed down around the turn of the year;[19] and the troops could keep the field in a campaign for a similar period. By the same token, though officially the first day of spring was also a very early date—7 February according to Varro [18]—and though the sun ripens crops of fruit, vegetables, and corn much earlier in the Mediterranean than in the north, the cold persists until late in the spring, especially in upland districts and at night, and it is usually well into May, if not later, before the Alpine passes are open. In some respects, therefore, and particularly in respect of campaigning, the whole

[18] Varro, *De Re Rustica*, I. 28. I and Pliny, *Historia Naturalis*, II. 47. 125 and xviii. 25. 222.

[19] See e.g. Aratus, *Phaenomena*, 264–7; Varro, *De Re Rustica*, I. 34; Virgil, *Georgics*, I. 207–11; also A. W. Mair, *Hesiod Translated*, 1908, pp. 130 and 144.

progress of the seasons as the Romans conceived it tended towards later dates in the year than we are accustomed to think of, and it is necessary to bear this in mind whenever we have to interpret a reference to a season of the year in Polybius or Livy.*

That the date here in question was a late rather than an early phase of the spring is confirmed by the second of Polybius' two references to the time of year. In a later book of his *History*, when he is correlating events elsewhere with the timing of Hannibal's march, he tells us that it was the beginning of summer, ἀρχομένης τῆς θερείας, when Hannibal, by setting out from Cartagena and crossing the Ebro, openly started warlike operations and embarked on the invasion of Italy.[20] Walbank, following De Sanctis[21] finds this expression vague, and says that it is not clear whether it refers to the departure from Cartagena or the crossing of the Ebro. 'It can therefore be neglected', he says,[22] thus coolly dismissing one of the few indications of dating provided by Polybius because it does not suit his own theory. But neither the expression itself nor its application is so very vague—not, at any rate, to an extent to justify such cavalier treatment. The first section of Hannibal's march, from Cartagena to the Ebro, a distance of about 480 kilometres through country under Carthaginian control, would have been accomplished in under four weeks, so that the whole of it could quite naturally be described as being 'at the beginning of summer'; and since there was clearly no longer delay after Hannibal had unfolded his plan of campaign to the troops than was needed to complete the final preparations for the march, there is no inconsistency in dating his address to the troops in the late spring and the march from Cartagena to the Ebro at the beginning of summer. No one, indeed, would have found

---

[20] v. 1. 3.   [21] p. 79.   [22] Note on Polybius III. 34. 2–6.

* It is tempting to adduce as an instance of this fact that the ancient version of the proverb made the spring, not the summer, the season which one swallow did not make, for in the Comtat Venaissin at least—around latitude 44° north—the swallows do not arrive noticeably earlier than they do in the north; but it seems that here too the Romans fixed an extraordinarily early date for the official opening of bird migration! Pliny says (*HN* II. 47. 122) that 22 February (usually known as *Favonium*) was called by some people *Chelidonia*, and by others *Ornithia*, from the sighting of the first swallow—though he was presumably quoting Greek authors who lived further south.

any difficulty here but for the fixed assumption that Hannibal must have started earlier, and that his address to the troops ὑπὸ τὴν ἐαρινὴν ὥραν must therefore have been in the early spring rather than the late.

What Polybius meant by 'the beginning of summer' can be gauged by the fact that both here and in another passage describing events of the year before,[23] in which he used the similar words, ἤδη . . . τῆς θερείας ἐνισταμένης, he made it follow after the entry into office of a new general of the Achaeans who had been elected, he said, at an election held 'around the rising of the Pleiades'—περὶ τὴν τῆς Πλειάδος ἐπιτολήν—and the rising of the Pleiades, according to various authors between the third century B.C. and the first A.D., was taken to be a date between 8 and 16 May.[24] Polybius' words in the one case plainly implied that an appreciable interval had elapsed after the new general of the Achaeans had been elected before a number of events which he proceeded to enumerate gathered momentum 'when summer was already coming in'. It seems reasonable to assume that he had in mind some similar interval when he dated the first stage of Hannibal's march 'at the beginning of summer'. I may not, therefore, be too far from his indication of the timing if I put the start of the march near the middle of June, which is the date I shall suggest when we come to examine the sequence of events before the start as described in his narrative and in that of Livy.

We shall see what they have to say about this in the next chapter. Thereafter we shall follow the narrative of the march itself. Then we shall look at their accounts of events in Rome and Italy during the same space of time. Finally we shall examine some facts mentioned by them as occurring in the period after the end of the march, to provide a closing bracket of the timetable.

[23] IV. 37. 2–3.
[24] *Scholia* on Aratus, *Phaenomena*, ll. 254 and 265; Varro, *De Re Rustica, Capitula Libri Primi* and I. 28. 2; Ovid, *Fasti*, v. 599–600; Pliny, *H.N.*, II. 47. 123 and XVIII. 25. 220–2.

II

BEFORE THE START

THE story begins with Hannibal's army in winter quarters at Cartagena after the fall of Saguntum, a town under Roman protection on the Spanish coast near Valencia.[1] Polybius says that the siege of Saguntum lasted eight months,[2] and in the passage to which I referred at the end of the last chapter about events in 219 B.C. 'when summer was already coming in'[3] he mentioned the beginning of the siege as one of a host of activities which began to move at that time. Though the dating of so many diverse events cannot have been exact, it seems clear from the two passages taken together that it must have been late in December before Saguntum fell. Livy says that Hannibal then moved into winter quarters and released his Iberian troops to their homes on parole to return in the early spring, so that they had 'the whole of the winter' for rest and refreshment of mind and body.[4] We may picture, therefore, the Numidian troops installed in winter quarters at Cartagena, and the Iberian ones dispersed to their homes, from about the New Year, 218 B.C.

Livy tells us that, having first numbered the tribesmen, Hannibal set out for Cadiz to pay his vows and bind himself by new ones at the temple of Hercules, after which he returned to the army's winter quarters at Cartagena.[5] There is no mention in Polybius either of the numbering of the tribesmen or of this religious pilgrimage, but Livy can hardly have invented them. The former must have taken some time, and the return journey to Cadiz and back of some 1,200 kilometres must have taken over a month even if Hannibal travelled light, quite apart from any time which he spent at the temple. It is likely, therefore, to have been near the end of February before he arrived back in Cartagena.

---

[1] Polybius III. 33. 5 and Livy XXI. 21. 1. [2] III. 17. 9. [3] IV. 37. 3–4.
[4] XXI. 21. 5–8. [5] XXI. 21. 9 and 22. 5.

He proceeded to take measures for the security of Spain, and also of Africa, during his absence on the intended expedition to Italy. These included some complicated exchanges of troops between Spain and Africa, the object being to separate the soldiers from their own people so as to hold them as hostages against possible sedition in either country, on a principle all too familiar in totalitarian countries today. Polybius and Livy are in agreement about the numbers involved, and Polybius gives full particulars of the movements, having, he says, read them in an inscription left by Hannibal himself.[6] This is the kind of thing which historians in their libraries tend to skim over without much interest as though it could all be done at the wave of a wand, but for those who were responsible for making the transport arrangements it must have been a major administrative problem; and since Polybius and Hannibal between them have taken the trouble to preserve the details, it is worth while pausing to see just what was involved.

It was not by any means a simple ferrying operation across the straits of Gibraltar as one might suppose. It comprised some quite long open-sea voyages, some of them, it would seem, triangular ones. First, about 15,000 troops were shipped from Spain to Africa, most of them to Metagonia, which corresponds to the Mediterranean coast of Morocco next to the Algerian frontier, and meant an outward voyage of about 200 sea miles from Cartagena; but some were sent also to Carthage (in modern Tunisia), a distance of about 600 sea miles, and, in addition, 4,000 troops were shipped coastwise to Carthage from Metagonia itself, a voyage of about 750 sea miles. About 14,000 troops were shipped in the reverse direction, most of them from Libya and Numidia (corresponding to modern Tunisia and the eastern part of Algeria), but some came from as far afield as Tripoli in the east and the Atlantic coast of Morocco in the west. The majority of them must have been embarked at or near Carthage for a voyage of some 600 sea miles across the Mediterranean to southern Spain.

The troops would have been carried in merchant sailing-ships which could keep the sea, in reasonable weather, night and day, and their average speed over a day's run would have

---

[6] Polybius III. 33. 8–18 and Livy XXI. 21. 11 to 22. 3.

been about 3 to 4 knots.[7] Very little information has come down
to us about the capacity of troopships in ancient times, but
A. Koester, whose father, grandfather, uncle, and great-uncle
were sea captains and who is probably the best authority on
the subject, thought it might have been about 200 men on
average.[8] On this basis some 160 voyages, or separate legs of
voyages, had to be performed to lift the total of 33,000 troops;
the outward voyages to Metagonia would have taken 2 to 3 days,
those from Metagonia to Carthage 8 to 10 days, and the voyages
across the Mediterranean between Tunisia and Cartagena
about a week each way. The operation cannot have begun
before the opening of the sailing season, which, according to all
the authorities, was rigidly fixed at 11 March,[9] and, however
much shipping Hannibal had at his disposal, the sheer exi-
gencies of administrative arrangements, and the capacity of
the ports to handle the embarkations and the loading of fresh
water and provisions, must have imposed some staggering of
the voyages. Making allowance for inevitable hitches and the
hazards of weather in the Mediterranean, which is not a
friendly sea at that time of year, it is likely to have been the
beginning of May before the whole operation was completed.

Even then Hannibal was still not ready to set out on his
march, for he had sent messengers to Cisalpine Gaul to ascertain the possibilities of crossing the Alps with his army and to
enlist the support of the tribes who were known to be in a state
of potential revolt against Rome; and he was anxiously awaiting
(ἐκαραδόκει) their return to Cartagena before coming to a
final decision.[10] Where and when did these messengers go, and
when did they return? Here is another problem of logistics
which has been totally ignored by the commentators, and
here again it was not by any means a simple journey.

The two chief tribes at enmity with Rome in Cisalpine Gaul
were the Insubres, whose capital was Milan, and the Boii, whose
capital was Bologna; and we know that Hannibal had been in
touch with both of them before he started on his expedition, for

---

[7] A. Koester, *Das Antike Seewesen*, 1923, pp. 179–81, and *OCD*², pp. 725 and 984.

[8] *Das Seekriegswesen bei den Roemern* in Mueller's *Handbuch*, Abt. 4. Tl. 3, Bd. 2,
p. 620.

[9] Vegetius, *Epitome Rei Militaris*, IV. 39; W. Kroll in Pauly-Wissowa, *Schiffahrt*,
Col. 410; H. S. Jones, *Companion to Roman History*, 1912, p. 50; *OCD*², p. 724.

[10] Polybius III. 34. 1–6.

a delegation of the Boii led by Magilus, one of their chieftains, came to meet him at the Rhône to guide him on his way into Italy,[11] and his first action on descending into Italy was to storm the chief town of the Taurini to cement his relations with the Insubres, with whom they had quarrelled.[12] The messengers therefore certainly went to Milan and to Bologna; but Polybius[13] also says that, in addition to visiting the disaffected tribes in Italy, they were sent by Hannibal to the Gallic tribes in the Alps themselves to solicit their aid in making his way through the mountains; and this must refer to the tribes on the French side of the frontier, for the Alps, as de Beer has pointed out, 'form a wide belt over two hundred kilometres deep between the Rhône and the frontier ridge',[14] whereas the descent from the passes on the Italian side is steep and short. Evidently, therefore, the messengers made a very considerable tour—and, whether or not the party split up to visit different tribes, it is clear from Polybius' account that they returned to Cartagena together.

To reach the tribes in the French part of the Alps, they had to make the outward journey by land, as, indeed, was inevitable in any case, for Hannibal cannot have sent them on their way before he had brought the long, hard siege of Saguntum to a successful conclusion in late December, and they could not have gone by sea at that time of year. It seems likely that they also took the opportunity, while on their way, to make the approaches to the Gallic tribes in Languedoc referred to by Livy when he tells how the Roman ambassadors who later came to solicit their goodwill found that these tribes too had been won over by gifts and promises from Hannibal.[15] Be that as it may, we can map out fairly distinctly the route which the messengers must have taken. They would have followed the ancient Iberian Way as far as the Rhône-crossing at Beaucaire–Tarascon;[16] from there they would have taken the shortest, best-known route to Italy, long frequented by the Gallic tribes, through Cavaillon to the upper reaches of the

---

[11] Polybius III. 44. 5–7 and Livy XXI. 29. 6.
[12] Polybius III. 60. 8 and Livy XXI. 39. 1–4.
[13] III. 34. 4.   [14] p. 34.   [15] XXI. 20. 8.
[16] G. de Manteyer, *La Voie fluviale du Rhône et ses chemins primitifs*, 1945, pp. 36–42.

Durance and the Col de Montgenèvre,[17] the lowest and easiest
of the Alpine passes, which somehow, snowbound though it
must have been, they managed to cross, no doubt with the
help of the neighbouring tribes. They descended into Italy
and made their way via Turin to Milan, and from there down
to Bologna, their last objective—about 1,800 kilometres in all
from Cartagena.

If they had set out on New Year's Day and travelled continuously at Herodotus' standard rate of about 35 kilometres a
day [18] without any intermission at all, it would have been near
the end of February by the time they got there; and since, even
if they started as punctually as that, they could not possibly
have kept up a flat rate of over 20 miles a day for nearly two
months on end on a journey in mid-winter, part of it through
the mountains, and since there must have been some halts for
discussions with the tribes they went to see, a date towards the
end of March seems a more probable date for their arrival at
Bologna. By then the sailing season would have opened and
they would have greatly shortened the return journey if they
could have taken ship from Pisa or Genoa, but there is no
mention of a sea passage in Polybius and it would not have
been easy for them to charter a vessel at either of those ports
under Roman control—or at Marseilles, which was on friendly
terms with Rome—for a voyage to Cartagena, the enemy base.
One is driven to assume, therefore, that they made the return
journey, like the outward one, by land, and the distance,
whether they retraced their steps by the way they had come
or crossed the Apennines and followed the curve of the shore
by the coast road through Liguria, would have been much
the same—about 1,800 kilometres. So it must have been near
the end of May by the time they got back to Cartagena—a
date which perfectly fits Polybius' description of Hannibal,
having completed his sea transport operation, 'anxiously
awaiting' their arrival, as though all else was by then in readi-
ness.

Shortly before the messengers arrived, Hannibal had received a report from Carthage informing him that his Government had rejected the peremptory demand of a Roman delegation to hand over himself and his senior officers as amends

---

[17] Strabo, IV. 1. 3 and I. 12.   [18] Herodotus, IV. 101.

for the attack on Saguntum, and had accepted a Roman
declaration of war.[19] This gave him the assurance he needed
that the home Government was behind him; and when he
heard soon afterwards the good news brought by the messengers about the possibilities of crossing the Alps and the
cooperation promised by the tribes in Cisalpine Gaul, the moment had at last come for action. It was then that he paraded
the troops, unfolded to them his plan of carrying the war into
Italy, and, on their enthusiastic assent, fixed a day on which to
start.[20] No doubt there were certain final preparations to be
made which could not be put in hand before he had divulged
his plan of campaign to the troops, and, if we are right in
putting the return of the messengers (and therefore the address
to the troops) at the end of May, the starting date of the march
itself can hardly have been earlier than mid-June.

This does, indeed, seem a late date in the year for the start
of a long and perilous march, but we have seen that there was
more than enough in the preceding events—the journey to Cadiz
and back, the trooping operations between Spain and North
Africa, the wait for the messengers from Cisalpine Gaul, and
the news from Carthage about the proceedings with the Roman
embassy—to show that it could not have been much earlier. It is
possible, even so, that Hannibal over-estimated his speed of
march and thought that, despite his late start, he would reach
the Alps before the autumn set in; and if any further reason
has to be looked for, it is likely to have been, as Marquion
pointed out,[21] that he knew that he would have to feed his
enormous army—consisting, at the start, of some 100,000 men,
12,000 horses, 58 elephants, and a multitude of pack animals[22]
—off the country as he went. Since he could not risk relying on
stores still left from the previous year's harvest, he had to wait
for the new one to be got in. In Spain the harvest would have
been gathered in by the end of May; in Languedoc and lower
Provence about three weeks later; in upper Provence, Dauphiné, and the Alps later still. If, therefore, Hannibal started
from Cartagena in mid-June, supplies from the new harvest
would have been available as he went along, and this may
well have been a factor in his calculations.

[19] Polybius III. 20. 8, 33. 1–4, and 34. 7.   [20] Polybius III. 34. 6–9.
[21] p. 63.   [22] Polybius III. 35. 1 and 42. 11 and Livy XXI. 22. 3.

III

THE SPEED OF MARCH

BEFORE setting out to follow Hannibal on his march, it will
be useful to consider what was likely to have been his
approximate rate of progress. Livy gives no direct information on the subject: he does once refer to a sortie of about
36 kilometres made by a detachment of Hannibal's forces
under Hanno as 'a day's march',[1] and we shall examine this
more carefully later;[2] for the moment I shall assume that it
was a cavalry contingent, in any case a flying column of some
sort, not a body of heavy troops, and no one has seriously
attempted to argue that such a high figure could have been the
average day's march of Hannibal's army.* Polybius' statement
that the whole march of some 1,500 kilometres from Cartagena
to north Italy took five months[3] is not in itself an indication
of the rate of progress on the march, for much time was spent
in subjugating the tribes in northern Spain before the march
across France began. He gives various intermediate distances
and some rather vague indications of time from which rates of
march can be roughly computed, but he specifically records
only one section of about 143 kilometres along a river covered
in 10 days, or an average of about 14 kilometres a day, which
seems too low at the other extreme.†

Some writers, however, including de Beer[4] and Devos,[5] have
taken it as an indication of Hannibal's rate of march in open
country, and Spenser Wilkinson[6] and R. L. Dunbabin[7] have

---

[1] XXI. 27. 2.   [2] pp. 98 ff.   [3] III. 39. 6–11 and 56. 3.
[4] pp. 25–6.   [5] p. 24.
[6] *Hannibal's March through the Alps*, 1911, pp. 16–17.
[7] *CR* 1931, p. 52.

---

* Camille Jullian, *Histoire de la Gaule*, Vol. 1, 1908, p. 474, did, regrettably,
commit himself to the view that the army averaged an even higher rate on one
section of the march which we shall examine in due course, but he is alone in this.

† 143 kilometres is the equivalent of Polybius' figure, 800 stades, which was
obviously a round number and may be taken to cover anything between 750 and
850 stades or, say, between 135 and 150 kilometres.

agreed with them about the length of a day's march, quoting it respectively as 9 English miles and 10 Roman miles. They can claim support from two French soldiers, Captain J. L. A. Colin and Colonel Perrin, who both wrote monographs on Hannibal's march before the days of motorized transport and paid particular attention to this question of his rate of progress. Colin,[8] discussing the distance of a 4-day march up the Rhône (which we shall consider in more detail later), said that 100 kilometres in 4 days was a maximum and Hannibal's speed must have been well below it. He accepted a distance of 56 kilometres 'as a first approximation' on the basis of Polybius' rate of 14 kilometres a day for the 10-day march along a river, and remarked: 'One very rarely finds, in military history, examples of armies doing more than 50 kilometres in four days outside critical periods preceding modern battles.' His predecessor, Colonel Perrin,[9] had shaded his own opinion a little more cautiously; 'Our armies', he said, 'do not exceed 20 kilometres in a day's march, and in that difficult country, and obliged to follow paths, an army with its baggage will not do more than 16 to 18 kilometres.' He allowed a slightly higher rate on the easier first stage of the march from Cartagena when he added: 'Hannibal's army, hugging the Spanish coast, with an effective of 102,000 men, certainly did not do more than 20 kilometres.'

The literary historians, however, untrammelled by military experience, have assumed distinctly higher figures for a day's march, the distances generally adopted by them, e.g. by Kahrstedt[10] and De Sanctis,[11] being something between 20 and 25 kilometres. Walbank[12] scales the rate up to an even higher figure for the 4-day march up the Rhône, where he thinks that Hannibal was forcing the pace to leave Scipio behind. J. Maissiat adopted a similarly high figure—26 kilometres a day—as Hannibal's average rate of progress.[13]

Maissiat, however, is one of an honourable trio of Frenchmen, the other two being Marquion and Devos, who have made serious efforts to visualize what the passage of Hannibal's

[8] *Annibal en Gaule*, 1904, pp. 336–7.
[9] *Marche d'Annibal des Pyrénées au Pô*, 1883, pp. 34–6.
[10] p. 378.   [11] pp. 70 and 80.
[12] Note on Polybius III. 49. 5 and *JRS*, 1956, p. 42.
[13] *Annibal en Gaule*, 1874, p. 143.

army through rough, uncivilized country must actually have been like. The army consisted, after the crossing of the Pyrenees (for it had suffered heavy losses in the fighting in Spain, and Hannibal left a considerable force behind as garrison under his brother, Hasdrubal), of 50,000 infantry, 9,000 cavalry and 37 elephants,[14] together with a baggage train which Colin[15] estimated at a factor of 500 pack animals for one day's rations of the men, apart from fodder for the animals, camp equipment, and treasure.* After the battle at the Rhône-crossing the strength of the infantry and cavalry had fallen to 38,000 and 8,000 respectively.[16]

Maissiat worked out the order of march in detail on the assumption that the foot-soldiers could not march more than two abreast on the narrow tracks, and arrived at the conclusion that, if the first elements of the infantry started at 5 a.m. and the baggage train followed the infantry, while the cavalry brought up the rear, the whole army would have completed the day's march of 26 kilometres (according to him) by about 4 p.m.[17] Marquion, however, says that, even if the army could have marched *three* abreast, the whole column would have stretched over a distance of 50 kilometres if it were all in movement at one time; and if the head of the column had started the day's march (which he puts at 25 kilometres on average) at 5 a.m., the tail would not have arrived in camp before 10 p.m. He concludes, therefore, that the army could not have marched in one long column of route (which would also have been extremely vulnerable to attack by unfriendly tribes), but must have advanced in what he calls 'approach formation', deployed in several parallel columns; and that it adopted this formation whenever possible until it was actually climbing the frontier range of the Alps.[18] Devos also allows that the army may have occupied a fairly broad front, which he puts at 100 metres, and reckons that on this basis the length of the column would

[14] Polybius III. 35. 4–8 and 42. 11, and Livy XXI. 22. 2–3.
[15] p. 364.   [16] Polybius III. 60. 5.
[17] op cit., pp. 136–42.   [18] pp. 84–6.

* It might be thought that the elephants served as pack animals, but apparently this was not so. Both Polybius and Livy make frequent mention of the pack animals, as distinct from the elephants, in their descriptions of the crossing of the Alps, and Polybius stresses both the number of them and their vital importance to the army.

have been some 4 to 5 kilometres. He gives a vivid picture of the amount of space that must have been required, and the time it must have taken, to get an army of this size in movement each morning, to negotiate the passage of rivers and defiles and to camp, forage, and feed men and animals each evening; and concludes that Polybius' rate of 14 kilometres for the 10-day march along a river was about the average distance covered in a day's march in open country.[19]

The curious thing is that all three writers, despite their careful evaluation of the modalities, have arrived at different answers about the average distance of a day's march. Devos's figure of 14 kilometres, in so far as it rests on Polybius' evidence about the 10-day march along a river, is demonstrably too low, for there must have been at least one rest day on the 10-day march, which at once raises the average for each day of actual march to 16 kilometres, while, if there were two rest days (as Polybius seemed almost to have implied when he thought it necessary to mention that on the previous march up the Rhône the army kept 'straight on'—ἐξῆς—for only *four* days[20]), the figure would be nearly 18 kilometres; and all the figures would be increased by anything up to a kilometre if Polybius' 800 stades was a round figure for something nearer 850 stades, or 152 kilometres. Devos himself had given an estimate of 15 to 20 kilometres a day before he was beguiled by the figure of 14, and his first thoughts were nearer the mark than his second.

On the other hand, the estimates of Maissiat and Marquion at 25 to 26 kilometres a day seem too high, and they are both equally surprising, though for different reasons. It is impossible to believe that an army of about 40,000 foot-soldiers, constrained to walk only two abreast as Maissiat assumed, together with 8,000 to 9,000 horses, plus the elephants and the mules, could have achieved his average of 26 kilometres a day along narrow paths. It is even less conceivable to anyone who has ever tried to pick his way up and down dale across the *garrigues* of southern France that it could have kept up a similar average *away* from the paths, as Marquion assumes. Yet Marquion claims that this method of advance across country in 'approach formation' would have enabled the army to keep up an average of 25 kilometres a day, and he actually steps the rate up to an

[19] pp. 22–4.   [20] III. 49. 5.

even higher average of just on 30 kilometres for three con-
secutive days of the march up the Rhône, where he thinks
that Hannibal was forcing the pace to escape pursuit by
Scipio.*

Let us, before trying to strike a balance between all these
different estimates, glance at what we are told about some
other marches in ancient history. Herodotus' evaluation of the
transit time from Sardis to Susa along the Royal Road, which he
reckoned at the rate of nearly 27 kilometres a day over a three
months' journey,[21] has sometimes been quoted as an index of
the speed of march of an ancient army, on the ground that it
was addressed to the possibility of a march by King Cleomenes
of Sparta, whereas elsewhere in his *History* Herodotus adopted
what I have called his 'standard rate' for an ordinary traveller
of about 35 kilometres a day as a basis for his measurements
of Scythia.[22] If this *was* Herodotus' intention, the mere fact
that he proceeded to tot up the number of days required to
cover the total distance of some 2,400 kilometres and arrived
at the arithmetical answer of about 90 days, without making
any allowance for rest days or other stoppages, shows it for
what it was—an armchair estimate. The march of Cleomenes
never, in fact, took place, and when Herodotus was dealing
with one that did, that of Xerxes and his army from the Helles-
pont to Attica, which is a distance of about 800 kilometres, he
mentioned without comment that the march took three months,
or an average of only about 9 kilometres a day.[23]

The six-month march of the younger Cyrus from Sardis to
Cunaxa described in the first book of Xenophon's *Anabasis*
works out at an average of 15 kilometres a day, inclusive of all
rests.[24] It might be thought that some of Alexander's marches
in the Middle East would afford a parallel to the march of
Hannibal, but Alexander was driving into the heart of an
established empire, and he was so much beset by fighting and
the demands of administration and diplomacy on the way that
no clear pattern of a direct line of march emerges. His biogra-

[21] Herodotus v. 53.   [22] Herodotus IV. 101.
[23] VIII. 51.   [24] The edition of C. E. Brownrigg, 1902, pp. xviii–xix.

---

*Marquion does not specify the figure of 30 kilometres a day, but he names a
starting-point and a destination on each of the three days, and the total distance
from start to finish is 90 kilometres (p. 125).

pher, Sir William Tarn, only once gives any particulars of his speed of march, when he records, with evident incredulity, that in northern Persia in midsummer 330 B.C. 'apparently the tradition made him cover the 400 miles to Sharud in 11 days, excluding rest days, based on the belief that he could maintain the extraordinary average of 36 miles a day', and that after an interval and a rest 'he then did the 52 miles to the Caspian Gates (so it is said) without a halt.'[25]

We have more realistic evidence to go on when we come to Roman marches. G. Veith estimated the average distance of a day's march in all Caesar's marches in Gaul at 20 kilometres,[26] and T. R. Holmes says that this was also the average daily distance, allowing 2 days for rest, on the famous march of about a fortnight from Besançon to the Belgic frontier.[27] (Devos's estimate for this particular march is only 15 kilometres a day,[28] but Holmes's authority here is surely to be preferred to his.)

The *locus classicus* on the required performance of the Roman legions on the march is the compendium of earlier military manuals compiled by Vegetius about 400 A.D., which specified 20 Roman miles as a normal day's march to be covered in 5 hours, with the explicit proviso, however, that these were to be *summer* hours, which (since the Romans divided the day into 12 hours between sunrise and sunset, regardless of the time of year) were in the ratio of about 12 to 15 of our equinoctial hours.[29] This does not mean that the march continued that much later in the day at other times of year to complete 20 Roman miles: on the contrary, it means that the distance was that much shorter at other times of the year, for the Roman marching routine was a rigid one, governed by the time of day, not by the distance. The day's march began after a very early breakfast at sunrise and continued, with periodical halts, until midday, but not thereafter. The afternoon was spent in constructing and fortifying a camp for the night, and the evening was left free for rest and recuperation and supper.[30]

---

[25] *Alexander the Great*, Vol. 1, 1948, p. 56.
[26] *Heerwesen und Kriegsfuehrung* in Mueller's *Handbuch*, 1928, Abt. 4, Tl. 3, Bd. 2, p. 422.
[27] *Caesar's Conquest of Gaul*, 1911, p. 635.
[28] p. 25.   [29] *Epitome Rei Militaris*, I. 9.
[30] Sir Frank Adcock, *The Roman Art of War under the Republic*, 1940, pp. 13–14, and G. Veith, p. 354.

In terms of our equinoctial hours, therefore, the standard day's march was only twelve-fifteenths of Vegetius' summer distance, i.e., 16 Roman miles, or about 23·7 kilometres. G. Veith, in his treatise on the Roman army, makes it clear that the norm for a day's march was a standard of time rather than distance, and concludes: 'The *justum iter* on good roads and in good marching weather amounted, as today, to 20 kilometres or more, and dropped in difficult mountain country, in soft going, or in excessive heat perhaps to less than ten.'[31] He adds later on—what is important for our consideration of Hannibal's march—that on marches lasting for a number of days the Roman legions took a complete rest day every 4 or 5 days.[32]

Let us now try to evaluate Hannibal's speed of march in the light of this collateral evidence. The Carthaginians may not have been as rigid as the Romans about constructing and fortifying a camp for each night's halt—Sir Frank Adcock calls this 'a habit to which no other ancient army was addicted'[33]— though Polybius does frequently mention a camp—στρατοπεδεία, χάραξ, or παρεμβολή, as he variously calls it[34]—in the course of his narrative. They may not, like the Romans, have taken a rest day as frequently as every 4 or 5 days: Devos has assumed only 1 day in 7 in his computation.[35] On the other hand, Hannibal's army was over twice the size of a Roman consular army, which, to take Scipio's as an example, numbered only 22,000 infantry and 2,200 cavalry,[36] and it must have been correspondingly less mobile; while the paths and tracks of southern Gaul in 218 B.C. were obviously nothing like the Roman military roads to which the *justum iter* applied.

Polybius said that the whole march of about 1,500 kilometres from Cartagena to the plains of the Po took five months; but on the section of about 285 kilometres from the Ebro to the Pyranees, through country which was not under Carthaginian sway and which Hannibal had to subjugate before he could proceed any further, there was heavy fighting; Polybius and Livy name four different tribes whom he conquered during this part of the march, and Polybius says that, though it was accomplished with unexpected rapidity, several towns were taken by storm, there were many severe battles, and Hannibal suffered heavy

---

[31] p. 354.   [32] pp. 422–3.   [33] op. cit., p. 13.
[34] e.g. III. 47. 2, 47. 3, or 52. 1.   [35] p. 24.   [36] Livy XXI. 17. 8.

losses.[37] There is good reason, therefore, to accept the view of Perrin,[38] Kahrstedt,[39] and De Sanctis[40] that this part of the march took at least two months; and if we allow three to four weeks, as we have previously assumed, for the first section of about 480 kilometres from Cartagena to the Ebro through country under Carthaginian control, we are left with about two months for the part of the march in which we are mainly interested, the length of about 750 kilometres—for, as Polybius observed, the Pyrenees marked the half-way stage in terms of distance, though not of difficulty[41]—between the Pyrenees and the plains of the Po.

Of this time span, Polybius says that 7 days were spent in the crossing of the Rhône,[42] and two other halts are mentioned by him and/or Livy—one at Elne after the crossing of the Pyrenees, where Hannibal paused for a parley with tribes,[43] the other at the place called the 'Island', where he was called to intervene in a dispute about the kingship of a local tribe and his army was comprehensively refitted[44]—which must have accounted for the best part of another week between them. We have, therefore, about seven weeks for the time actually spent on the march of rather more than 750 kilometres between the Pyrenees and the plains of the Po, or an average of between 15 and 16 kilometres a day, inclusive of fights on the way with local tribes (of which there were several), normal rest days on the march, and the crossing of the Alps.

If we allow, to split the difference between Veith and Devos, for, say, one rest day in six, this gives an average distance of between 18 and 19 kilometres for the days of actual march, which, considering that between a fortnight and three weeks was spent in crossing the Alps,* seems reasonably in line with Vegetius' 23·7 kilometres and Veith's '20 kilometres or more' for marches of the Roman legions on good roads and in good marching conditions. The one section of the march in which Hannibal was following the line of a main highway (whether or

[37] Polybius III. 35. 2–3 and Livy XXI. 23. 2.
[38] p. 37.   [39] p. 375.   [40] pp. 9 and 80.   [41] III. 39. 12.
[42] III. 43. 1, 44. 3, and 45. 5.   [43] Livy XXI. 24.
[44] Polybius III. 49. 8–12 and Livy XXI. 31. 6–8.

* Polybius' figure (III. 56. 3) was 15 days, but, as we shall see later, this seems to have been an understatement.

not the whole army kept to the road) was the section of about 290 kilometres along the ancient Iberian Way between the Pyrenees and the Rhône,[45] and here he may be presumed to have made his best speed, especially as he had been promised free passage by the local tribes.[46] Marquion,[47] curiously enough, though he put his normal average much higher, credits him with only 20 kilometres a day on this section, perhaps because he includes in it the passage of the Pyrenees; he puts the distance at some 300 kilometres and the time taken at about a fortnight (as Perrin also did),[48] but he ignores the incidence of rest days, of which there must have been at least one on a march of that length; so that his figure of 20 kilometres a day implies an average distance of 22 to 23 kilometres on the days of actual march. Such a figure is close enough to those of Vegetius and Veith for the performance of the Roman legions under good marching conditions, and it seems to strike about the right balance between the various estimates we have discussed.

To sum up the discussion, therefore, we might conclude that something of this order—or, to put it more usefully for our purpose (since we do not know how often Hannibal's army took a rest day), an average of about 20 kilometres a day *inclusive* of rest days—can be accepted as a norm for the army's rate of progress in open country along the route of a main highway when unmolested by local tribes; and this can be regarded as a standard by which to judge the probable rate on other sections of the march where the conditions were less favourable.

[45] Strabo IV. 1. 3 and G. de Manteyer, *La Voie fluviale du Rhône et ses chemins primitifs*, 1945, pp. 36–42.
[46] Livy XXI. 24. 5.   [47] p. 63.   [48] p. 71.

IV

FROM CARTAGENA TO THE PLAINS
OF THE PO

LET us now, using our findings about the army's probable rate of progress as a check, trace the timetable of the march from its start at Cartagena, which I have put about the middle of June, to its finish on the plains of the Po. For the first section of about 480 kilometres from Cartagena to the river Ebro through territory already subjugated by the Carthaginians we can reasonably allow the standard rate of 20 kilometres a day, inclusive of rest days, so that this section of the march would have taken between three and four weeks, as I have previously assumed. Hannibal would thus have crossed the Ebro—the critical action of open hostility from the point of view of the Romans—by the middle of July. For the hotly contested march of some 285 kilometres from there to the Pyrenees I have allowed at least two months, and, in case this should be thought excessive, it must be added that the period included, not only the march itself and the fighting to which I have referred, but a pause at the Pyrenees for consolidation and regrouping of forces. Polybius and Livy say that at this point Hannibal detached 11,000 troops, together with 21 elephants, under the command of his brother, Hasdrubal, as garrison for the territory between the Ebro and the Pyrenees; he also dismissed an equal number of the Iberian troops to their homes and lightened his remaining army, consisting now of 50,000 infantry, 9,000 cavalry and 37 elephants, by leaving the heavy baggage with Hasdrubal.[1] Only then did he set out from Ampurias on the Spanish side of the frontier for the next stage of the march, and it must have been near the middle of September before he did so.

He crossed the Pyrenees either by the coast road or by the easy Col de Perthus a little way inland and pitched camp at

[1] Polybius III. 35. 4–8 and 42. 11 and Livy XXI. 22. 2–3.

Elne, about 35 kilometres beyond the frontier. There he sent messengers to a concourse of Gallic tribes gathered near Perpignan a few miles further on, inviting them to a parley at his camp. The chieftains came, accepted his fair words (and his gifts), and promised free passage through their territory; and Hannibal set off on the march to the Rhône.[2] It is some 250 kilometres along the route of the ancient Iberian Way (which later became the Roman *Via Domitia*) from Elne to the Rhône-crossing at Beaucaire–Tarascon, and we shall see when we discuss the geography of the march in Part II that there are strong reasons for thinking that this must have been Hannibal's route. We have already accepted the standard rate of 20 kilometres a day, inclusive of rest days, for this section of the march and allowed about a fortnight for the army's movements from Ampurias to the Rhône, so that, if we allow an extra day or so for the parley with the Gallic chieftains at Elne, it must have been near the end of September when Hannibal arrived on the banks of the Rhône.

From there to his arrival on the plains of the Po we have practically a day-to-day narrative from both Polybius and Livy, and though their indications of time do not tally in every detail, and are not entirely self-consistent, the timetable they present is fairly clear. First, 7 days were spent in the crossing of the Rhône;[3] the army then marched upstream for 4 days without a break to the place called the 'Island' formed by the confluence of the Rhône and another river;[4] Hannibal's aid was invoked, when he arrived there, to settle a dispute between two brothers over the kingship of a neighbouring tribe, as a result of which he was rewarded with a comprehensive refitting of the clothing and equipment of his army:[5] we are not told how much time was spent at the 'Island', but it must have been 3 or 4 days; the army then marched for 10 days 'along the river' (so Polybius put it) to a point at which it 'began the climb to the Alps'—ἤρξατο τῆς πρὸς τὰς Ἄλπεις ἀναβολῆς.[6]

Where this point was, not in geographical location, but in Polybius' scheme of the march, is a question on which there are different views. In a preliminary conspectus of the geography,

[2] Livy XXI. 24.   [3] Polybius III. 43. 1, 44. 3, and 45. 5.
[4] Polybius III. 49. 5 and Livy XXI. 31. 4.
[5] Polybius III. 49. 8–12 and Livy XXI. 31. 6–8.   [6] Polybius III. 50. 1.

with which he prefaced his account of the march to give his
readers an idea of the distances involved before he embarked
on the detailed narrative, he had divided the march from the
Rhône-crossing into two lengths, the first of which he said was
250 kilometres 'as far as the climb of the Alps into Italy'—ἕως
πρὸς τὴν ἀναβολὴν τῶν Ἄλπεων τὴν εἰς Ἰταλίαν—[7] and the view
generally taken is that he meant by this the same point as the
one designated by the expression I have just quoted, i.e. that
the march 'along the river' was conterminous with the 250
kilometres from the Rhône-crossing, and therefore that the end
of it coincided with the beginning of Polybius' second length,
which he gave as 214 kilometres for 'the crossing of the Alps'
—αἱ τῶν Ἄλπεων ὑπερβολαί.[8] I shall discuss this question more
fully when we come to the geography of the march in Part II,
and I shall argue that there are cogent reasons for holding that
the march 'along the river' was *not* conterminous with the 250
kilometres from the Rhône-crossing, but fell perhaps 40 kilometres short of it. Here I am only concerned with the crux in
so far as it affects the timetable; and in this aspect of it
Polybius himself seems to have confirmed that the two points
were different, for he assigns different time spans to the sectors
of the march which followed them.

In a retrospective summary of the march after it was over
he said that the 'crossing of the Alps'—ἡ τῶν Ἄλπεων ὑπερβολή
—had taken 15 days,[9] and Livy repeated the same figure on his
authority;[10] but the days enumerated in Polybius' narrative
from the beginning of the 'climb to the Alps' to the arrival on
the plains of the Po add up to 18.[11] Philip Cluver long ago
noticed what he took to be a discrepancy between the two
figures and found fault with Livy for not having spotted it.[12]
But there is no discrepancy if Polybius meant that 'the crossing
of the Alps' started somewhere *beyond* the point at which the
army 'began the climb *to* the Alps'; and the fact that he reported different times for the two lengths of march confirms
that this is what he did mean.

It must be admitted, however, that the conventional interpretation makes better sense in terms of the rate of march—
though only if Polybius' summary figure of 15 days is regarded

[7] III. 39. 9.   [8] III. 39. 10.   [9] III. 56. 3.   [10] XXI. 38. 1.
[11] III. 50. 3 to 56. 1.   [12] *Italia Antiqua*, 1624, p. 379.

4—H.M.I.H.

as a mistake and the true figure is taken to be 18—for this gives an average of just under 12 kilometres a day for the 214 kilometres across the Alps, which strikes one as a realistic estimate; whereas if, as I think, the 'climb to the Alps' began some 40 kilometres further back, the same figure for the time produces an average of 14 kilometres a day, or almost exactly the same as that recorded by Polybius for the much easier section 'along the river' (If Polybius' figure of *15* days is adopted for the distance of 214 kilometres, the resulting average for the 'crossing of the Alps' is practically the same unrealistic rate.) But even on this interpretation the resulting rate of progress on the days of actual march is unsatisfactory, for Polybius' narrative of 18 days includes 6 days of stoppages for one reason or another,[13] and an average daily march of nearly 18 kilometres across the highest part of the Alps—faster than the daily average 'along the river'—cannot be regarded as realistic; and it has to be admitted that the figure of 21 kilometres a day resulting from my hypothesis that the distance was more like 254 kilometres is even more untenable.

Some modern writers, while adopting the conventional view that Polybius meant the whole length from the end of the march 'along the river' to the plains of the Po when he gave the *distance* for the 'crossing of the Alps' as 214 kilometres, have somewhat arbitrarily supposed that he meant a different and shorter length when he used the same expression for the *time* of 15 days. Marquion, for instance, suggests that he must have meant this to refer merely to the really severe part of the climb and the difficult first part of the descent, and this would certainly make better sense of the rate of march. Marquion, however, posits an arbitrary figure of 25 days for the whole distance after the end of the march 'along the river',[14] and Dunbabin purports to read the narrative of Polybius himself as adding up to 21 days.[15] But neither figure can be extracted from the text on a careful reading, and I agree with Cluver that the total indicated by Polybius' narrative was 18 days.

It has seemed right to mention these anomalies about the rate of march. The only explanation for them one can proffer is that Polybius did not carry in his head the estimates he had given in his geographical conspectus ten chapters earlier when

[13] III. 52.1, 53. 9, 55.7, and 55. 8.   [14] pp. 63–4.   [15] p. 122.

he was describing the actual course of the march, and that something was wrong with his figures for the distances— which may not be surprising when one reflects that he was dealing here with a part of the march in which Hannibal had departed far from the direct route to Italy. But the anomalies, puzzling though they are, do not seriously affect the question of the timetable, which is our present concern; and even the inflated figures adopted by Marquion and Dunbabin would not alter it materially.

Let us adopt, therefore, as Cluver did, the plain reading of Polybius' text, that the time taken from the end of the march 'along the river' was 18 days, which gives a total of about six weeks from Hannibal's arrival on the banks of the Rhône to the end of the march on the plains of the Po—7 days over the crossing of the Rhône, 4 days to the 'Island', say 4 days' halt there, 10 days 'along the river', and a final 18 days after that. Since we have put Hannibal's arrival on the banks of the Rhône near the end of September, we can conclude that the end of the march was not far from the middle of November, or about five months, as Polybius said, after the departure from Cartagena near the middle of June.

V

THE SETTING OF THE PLEIADES

WE have followed the story of Hannibal's march and the events that preceded it stage by stage, evaluating each instalment in terms of the time it must have taken and an approximate calendar date; and we have found that the march must have ended near the middle of November, which means (since the descent from the pass to the plains of the Po took about a week) [1] that the army was on the pass sometime in the first week of November. It was about then that the Pleiades were setting in 218 B.C., as Polybius and Livy said; [2] and de Beer, [3] Marquion, [4] and Devos [5] have accepted this as evidence that the date was at least not earlier than the end of October. But those historians who have placed it some six or seven weeks earlier have denied that the expression 'the setting of the Pleiades' implied any such limitation. We shall have to examine the matter more closely, therefore. There are really two questions to be considered: first, what was the date denoted by the expression itself? secondly, how much latitude is implied by Polybius' words that it was *close* to the date in question—συνάπτειν—when the army was on the pass?*

Mommsen gave a lead to the latitudinarians when he pronounced in his magisterial way that the expression did not mean anything more than the approach of winter, 'least of all the day of the heliacal setting of the Pleiades (about 26 October)', and he put the date at the beginning of September. [6] De Sanctis [7] and Walbank [8] fell in behind, though lagging 10 days to a fortnight later, and Walbank, echoing De Sanctis, makes the following assertion about the meaning of the phrase:

[1] Polybius III. 54. 4 to 56. 1.　　　[2] Polybius III. 54. 1 and Livy XXI. 35. 6.
[3] pp. 70 and 103.　　　[4] p. 63.　　　[5] p. 123.
[6] *History of Rome*, 1854–6, tr. Dickson, Vol. 2, p. 263.
[7] pp. 76 and 79.　　　[8] Notes on Polybius III, 34. 6 and 54. 1.

---

* Livy (XXI. 35. 6) said that the Pleiades 'were already setting'—*occidente iam sidere Vergiliarum.*

The reference to the setting of the Pleiades is a general expression for
the approach of the bad season. . . . The morning setting of the
Pleiades is calculated as 7 or 9 November. . . . But from the time of
Hesiod (*Op.* 383 ff.) the setting of the Pleiades was an indication of
the approach of winter . . . and the fact that new snow had just
fallen suggests that Hannibal was on the summit about the third
week in September.

Now, the passage of Hesiod to which Walbank and De
Sanctis both refer, which is a *locus classicus* on the subject, so far
from supporting the assertion that 'the setting of the Pleiades'
was 'a general expression for the approach of the bad season'
which could be equated with the third week in September,
shows that, on the contrary, a much later date was specifically
denoted. Hesiod was giving a 'farmer's calendar' of the operations to be put in hand at different times of the year, and the
directions he gave as to timing were quite specific: they were
not couched loosely in terms which could be stretched six or
seven weeks either way, as Walbank and De Sanctis imply.
Both in this passage and again at line 616 he quoted the setting
of the Pleiades as the signal to begin the major operations of
ploughing and sowing the grain for the next year's harvest.
These operations, as A. W. Mair showed in a fascinating study
of the whole subject,[9] were quite distinct from the threefold
turning of the soil during spring and summer, and they were
not put in hand before the end of October or beginning of
November after the vintage had been got in. It is therefore
quite absurd of Walbank and De Sanctis to quote this passage
of Hesiod in support of a theory that the date in question here
was the third week in September.

But in any case there was no need for them to fetch their
example from Hesiod, nor is there very much point in mentioning a date on which the setting of the Pleiades is now calculated
to have occurred in 218 B.C. except as confirmatory evidence
of the facts. The more relevant question is what the date was
taken to be at the time, and about this there are plenty of
references much nearer in time to Polybius which give perfectly
specific information. Naturally the dates quoted by different
authors of different periods, expressed in different time scales,
are not precisely the same, but not one of them, in terms of our

[9] *Hesiod Translated*, 1908, pp. 128–30 and 145–6.

calendar, is earlier than the second half of October, and the majority of those nearest in time to Polybius (some of them quoted by de Beer in his appendix on the subject) [10] are sometime in November.

The earliest recorded dates are those of the Milesian philosophers of the sixth century B.C., Thales and Anaximander, who, according to Pliny,[11] specified the setting of the Pleiades as occurring 25 and 31 days respectively after the autumnal equinox, corresponding (by Roman method of counting) to 17 and 23 October on the basis of our date for the equinox, 23 September. Since Thales' computations (whether his own or taken from a Babylonian table) were sufficiently accurate to predict an eclipse of the sun, his date would have been that of the true setting, i.e. the day on which the Pleiades set at precisely the same moment as the sun rose. Since, however, for nearly an hour before sunrise there is too much light in the sky for the stars to be visible, the normal meaning of 'the setting' of a star for practical purposes was the first day on which, setting 4 minutes earlier each day, it could actually be *seen* setting before sunrise, which is about a fortnight later, and this was the accepted meaning of 'the setting of the Pleiades' in later times.[12]

Democritus gave the date as 26 October, according to a calendar compiled by Geminus in the first century B.C.;[13] and this too must have referred to the true setting, since he specified it explicitly as 'simultaneous with sunrise'—ἅμα ἡλίῳ ἀνίσχοντι. Mommsen, it may be remembered, quoted the same date, though he was mistaken in calling it the 'heliacal' setting, which means the setting of a star at sunset, whereas we are concerned here with the morning or 'cosmical' setting of the Pleiades at *sunrise*.* Euctemon and Eudoxus, according to Geminus,[13] gave the date as the 15th and 19th day respectively of the month Scorpion, which began in those days (as it still does for astrologers, who ignore the precession of the equinoxes) on 23 October—in other words, 6 and 10 November in our

---

[10] pp. 100–3.   [11] *HN* xviii. 25. 213–14.

[12] Autolycus, Περὶ ἀνατολῶν καὶ δύσεων, i. 1; and F. Boll, *Fixsterne*, Pauly-Wissowa, Vol. 6, 1909, Cols. 2423 ff.

[13] Ἐισαγωγὴ εἰς τὰ φαινόμενα under the month Σκόρπιον.

---

* Devos makes the same mistake (p. 35) when he quotes Polybius as speaking of 'the *heliacal* setting of the Pleiades': there is no such word in the Greek.

the setting of the Pleiades fell in the month Scor⎵ which', ⎵ed that
he said, 'was for the Romans November'.[14] Varro he first
century B.C. said that it occurred 32 days after the autumnal
equinox;[15] and since he seems to have dated the equinox at
27 September,[16] this probably meant for him a date around
28 October; but an early editor who annotated this passage in a
summary at the beginning of the book gave the calendar date
as 8 November.[17] Pliny in the first century A.D. twice specified it
as 11 November.[18]

Both Aratus in the same passage and Varro a little further on
repeated Hesiod's precept that the setting of the Pleiades was
the time to start ploughing and sowing the grain for the next
year's harvest, and Varro added that the grapes should be
picked and the vintage done between the autumnal equinox and
the setting of the Pleiades,[19] which confirms, if any further
confirmation is needed, that no earlier date for the latter can
possibly have been meant. In short, there is an impressive array
of evidence from writers between the fifth century B.C. and the
first A.D. that 'the setting of the Pleiades' meant for Polybius
and the Romans a date in the first fortnight of November or
the end of October at the earliest, and I have not been able to
find any justification for Walbank's assertion that the meaning
of the expression could be stretched to denote a date some six
or seven weeks earlier.

R. L. Dunbabin was equally positive that this was the accepted meaning of the phrase. 'There can be no doubt', he said,
'that Polybius and Livy thought of the Pleiads as setting about
November 9', but he went on to say that the whole phrase,
διὰ τὸ συνάπτειν τὴν τῆς Πλειάδος δύσιν, showed that 'Polybius
certainly meant a date sometime before', and this brings us
to the second of our two questions. Dunbabin thought that
Hannibal's crossing of the pass could not be put 'much more
than two or three weeks before November 9'; and his date for
it was 'about October 19',[20] which is a good fortnight earlier
than my date in the first week of November.

[14] Scholium on Phaenomena, 264.   [15] De Re Rustica I. 28. 2.
[16] De Re Rustica, Capitula Libri Primi.   [17] Ibid.
[18] HN II. 47. 125 and XVIII. 25. 225.
[19] De Re Rustica, I. 34. 2.   [20] pp. 122–4.

It is, however, much closer to it than those of Mommsen, De Sanctis, and Walbank: the difference between them is barely beyond the margin of error which must attach to all such estimates; and too much should not be made of the fact that my date in the first week of November coincides so closely with some of those mentioned for 'the setting of the Pleiades' in Roman times. I do nevertheless take issue with Dunbabin about his interpretation of the word συνάπτειν, for he does seem to allow more latitude to Polybius' expression than is warranted. It is not clear why he should have said that 'Polybius certainly meant a date before' the accepted date, for the plain meaning of συνάπτειν here is 'coinciding with'; and the fact that Polybius not only chose to use the word, but combined it with a sharply defined noun in a substantival construction, when he might have used a participle or a verb in the imperfect tense if he had merely wanted to say that the Pleiades were on their way towards setting, suggests that he meant a date quite close to the setting, not some rather vague period beforehand. His use of the verb συνάπτειν in other places certainly seems to confirm this. He had used it, for instance, to describe how Hannibal *rejoined* his cavalry and baggage train after being separated from them for a night in a gorge on the way up to the pass,[21] and later he used it twice in the same passage to relate, first, how Sempronius *arrived* at Rome with his legions,[22] and afterwards how he hurried on from Ariminum to *join* Scipio,[23] none of which could possibly denote mere convergence or approximation. It does seem, therefore, that Dunbabin has stretched the meaning of the phrase too far in allowing a period up to three weeks beforehand. However, his timetable, as I have said, is only marginally different from mine; but Walbank dismisses it, without further comment, as 'unacceptable'.[24]

U. Kahrstedt, who shared with Dunbabin a becoming humility before the ancient authorities, drew attention to a further significant point—the fact that there had been a recent fall of snow when Hannibal and his army were on the pass.[25] Kahrstedt said that he would have liked, because of this, to put the date sometime in September, 'but', he continued, with a

---

[21] III. 53. 6.   [22] III. 68. 12.   [23] III. 68. 13.
[24] Note on Polybius III. 68. 14.   [25] Polybius III. 54. 1 and Livy XXI. 35. 6.

candour that did him credit and should have put some others
to shame, 'Polybius' astronomical indication is not to be treated
as inaccurate and approximate without compelling reasons';[26]
and he therefore concluded that Hannibal was on the pass in
October—probably, he thought in the first half of the month.
Kahrstedt had lighted on the right clue, but only his modesty
saved him from drawing the wrong conclusion; for he had
misread it, as Walbank also did.

The fact that the first snowfall on the Alpine passes frequently
occurs in September, which Walbank and others have quoted
as a reason for advancing the date of Hannibal's transit, tells
in precisely the opposite direction; for the setting of the Pleiades,
as Dunbabin pointed out,[27] was only mentioned by Polybius
and Livy (and therefore presumably by their common source)
to explain the recent snowfall; and if the transit had taken place
in mid-September, when a snowfall could normally be expected,
there would have been no point in referring to the setting of the
Pleiades some seven weeks later. It was only relevant to mention
it if this was in fact the time of the transit. This brings us to the
simplest, and perhaps the most cogent, of all the answers to this
unnecessarily complicated question: if Polybius or Livy, or
their common source, *had* meant to say that Hannibal was on
the pass in the third week of September, they would not have
referred to the Pleiades at all; they would have dated it by the
autumnal equinox, the method of dating which both authors
employed elsewhere for events at that time of year.[28]

If any further proof is needed that it was a much later date, it
is sufficient to read their descriptions of conditions on the pass
during the transit. Not only had there been this recent fall of
snow, but the snow was lying and already packing ($ἤδη$
$ἀθροιζομένης$),[29] there were drifts everywhere (*omnia nive
oppleta*),[30] and there was another fall of snow to add to the
army's difficulties when it was beginning the descent.[31] It is
a picture of wintry conditions on the mountain pass grimly set
in, not of a transient snowfall in mid-September.

[26] p. 370.   [27] p. 122.   [28] e.g. Polybius IV. 37. 2 or Livy XXXI. 47. 1.
[29] Polybius III. 54. 1.   [30] Livy XXI. 35. 7.   [31] Polybius III. 54. 8.

PREPARATIONS IN ROME

WE have seen how all the direct evidence of Polybius and Livy on Hannibal's activities before and during the march—their narratives of the events themselves, Polybius' dating of the start at 'the beginning of summer' and of the crossing of the Alps 'close to the setting of the Pleiades', and their description of conditions during the crossing—supports the conclusion that the five-month march began in mid-June and ended near the middle of November. We now have to consider how far this timetable is consistent with what we are told about events in Rome during the same period.

The news of the fall of Saguntum (which I have dated in late December 219 B.C.)[1] must have reached Rome early in the New Year, and Livy says that it arrived at about the same time as the return of two ambassadors who had been sent, first to Saguntum, and then on to Carthage, to protest against Hannibal's attack on that town under Roman protection.[2] Livy also says that the commands of the consuls due to take office on 15 March had previously been nominated, namely, Spain and Africa, and that they were now allotted between them—Spain to Scipio, Africa (with Sicily) to Sempronius— together with an allocation of forces. Three standard consular armies, each consisting of two Roman legions of 4,000 men each, 600 Roman cavalry, and considerably larger numbers of allied infantry and cavalry, were voted in all. The third army was assigned to the praetor, L. Manlius, as a garrison of Cisalpine Gaul, where it was also regarded as backing up Scipio's army in the war against the Carthaginians, although, as we shall see, the result turned out exactly the opposite.[3]

But this highly specific passage in Livy is preceded by a chapter in his best rhetorical style describing the mixture of shame,

---

[1] p. 20 above.   [2] XXI. 16. 1.   [3] Livy XXI. 17. 1–8.

consternation, and anger, with which the news of the fall of
Saguntum was received in Rome; and the disarray of the Senate
facing the prospect of a new war with its formidable old
enemy under a brilliant young leader, at a moment, so he said,
when the Roman nation was more sunk in lethargy and more
unwarlike than it had ever been; and in the course of this splen-
did diatribe he lets fall the remark that Hannibal was already
crossing the Ebro.[4] Now, not only have we seen, on examination of the timetable, that Hannibal cannot have crossed the
Ebro much before the middle of July,[5] but we know from
Polybius that he did not even set out from Cartagena before
he had received a report on the proceedings at Carthage
during a visit of a *second* Roman embassy (to which we shall
come in a moment), which arrived while he was still waiting
for the return of the messengers from Cisalpine Gaul towards
the end of May;[6] and Livy himself contradicts this reference to
the crossing of the Ebro when he tells us later on that the rumour of it was current at the time when the *second* embassy
returned to Rome.[7]

It is clear, therefore, that Livy has mingled in this highly
wrought passage about the news of the fall of Saguntum a
description of reactions and decisions at Rome which properly
belonged to a much later date. And, indeed, the whole passage
is anachronistic; for the Romans certainly did not envisage at
that early stage, as Livy says they did,[8] that the war would be
waged in Italy: on the contrary, they had just nominated Spain
and Africa as the commands of the two consuls in the expecta-
tion that the war would be waged there;[9] and even when
Scipio sailed from Pisa much later on he was still under orders
for Spain, and only anchored off the mouth of the Rhône as a
port of call until he heard that Hannibal was already crossing
the Pyrenees.[10] So there is no doubt that we must assign to a
later date in the year the decisions and military dispositions
described by Livy (despite his remark at the beginning of the
next chapter that the arrangements had been made before the
second embassy was dispatched to Carthage);[11] for the plain
fact is that, until the second embassy reported, no one knew

---

[4] XXI. 16.   [5] p. 35 above.   [6] III. 34. 7.   [7] XXI. 20. 9.
[8] XXI. 16. 6.   [9] Livy XXI. 17. 1.
[10] Polybius III. 40. 2 and 41. 2–6.   [11] XXI. 18. 1.

whether the issue was to be war or peace, and no orders could have been given for sending expeditionary forces to Spain and Africa.

Livy also says that it was at this juncture that the issue of war or peace was referred to the people and the people voted for war.[12] Walbank, in a note on Polybius III. 20. 6, quotes this passage, which he calls 'Livy's reliable account', in support of his view that the *comitia centuriata* passed its final vote for war on this occasion and that no further ratification was needed if the Carthaginians rejected the ultimatum which the second embassy was to deliver. He says that 'at this time and throughout the second century the war motion went through the Comitia in a conditional form', though only one of the references he quotes in support of this seems a wholly unmistakable instance of it—the vote of the people for war with Perseus of Macedon in 171 B.C.[13] He may be right, though it seems more likely that Livy's account of the people's vote on this occasion was as anachronistic as the rest of the passage. In any case, it does not affect the timetable of the Roman military preparations, which cannot have been effectively put in hand before the second embassy reported.

We must now consider more closely the timing of this second embassy to Carthage, which was the first overt action by the Roman Senate after the fall of Saguntum. Livy gives no indication of the date on which it was sent: he merely records that the intention was to put the Roman cause in a good juridical posture before war began, and that the embassy consisted of five senior senators, who were to put the straight question to the Carthaginian Government whether it accepted responsibility for Hannibal's attack on Saguntum, and, if the answer was 'Yes', to declare war.[14] Polybius gives substantially the same account, except that he puts the ambassadors' challenge in the form of a demand to surrender Hannibal and his chief officers, failing which war would be declared.[15] But he gives an indication of dating which is almost as misleading as Livy's dating of the military preparations and dispositions. He was anxious, as he himself makes clear, to vindicate Roman honour and to dispel any impression of wavering after their allies at Saguntum

---

[12] XXI. 17. 4.   [13] Livy XLII. 30. 10–11.
[14] XXI. 18. 1–2.   [15] III. 20. 8.

had been left in the lurch,[16] so he relates that, *directly after* learning of the fate of Saguntum, the Romans sent the ambassadors *post-haste* to Carthage ($\Pi\alpha\rho\alpha\chi\rho\tilde{\eta}\mu\alpha\ldots\kappa\alpha\tau\grave{\alpha}\ \sigma\pi ov\delta\acute{\eta}v$),[17] which is contradicted by his own subsequent statement, confirmed by Livy, that their return to Rome coincided with the arrival of the news that Hannibal had just crossed the Ebro,[18] which, on any timetable, was several months later.*

The historians have differed widely about the explanation of this crux. Kahrstedt seems to accept something near to Polybius' account when he says that the ambassadors had been to Carthage and returned to Rome by the middle of March. But since he goes on to say a few pages later that Hannibal crossed the Ebro about the end of May,[19] without making any attempt to reconcile this with the agreed statement of the two historians that the news of his crossing the Ebro reached Rome at about the same time as the ambassadors did, or with Polybius' statement that Hannibal only received a report on the proceedings at Carthage a short time before he set out on his march,[20] it is not a tenable account of the sequence of events.

Kahrstedt also rejects as absurd and unhistorical the story recorded by Livy (though not by Polybius) that the ambassadors went on from Carthage to tour through Spain and southern Gaul on a mission to win over the tribes before returning to Rome: he thinks they must have come straight back to Rome to report after their declaration of war in Carthage.[21] This certainly sounds like the voice of common sense. But Livy's account of the ambassadors' tour is so detailed and circumstantial that it cannot be dismissed as pure invention. Not only does he expressly say that the ambassadors had been given orders at Rome, before they set out, to make the tour after leaving Carthage, but he gives the names of two separate tribes to whom they made approaches in Spain, records the words of the dusty answers they received both there and in Gaul, and tells how, when they reached the friendly Greek

[16] III. 20. 1–2.   [17] III. 20. 6.
[18] Polybius III. 40. 2 and Livy XXI. 20. 9.   [19] pp. 372 and 375.
[20] III. 34. 7.   [21] p. 371.

---

* Walbank has also pointed out (note on Polybius III. 20. 6) that two of the ambassadors named by Livy were the consuls for 219–18 B.C., who could not have left Rome before the expiration of their year of office on 14 March.

city of Marseilles, they learnt the reason—that Hannibal had got in first and won the tribes over before they came.[22] It has to be remembered that the Romans at this stage believed they had the initiative; they were still thinking in terms of offensive operations in Africa and Spain, as they continued to do right up to the time of Scipio's landing at the mouth of the Rhône. It is therefore not as surprising as it seems at first sight that they should have wanted to enlist support among the tribes in Spain and Gaul before taking the offensive, and thought that they still had plenty of time in which to do so.

Walbank, in agreement with W. Hoffmann, goes to the other extreme about the timing of the second embassy to Carthage, and thinks that it was not even dispatched until after the news of Hannibal's crossing the Ebro had reached Rome (which he puts early in June).[23] But this cannot be right either, for it is contrary to the plain statements of both Livy and Polybius that the ambassadors had returned to Rome by the time the first authentic report of it arrived there—and if Livy's account of their tour among the Spanish tribes is accepted, as it surely should be, they could not have perambulated at large in territory which Hannibal was already invading. Moreover, if the crossing of the Ebro rather than the attack on Saguntum had been the occasion of the Roman ultimatum, the ambassadors would have held quite different language in Carthage from that recorded by both Polybius and Livy.[24] It seems certain, therefore, that they had left Spain and were on their way back through southern France by the time Hannibal crossed the Ebro, and the news that he had done so reached Rome at about the same time as they did.

There can be no precise dating of this second embassy, but a timetable such as the following seems to fit all the facts recorded by Polybius and Livy and looks reasonable in itself. Let us put the dispatch of the embassy from Rome in early May and the colloquy with the Carthaginian Senate, ending with the dramatic declaration of war vividly described by Livy,[25] and prosaically by Polybius,[26] in mid-May: the news of the discussion would then have reached Hannibal in Cartagena

[22] XXI. 19. 6 to 20. 9.   [23] Notes on Polybius III. 20. 6 and 40. 1–2.
[24] Polybius III. 20. 6–10 and Livy XXI. 18. 1–7.   [25] XXI. 18.
[26] III. 33. 1–4.

towards the end of May, as I have previously suggested. The Roman ambassadors went on from Carthage to northern Spain, arriving there at about the same time as the report from Carthage reached Hannibal. They toured homewards through Catalonia and Languedoc to Marseilles, and returned from there to Rome, to find the city in a high pitch of war fever on account of a rumour that Hannibal had crossed the Ebro—a rumour that was confirmed shortly afterwards by envoys from Marseilles, who must have followed hard on the heels of the ambassadors.[27]

It is some 600 kilometres from the Ebro to Marseilles by land, which would have taken perhaps three weeks in travelling time; and allowing for halts along the route for negotiations with tribes, for a further halt for discussion with the allies at Marseilles, and for the voyage from there back to Rome, it is likely to have been at least six weeks after they landed in Spain towards the end of May before the ambassadors got back to Rome. Obviously there can be no exactitude about such guess-work, but it is not too far out of line, on our timetable, with the evidence of Polybius and Livy that a rumour of Hannibal's crossing the Ebro, which I have dated near mid-July, was current in Rome when the ambassadors arrived there and was confirmed by the news from Marseilles soon afterwards.

[27] Livy XXI. 20. 9 and 25. 1, and Polybius III. 40. 2.

VII

THE REVOLT OF THE BOII

I F I have seemed to labour unduly the question of the timing of the second embassy to Carthage, it is because the Roman preparations for war only began effectively after its return, and it marks, therefore, a critical point of departure in our timetable. Polybius makes it clear that no final decisions were taken at Rome until the ambassadors had returned and reported in person on the language they had held in Carthage and the decision which resulted; and it was only then, according to him, that the Romans decided to send Scipio to Spain and Sempronius to Africa with their consular armies.[1]

Though, as we have seen, Walbank cannot be right in dating the *dispatch* of the embassy after Hannibal's crossing of the Ebro, he is certainly right in taking the latter—or rather, the news of it in Rome—as the starting-point of the Romans' preparations for war and in referring to this as their 'late decision to declare war'.[2] His own dating of the decision to send the consuls to Spain and Africa is 'late June or early July', because, according to him, news of Hannibal's crossing the Ebro was already at Rome in early June;[3] but, as we have seen, this is at least a month too early. Hannibal crossed the Ebro, according to my timetable, sometime in the first half of July, the authentic news of it reached Rome later in the month (shortly after the return of the ambassadors), and it was near the end of July before the executive arrangements were put in hand which culminated in Scipio just missing Hannibal on the banks of the Rhône. But the preparations were not allowed to continue without interruption, and the actual date of Scipio's departure was determined by other events, to which we must now turn.

The news of Hannibal's crossing the Ebro was not only the

[1] III. 40. 2.   [2] Notes on Polybius III. 40. 1–2 and 41. 2.
[3] Note on Polybius III. 40. 1–2.

signal for war preparations in Rome: it triggered off a revolt of the Boii (no doubt previously concerted with Hannibal's messengers), which brought fresh complications and delays. The Romans, while enrolling the legions and making the rest of the preparations for the expeditions to Africa and Spain, were in a hurry to finish another project on which they had previously decided: that of establishing two colonies, Placentia and Cremona, in Cisalpine Gaul, one on each bank of the Po. They had given 30 days' notice to the 6,000 colonists of each of them to report there, and they were energetically fortifying the two towns.[4] At this juncture, which must have been near the end of July, the Boii attacked the new colonies, and Polybius and Livy are in substantial agreement about the operations which ensued, first against the colonists, and then against the praetor, L. Manlius, who came to their help with the garrison troops;[5] and since the sequence of events in these operations is important for our evaluation of the timetable, I will paraphrase their account of them at some length.

The Boii, having first asked the Insubres to join them, raided the lands of the two new colonies while the triumvirs were still parcelling out the holdings, forced the colonists to flee with the triumvirs as far as Mutina (the modern Modena) about 100 kilometres along the road to Ariminum (the modern Rimini), and there laid siege to them. They treacherously entrapped the triumvirs into a discussion of peace terms and took them prisoner. The praetor, L. Manlius, who was stationed with the garrison troops at Ariminum about 150 kilometres further on, hurried to the rescue as soon as he heard the news, but he allowed his men to straggle and lost about 600 of them in an ambush in the woods. The rest got away into open country and succeeded in fortifying a camp. They set out afresh on the road to Mutina, but again when they were making their way through woods the Boii attacked the rearguard, and they lost 700 more men and six standards. Manlius seems somehow to have succeeded in relieving the siege of Mutina—or else the Boii, who, according to Livy, had no heart for siegecraft, raised the siege themselves—for the next we hear of him is that he had passed some 60 kilometres beyond Mutina on his way to Placentia and Cremona. But while he was still some 40 kilo-

---

[4] Polybius III. 40. 3–5.   [5] Polybius III. 40 and Livy XXI. 25.

Cisalpine Gaul.

metres short of his objective, he was forced to take refuge in the village of Tannetum (near Parma), where he threw up hasty defences, got in supplies by river (receiving also some reinforcements from the Gauls of Brescia), and remained cooped up watching the multitude of enemies growing every day. When the news of these misfortunes reached Rome, some 600 kilometres from Tannetum by the normal route,[6] and the Senate heard that a full-size consular army under the praetor was shut up in a small village in Cisalpine Gaul, they decided that one of Scipio's legions (or both of them according to Polybius), together with 5,000 of his allied troops, all newly raised by him for the expedition to Spain, must be detached to go to the help of Manlius, and they ordered Scipio to raise new levies to take their place. So Scipio had to start again enrolling one or both of his Roman legions and recruiting more forces from the allies before he could set out for Spain.[7]

Such is the sequence of events described in detail by Livy, and rather more summarily by Polybius. All the movements described took place up and down a straight line about 250 kilometres long between the two new colonies of Placentia and Cremona at one end and the Roman frontier station of Ariminum at the other, the line along which the *Via Aemilia* was constructed a generation later to become the strategic artery of Cisalpine Gaul. I have inserted the various intermediate distances in the above summary so that the reader can form his own estimate of the time it must all have taken. It would be spurious accuracy to attempt to pin-point a time span for each of the separate transits from one place to another, whether of messengers, fugitives, marauding hordes, or an army on the march, or to estimate precisely the delays implied by the abortive siege of Mutina, the various halts of Manlius' army, or the time during which he was beleaguered at Tannetum before the news reached Rome and the Senate took the decision to divert some of Scipio's troops. It should be borne in mind, however, that, as I have previously mentioned, a Roman army stopped marching at midday: the rest of the day was spent in constructing and fortifying a camp, and Manlius would certainly not have neglected this routine precaution on a march

[6] According to Dunbabin, p. 124.
[7] Livy XXI. 25.1 to 26. 2 and Polybius III. 40. 6–14.

through country infested by enemies; nor could his army have achieved a *justum iter* of 20 kilometres on its marching days, when the *Via Aemilia* had not yet been built and we are told that on at least two occasions it was making its way through woods.

It seems an inescapable conclusion from any realistic evaluation of this evidence that from the moment when the signal was given for the first attack of the Boii on Placentia and Cremona to the issue by the Roman Senate of the revised orders to Scipio the time that elapsed cannot have been less than a month. This tells us two things: first, that at least that amount of time had already passed since the news of Hannibal's crossing the Ebro was received in Italy; secondly, that, though Scipio's army was in being, it was still not ready for embarkation after at least a month of recruitment and preparation. The process may have been going on longer, for we do not know whether the Boii attacked directly they heard the news of Hannibal's crossing the Ebro—De Sanctis thought they might have waited a month before doing so[8]—nor do we know how much longer the preparations would have taken if they had not been interrupted. But, since they *were* interrupted and Scipio had to enroll replacements for half, if not all, his Roman citizens and a third of his allied soldiers on top of the recruitment of two other consular armies besides his own which had just taken place, it would be very surprising if he got his army complete and ready to sail in under another month from then.

That this is by no means an exaggerated estimate of the time required to raise and train an army is confirmed by a letter of Pompey the Great to the Senate in which he recorded, with evident pride, that he had got an army ready to start on an expedition to Spain—the same objective as Scipio's—in *40* days from the day on which he was granted the *imperium*.[9] Yet the historians, if they have noticed the matter at all, have minimized it. Walbank even denies that the diversion of Scipio's troops for the campaign against the Boii had any effect at all on the date of his embarkation, for, he says, this would not explain the late start of his colleague, Sempronius, for Sicily.[10] But Polybius did not say that the two consuls sailed for their repective theatres on the same day, but only in the same season

[8] p. 81.   [9] Sallust, *ex Historiis*, Frag. 98. 4.   [10] Note on Polybius III. 41. 2.

of the year, ὑπὸ τὴν ὡραίαν,[11] and this was a very loose expression, as we shall see later.[12] De Sanctis did recognize the diversion of Scipio's troops as a cause of delay, but he did not allow enough time for it: he thought that Scipio sailed from Pisa within a month after the outbreak of the revolt of the Boii,[13] whereas, as we have seen, at least that amount of time must have elapsed before he was even given the order to raise new troops.

We may take it, therefore, as a conservative estimate that Scipio cannot have sailed with his newly raised troops from Pisa sooner than a good two months after the news of Hannibal's crossing the Ebro was received in Rome, in other words, near the end of September. The coasting voyage as far as the mouth of the Rhône took 4 to 5 days,* and when Scipio heard, on arrival there, that Hannibal was already crossing the Pyrenees, he disembarked his troops instead of continuing on the voyage to Spain, thinking that he still had plenty of time in which to confront him on the Rhône.[14] This is the point at which our two timetables, the one of Hannibal's march and the other of events in Rome and Italy, begin to converge, and the dates fit together, for I have put Hannibal's crossing of the Pyrenees near the middle of September, and the news of it would have reached Fos or Port St. Louis at the mouth of the Rhône shortly before Scipio's arrival at the end of the month. Scipio was mistaken, however, in thinking that he had plenty of time before Hannibal could get as far as the Rhône, for Hannibal and his army followed quickly behind the news itself, and a day or two later Scipio heard, to his amazement, that he was already crossing the river. He sent 300 of his cavalry up-country to reconnoitre. They met 500 of Hannibal's cavalry, sent out on a similar mission, not far from the Carthaginian camp and fought a bloody battle with them.[15] The next day Hannibal raised camp and marched upstream along the Rhône, and when Scipio arrived at the camp with his army he found that Hannibal had left 3 days before.[16]

[11] III. 41. 2.　　[12] pp. 59–62, below.
[13] pp. 80–1.　　[14] Polybius III. 41. 4–6.
[15] Polybius III. 41. 9, 44. 3, 45. 1–2 and 5, and Livy XXI. 26. 5, 29. 1–3, and 31. 2.
[16] Polybius III. 45. 5 and 49. 1, and Livy XXI. 32. 1.

* Polybius III. 41. 4. Polybius says that Scipio arrived 'on the fifth day', πεμπταῖος, reckoned inclusive of the day of departure on his method of counting.

I have put Hannibal's arrival on the banks of the Rhône near the end of September,[17] i.e. at about the same time as Scipio's voyage from Pisa, and the events that followed show that they must have been close to each other at the Rhône before either of them knew of the other's presence. Hannibal spent 5 days effecting his crossing of the Rhône before he heard that a Roman fleet had anchored off the mouth of the river and sent his cavalry out to reconnoitre;[18] and Scipio did not know that Hannibal had got as far as the Rhône until after he had disembarked, though he must have had a report of it very soon afterwards, for both Polybius and Livy say that one of his reasons for sending out a cavalry contingent to reconnoitre instead of advancing at once with his whole army was that his troops were still feeling the effects of the sea voyage.[19] Hannibal, in fact, must have reached the Rhône before Scipio arrived at the mouth of the river, though the news had not yet got there, for the effects of the 5-day voyage on Scipio's men cannot have lasted more than a day or two, and he evidently sent his cavalry out before they had worn off; the cavalry must have encountered Hannibal's cavalry, moving towards them, on the next day; and Hannibal had already been at the Rhône for 5 days by that time. The battle between the cavalry forces must therefore have been in the first days of October, and this is the point of junction between our timetable of Hannibal's march and that of the concurrent events in Italy.

[17] p. 36 above.   [18] Polybius III. 43. 1 and 44. 3.
[19] Polybius III. 41. 6–9 and Livy XXI. 26. 4–5.

VIII

SCIPIO'S SAILING DATE

E have seen that our two timetables, one of Hannibal's march, the other of events in Rome and Italy, dovetail together, and they are both consistent with the evidence in Polybius and Livy which we have so far considered. But now we come up against a difficulty of which the best that can be said is that all the other commentators who have noticed it have found it to be such. Polybius says that the two consuls sailed for their respective theatres ὑπὸ τὴν ὡραίαν,* which the Loeb translator, *more suo*, renders 'early in summer',[1] whereas I have put Scipio's departure from Pisa near the end of September. Let us see, first, how these three Greek words have fared at the hands of other commentators, and we shall take the opportunity to glance at some of their timetables and see how they compare with ours.

Mommsen took the words in the same sense as the Loeb translator, and accepted them at their face value: 'Scipio', he said, 'embarked at the beginning of summer and so at latest by the commencement of June.' But he then had to admit (since, even on his timetable, the encounter between the cavalry forces on the Rhône did not take place until early in August) that Scipio 'must have spent much time on the voyage or remained for a considerable period in singular inaction at Massilia',[2] which seems a distinctly lame conclusion. It is, in fact, quite untenable, for Polybius explicitly says that the voyage

---

[1] III. 41. 2.   [2] *History of Rome*, 1854–6, tr. Dickson, Vol. 2, p. 263.

* I have adopted the reading, ὑπὸ τὴν ὡραίαν (Reiske's emendation), which is to be found in most editions. It is supported by the occurrence of the same phrase at III. 16. 7, where this is the reading in all MSS. Here, however, all the MSS. have ἐπὶ τὴν ὡραίαν, and the Teubner editor retains this reading, which is also adopted by Walbank in his *Historical Commentary*. They may claim the support of certain other places in Polybius (e.g. III. 83. 7, X. 8. 7, and XVI. 18. 5) and one in Thucydides (II. 84. 2) where ἐπί with the accusative in a similar temporal sense is also the unanimous reading of the MSS., although there too it has generally been emended to ὑπό by editors.

did not take more than 5 days,[3] and Scipio would not have missed Hannibal by 3 days on the Rhône if he had been stationed at the mouth of the river since early June; nor would his men still have been suffering from the effects of the voyage, as Polybius and Livy both said they were, when he first heard that Hannibal was there.[4]

De Sanctis seems to agree with Mommsen about the *meaning* of the words, but he is more circumspect about their interpretation. After remarking that ὑπὸ τὴν ὡραίαν 'is not a precise date' and that 'the expression should neither be pressed too much nor disregarded to the extent of holding it possible, as Kahrstedt does, that Scipio sailed, at the earliest, at the end of August', he delivers his own judgement that the date in question was about the end of July, which is still some two months short of my date at the end of September. It is based on his estimate that a period of about two months after the official foundation of the colonies of Placentia and Cremona on 31 May 'seems neither too little nor too much' to leave room for the intervening events, particularly the revolt of the Boii and the diversion of Scipio's troops, with the consequent necessity for him to raise new levies before he could set out.[5]

Thus De Sanctis did, as I have previously mentioned, admit the diversion of Scipio's troops to help in quelling the revolt of the Boii as a factor in the timetable, but he made quite insufficient allowance for it. It is not clear, in the first place, why he made his two months run from the official foundation of the two new colonies when he himself says that this was 'a religious ceremony which in that period had a ritual and symbolical significance rather than any practical meaning'.[6] It might possibly have been the day on which the new colonists were given the 30 days' notice of which Polybius speaks,[7] but, if so, it would tend to support my date for the attack of the Boii near the end of July; for the work of fortifying the two new colonies, which Polybius says was in full swing when the attack came, could not have begun before the colonists assembled at the expiration of the notice on 30 June. In the second place, De Sanctis himself allowed that the revolt of the Boii might not have begun before the end of June;[8] in which case his period of

---

[3] III. 41. 4.   [4] Polybius III. 41. 8 and Livy XXI. 26. 5.
[5] p. 80.   [6] p. 81.   [7] III. 40. 4.   [8] p. 81.

only a month thereafter before Scipio sailed was certainly *not* enough for the military operations which ensued before the decision was taken to divert his troops and the subsequent delay in raising new levies.

But the whole of De Sanctis's timetable is, in fact, too schematic. He begins by fixing a date around 20 September for Hannibal's arrival in Italy (brushing aside, as we have seen, the plain meaning of 'the setting of the Pleiades'); he infers from this, and from Polybius' statement that the whole march took five months, that the starting-date was about 20 April (dismissing also Polybius' reference to the start of the march at 'the beginning of summer');[9] and he fits all the intervening events into a framework within those two limits, without making any serious effort to verify that his dates can be reconciled with the accounts in Polybius and Livy of what actually happened.

Walbank, while constructing his timetable in essentially the same way as De Sanctis, and adopting his arguments to dispose of 'the beginning of summer' and 'the setting of the Pleiades', makes all the dates somewhat later, and puts Scipio's sailing date at 15–20 August; but he evidently takes the same view as Mommsen and the Loeb translator about the meaning of ὑπὸ τὴν ὡραίαν, for he begins his note on the passage with the words 'despite this phrase',[10] and that is all he has to say about it— thus quietly relegating Polybius' description of Scipio's starting-date to the same limbo as his dating of Hannibal's departure.

Kahrstedt, who was taken to task by De Sanctis for stretching too far the meaning of ὑπὸ τὴν ὡραίαν, showed more respect than he did, as we have seen, for that more definite of Polybius' dates, 'the setting of the Pleiades', and his timetable approaches nearer to mine. He thinks that Hannibal was on the pass in the first fortnight of October, and, working backwards from there, he puts Scipio's sailing date at the end of August, 'which', he remarks—a trifle blandly— 'Polybius called ὑπὸ τὴν ὡραίαν'.[11]

Dunbabin's timetable, as we have seen, is not very different from mine. His date, 19 October, for Hannibal's crossing of the pass[12] would imply, though he himself has not filled in this part of the timetable, that Scipio sailed from Pisa in the second week

[9] p. 79.   [10] Note on Polybius III. 41. 2.
[11] pp. 370–3.   [12] p. 124.

of September, compared with my date near the end of the month. Dunbabin, however, not being concerned primarily with Scipio's movements at this point of time, does not deal with Polybius' phrase ὑπὸ τὴν ὡραίαν, and we must now come to grips with it—though, when most of the historians have discounted it as they have, I may perhaps be forgiven if I do not view it too gravely as a lion in our own path. It will be observed, moreover, that, except for the Loeb translator, who had no option, and the bulldozing Mommsen, none of them have committed themselves to a translation, and all of them shaded its meaning, by implication, away from the rendering 'early in summer'.

What, then, are we to make of the phrase? In the first place, it is obviously not a very precise expression in itself—much less precise than Polybius' other indications of dating which we have considered. Secondly, it embraces here the embarkation of two separate expeditionary forces (that of Sempronius as well as Scipio's) from different ports, so that no one specific date can have been intended. Thirdly, every commentator and historian except Mommsen agrees that, whatever the actual date was, it cannot have been early in summer, leaving it to be inferred that, if this *is* the correct translation of the phrase, Polybius was here in error. But, lastly, it is most unlikely that Polybius himself had any clear idea in his mind as to what the date was. He does not seem to have been recording at this point information drawn from some previous source: one has the impression that he was merely filling in a sentence which would have been rather bare without some indication of timing, and that the phrase was no more than a grace-note in his prose, meaning 'during the season'. In short, I have already spent too much time over a difficulty which has received short shrift from almost every other commentator; the phrase carries far less weight than the other, more specific dates in Polybius' narrative; and, if it did mean what most of the commentators seem to think it meant, we can safely follow their example and disregard it.

[13] III. 16. 7.   [14] III. 19. 12.

IX

AFTER THE MARCH

W E have now examined all the points which call for consideration up to the end of the march and found nothing so far which need upset our timetable, and it might be supposed that our task was done; but unfortunately there is still an 'after-sale' period which has to be serviced. Historians have argued, on one ground or another, that the events which followed Hannibal's arrival in Italy could not have been contained within the periods indicated by Polybius and Livy unless the date of his descent from the Alps was a good deal earlier than I have made it. It is necessary, therefore, to examine the various questions which arise during this period. I shall summarize first the narratives of Polybius and Livy, and consider the difficulties raised by the historians afterwards.

After Scipio had missed Hannibal by 3 days on the Rhône, he hurried back to the mouth of the river, sent his brother on to Spain with the army, and returned himself to Pisa with a few men to take command of the troops in Cisalpine Gaul, so as to confront Hannibal in Italy on his descent from the Alps.[1] He is said to have surprised Hannibal by the speed with which he made the journey,[2] and he fought his first engagement with him on the river Ticinus, a northern tributary of the Po, where he himself was so badly wounded that he was unable to take any further part in the fighting that year. He was present in his tent at the disastrous battle on the river Trebia around the turn of the year; but the effective command of the two consular armies had passed to his colleague, Sempronius, who had joined him with his army just before the battle, and it is to him that we must now turn.

Sempronius was with his army at Lilybaeum, on the extreme western tip of Sicily, when the order from the Senate reached him that he was to return with all speed to help his colleague

---

[1] Polybius III. 49. 3–4 and 56. 5–6.   [2] III. 61. 8–9.

repel the invasion of Hannibal in north Italy. Livy gives no indication of the timing of this order or of its reception by Sempronius: he merely says that it reached him on his return to Lilybaeum from a naval expedition to the Lipari Islands; that, after detaching part of his fleet under the praetor, M. Aemilius, and one of his own officers to guard the coasts of Sicily and south Italy, he sent the army off by sea to Ariminum and followed himself with another ten ships after settling affairs in Sicily. From Ariminum (the modern Rimini) he joined Scipio with his army on the river Trebia near Placentia (the modern Piacenza).[3]

Polybius, however, gives quite a different account. He says, in the first place, that it was only after Hannibal had actually arrived in Italy and Scipio was facing him on the Po that the Senate ordered Sempronius' recall.[4] And he tells a curious story, quite different from Livy's, about the way in which Sempronius brought his army back. He says that he sent the fleet home separately, but put the troops on oath, through the tribunes, to report at Ariminum, some 1,300 kilometres away, on an appointed day before bedtime;[5] that he and his troops passed through Rome on their way (thereby giving much encouragement to the populace); and that the troops, having walked continuously for 40 days from Lilybaeum, duly collected according to their oath at Ariminum, where Sempronius took them over and hurried on to join forces with Scipio at Placentia.[6]

From there on to the battle of the Trebia the accounts of Polybius and Livy are substantially in agreement. After joining forces with Scipio and giving his men a rest from their long journey, Sempronius had a successful skirmish with some of Hannibal's forces. This encouraged him to disregard the strong advice of the wounded Scipio, who thought it better to avoid any major engagement until after the winter, when the troops would have had more training and the fickle Cisalpine Gauls would have had more time to turn against Hannibal. Sempronius preferred to force the issue there and then. He was an ambitious man and he was anxious, so Polybius and Livy both tell us, to gain the personal credit for a decisive battle while his

---

[3] XXI. 51. 5–7.   [4] III. 61. 8–9.   [5] III. 61. 10.   [6] III. 68. 12–14.

colleague was *hors de combat* and while he himself was still consul, for he was coming to the end of his consular year, the consuls for the following year had already been nominated by the Senate, and the elections to confirm their appointment were pending.[7] He therefore allowed Hannibal to lure him into a trap at the battle of the Trebia, which took place around the turn of the year—περὶ χειμερινὰς τροπάς—according to Polybius, or the time of the shortest day—*brumae tempus*—according to Livy, in appalling weather of bitter cold, rain, and snow, and ended in utter defeat for the Romans.[8] The survivors of the two consular armies retired after the battle to winter quarters at Placentia and Cremona. Sempronius himself made a risky journey through enemy patrols to hold the consular elections in Rome, and returned, having done so, to winter quarters at Placentia.[9]

After this, the accounts of Polybius and Livy diverge again. Polybius, who does not record the journey of Sempronius to Rome to hold the elections, makes no further mention of him. His next reference to military activities in Italy is to record that the consuls nominated for the following year were mustering the allies and enrolling their own legions,[10] and that in the early spring—ἐνισταμένης τῆς ἐαρινῆς ὥρας—they began fresh operations against Hannibal.[11] Livy, however, says that Sempronius was still in command after an uneasy period in winter quarters and fought an indecisive battle with Hannibal once again at the first dubious signs of spring—*ad prima ac dubia signa veris*[12]—before the new consul, Flaminius, took over the command of his army on the first day of his year of office, 15 March.[13]

Such are the dry bones of the story as told by Polybius and Livy. But the historians who have picked them over have left them so utterly disjointed that the only way to get through the meal is to gnaw them one by one. We are spared, however, one difficulty which they might have raised at the outset—Polybius' statement that the order of recall to Sempronius was only dispatched after Hannibal had actually arrived in Italy. For, if this were the case, Sempronius certainly could not have brought his army back in time to fight the battle of the Trebia 'around

---

[7] Polybius III. 70. 7 and Livy XXI. 53. 6.
[8] Polybius III. 72. 3–4 and Livy XXI. 54. 7–8 and 56. 6–8.
[9] Livy XXI. 57. 4.   [10] III. 75. 5.   [11] III. 77. 1.
[12] XXI. 58. 1–2 and 59. 2–9.   [13] XXI. 63. 1.

the turn of the year' unless Hannibal had arrived in Italy a
good month earlier than my date near the middle of November.

But no one has taken this statement seriously, and it is certainly right not to do so. It occurs in a curious passage quite
unlike Polybius' usual manner. It seems as though, having
brought his two chief actors face to face in Italy (as he himself
remarked),[14] Polybius felt that he was nearing a climax in his
story and that some heightening of the tone, some drama was
called for, so that he embarked on a set rhetorical piece quite
foreign to his temperament. It is almost reminiscent of Livy's
set piece, written perhaps 120 years later, about the reception
of the news of the fall of Saguntum in Rome; and indeed Polybius actually mentions the fall of Saguntum and pretends that
nothing had been heard of Hannibal's movements in Rome
since his capture of the town—as though he himself had not
recorded the Roman reactions to the subsequent news of his
crossing the Ebro and the measures that were taken to meet it.
In the same histrionic vein he proceeds as though nothing had
been reported back by Scipio, and makes out that it was only
after Hannibal had actually arrived in Italy that the Senate,
thunderstruck by the news, ordered the recall of Sempronius.[15]

The whole passage is a tissue of falsities, and every historian
has discounted it in favour of the common-sense view that the
Senate did not wait until Hannibal had arrived in Italy, but
acted as soon as it received Scipio's report that he was on his
way there. The critical point for the timetable, therefore, is not
when *Hannibal* arrived in Italy, but when Scipio got back with
his report. Dunbabin worries quite unnecessarily over the
words, κατὰ τοὺς αὐτοὺς καιρούς, with which Polybius, having
completed his account of Hannibal's crossing the Alps, reverts
to Scipio's actions after he had missed Hannibal on the Rhône,
and tells how he returned by sea to Pisa to take over the command of the garrison troops in Cisalpine Gaul.[16] Dunbabin
goes so far as to calculate that, if the words had to be taken
literally, i.e. if Scipio arrived in Italy at the same time as
Hannibal, he must have taken 28 days on the homeward voyage, although the outward one had taken only 5 days.[17] He
himself recognizes that this cannot have been the case; and it
is obvious that, even if such a loose expression were capable of

[14] III. 57. I.   [15] III. 61. 1–9.   [16] III. 56. 5.   [17] pp. 122–3.

meaning anything so precise, Polybius had no such intention:
he merely inserted the words to make a retrospective transition
in his story from the one topic to the other—as we might say
'meanwhile'. Indeed, he himself makes it plain that Scipio
arrived in Italy well before Hannibal when he records that,
after travelling through Etruria and taking over the frontier
troops who were engaged with the Boii, he marched with
them to the plains of the Po and remained in camp there *waiting*
for the enemy—καταστρατοπεδεύσας ἐπεῖχε τοῖς πολεμίοις.[18]

What, then, does this imply in terms of the timetable?
Scipio had missed Hannibal on the Rhône, according to my
dating, at the beginning of October; since he left the army and
the naval galleys behind and sailed on the return voyage with
only a few men,[19] he would have embarked on a merchant
sailing-ship which could keep the sea night and day, and there
is no reason to suppose that the homeward run of 300 sea miles
in a single vessel—with the prevailing wind in his favour—took him
longer than the outward voyage of 4 to 5 days by a large fleet
keeping company, including sixty naval galleys which probably
had to put into shore each night.* He would therefore have got
back to Pisa by the middle of October; his report would have
reached Rome in a day or two; the Senate would have acted
at once in such an urgent matter; and the order of recall would
have taken perhaps another 10 days to reach Sempronius at
Lilybaeum. We may conclude, therefore, that Sempronius had
received the order and was in a position to send his troops off
on their homeward journey before the end of October.

If this, then, is accepted as the datum-line for subsequent
stages of the timetable, the next question we have to ask is:
how did Sempronius move his army from Lilybaeum to Ariminum? Are we to accept Livy's version that they went by sea
or Polybius' story of the journey by land? Dunbabin thinks the
former, chiefly because he finds the timetable for a land journey
too tight, whereas the sea voyage could have been made,
according to him, in 19 days;[20] and Sempronius could have
joined forces with Scipio at Placentia before the end of Novem-

---

[18] III. 56. 6.   [19] Polybius III. 49. 3–4 and 56. 5.   [20] p. 125.

* The question of Scipio's fleet on the outward voyage will be discussed more fully
in Part II.

ber. But Sempronius, it is clear, was in a hurry to force the issue
as soon as he arrived, and there is nothing in the narrative to
suggest that he had been at Placentia for nearly a month before
he fell into Hannibal's trap and fought the battle of the Trebia
around the turn of the year. Moreover, it was very near the
close of the sailing season on 11 November, and the seas at that
time of year were already considered dangerous,[21] as Dunbabin
himself admits.[22] It is not likely that Sempronius would have
run the risk of losing the whole of his army by shipwreck in the
stormy Adriatic so late in the season. But the strongest argument
against Livy's version is Polybius' story of the soldiers being put
on oath to report at Ariminum on a certain day, which is too
curious and too circumstantial to have been invented. Everything points, therefore, to accepting his rather than Livy's
version, and we will now examine it more closely.

Dunbabin says that the distance by land from Lilybaeum to
Ariminum is about 1,330 kilometres, and he remarks that, if the
troops really covered the distance in 40 days, 'no historian seems
to have noticed that it was one of the greatest marches in
history.'[23] But the truth is, it was not a march at all: it was a
mass walk, and, as such, it was perfectly feasible, given the
urgency. Once Sempronius had decided against sending the
army by sea, he knew very well that the quickest way of getting
his soldiers to Ariminum was to let them travel as individuals
with a time limit on the journey. Anyone who has ever taken
part in a route march knows that it is far from the fastest way
of getting from one place to another on foot, and the Roman
marching routine was a particularly rigid one, as I have several
times pointed out. The requirement of a fortified camp for
each day's halt might have been relaxed on a march through
Italy, but the authorities would still have been responsible for
victualling and accommodation, whether in camp or in billets.
It was far simpler, and quicker, to let the men fend for themselves for board and lodging on the journey and make their own
way to the destination.

The norm for a day's march, as I have previously mentioned,
was 20 kilometres, or rather more on good roads and in good
conditions; to cover a distance of over 1,300 kilometres in 40
days (or only 32 if a rest day was taken every 4 or 5 days, as

[21] Vegetius, *Epitoma Rei Militaris*, IV. 39.   [22] p. 125.   [23] p. 124.

Veith thinks was normal)[24] would indeed have been impossible
for a Roman army; but for an individual pedestrian an average
of 33 kilometres a day is within Herodotus' standard of 35
kilometres a day for an ordinary traveller.[25] It is, admittedly, a
fast rate to keep up for 40 days on end, but it is clear from the
context that Sempronius' men were being stretched to do it,
and that it was regarded as a feat to achieve it. That they did
travel individually, not as a body, is made quite clear, not only
by the story of their being put on oath, which would have made
little sense if they were marching under discipline, but also by
the words which Polybius uses to describe the end of the
journey: he speaks of their having 'collected'—ἀσθροισθέντων—
on the due day and of Sempronius then 'taking them over'—
ἀναλαβών—and the word he uses to describe their 40-day walk
is the unusual one, πεπεζοπορηκότων, which means simply
'travelling on foot' and is not a word he would have used if they
had been marching in military formation.[26] It is therefore quite
extraordinary that the commentators should have missed
what was staring them in the face and boggled over this so-
called march.

De Sanctis, however, as well as Dunbabin does so, and invents a totally fictitious timetable of his own to account for it.
Since the troops could not have marched as a body from Lilybaeum to Ariminum in 40 days, he says that Polybius must have
meant the 40 days to count from Rhegium,[27] though why this
should be so when Polybius distinctly said it was from Lilybaeum,[28] or why De Sanctis should have chosen to fasten the
40 days on Rhegium rather than any other place on the route,
he does not explain. Walbank, however, echoes the master's
voice and proclaims De Sanctis's conclusion that it was 40 days
from Rhegium and therefore, by a proportion sum, 60 days
from Lilybaeum.[29]

It is true that Polybius neglected the ferry across the straits
of Messina when he spoke of the men walking 40 days on end
from Lilybaeum, and this, no doubt, was De Sanctis's reason
for making his 40 days start from Rhegium on the Italian shore
of the straits. But the ferry was an incident of the journey

---

[24] pp. 422–3.   [25] Herodotus iv. 101 (see p. 30 above).
[26] iii. 68. 13–14.   [27] pp. 27 and 85.
[28] iii. 68. 14.   [29] Note on Polybius iii. 68. 14.

whatever time is allotted to it; the soldiers had already walked from one end of Sicily to the other before they got there; and Polybius expressly included this in his total. Difficulties have also been felt about his statement that Sempronius and his troops passed through Rome on their way,[30] in view of the fact that a consul was not allowed to march through Rome with his army except in a duly authorized triumph; but these too evaporate, once it is realized that Sempronius was merely travelling with his men, not marching at their head.

There is no reason, therefore, why we should not accept Polybius' version of the 40-day walk, which would have brought Sempronius and his army to Ariminum early in December on our timetable, and to Placentia 250 kilometres further on within the next fortnight. This is quite in harmony with the statement of Polybius and Livy that the battle of the Trebia took place around the winter solstice, provided the expression is not taken too literally. But since there has been a tendency to do so, it is necessary to say something about this.

De Sanctis, in his schematic way, enunciates the proposition that, since there must have been, according to him, an interval of two and a half months (on one assumption) or three and a half (on another) between Hannibal's crossing of the Alps near the setting of the Pleiades and the battle of the Trebia around the winter solstice, 'of the two astronomical dates given by Polybius one at least should not be interpreted with too much rigour'; and he proceeds to argue that, of the two, it is 'the expression συνάπτειν of the setting of the Pleiades which is to be understood in an approximate sense',[31] thereby making precisely the wrong choice of the one to discount. I have already given my reasons for not granting too much latitude to the word συνάπτειν in this context; and, as for the setting of the Pleiades itself, this is a definite event which can be verified by anyone who looks at the stars in a clear sky just before sunrise, whereas there is absolutely no way of telling which is the shortest day of the year by observation.

The change in the length of the day at that season of the year is imperceptible; the difference between 15 December and 15 January is only 25 minutes even in our latitude, and in the

---

[30] III. 68. 12 and Walbank's note thereon.   [31] p. 86.

Mediterranean it is less. Nor could the winter solstice be assigned any fixed date in the calendar at that period; for the calendar years before the reform of Julius Caesar consisted alternately of 355 and 377 or 378 days, with a further adjustment to bring them into line with the sun over a 24-year cycle.[32] Even after the Julian Calendar had been introduced the Romans put the winter solstice rather later than we do: both Varro[33] and Pliny[34] gave the calendar date as 25 December. Polybius' reference to 'the turn of the year' and Livy's to 'the time of the shortest day' could have applied equally well at any time between mid-December and mid-January, and, as far as this is concerned, the battle of the Trebia could have taken place on any day within that period; indeed, the description of the bitter cold, rain, and snow suggests that, if anything, it was in early January rather than December.

But now, with the mention of the Roman calendar, we have another obstacle to surmount. The intercalary month of 22 or 23 days, which the *pontifices* were supposed to proclaim every other year at the end of February to bring the months roughly into line with the sun, sometimes got omitted—to such an extent that by the time of Julius Caesar, when the calendar had become a political cat's paw, three such months altogether had been omitted, and Caesar had to add 67 days to the year before introducing the new one. Some such disorder must have been developing at the time of the Second Punic War, for in 191 B.C. a law was passed giving the *Pontifex Maximus* sole power to rectify it. There is a school of thought, therefore, which holds that the calendar in 218–17 B.C. was already over two months ahead of the sun, and that the winter solstice fell on a calendar date at the beginning of March; or, as H. J. Mueller put it the other way round, that the Ides of March, the date on which the new consuls took office, 'fell in the middle of January a few weeks after the elections'.[35] And it is argued that this is why Livy said 'the time of the elections was near'—*tempus propincum comitiorum* —[36] and Polybius said 'this was the time'—οὗτος γὰρ ἦν ὁ χρόνος[37]—for the consuls' change of office, to explain why

[32] J. E. Sandys, *Companion to Latin Studies*, 1921, p. 93.
[33] *De Re Rustica, Capitula Libri Primi.*   [34] *HN* XVIII. 25. 220.
[35] Note on Livy XXI. 53. 6 in his recension of Weissenborn's edition, 1885, etc.
[36] XXI. 53. 6.   [37] III. 70. 7.

Sempronius wanted to force the issue at the battle of the
Trebia around the turn of the year.

This was Kahrstedt's view of these particular events.[38] But
De Sanctis would have none of it, and rebuked Kahrstedt for
accepting it. 'The testimony of Polybius', he said, 'presupposes
that the calendar year was in order, or in arrear, at the most,
by one or two months'.[39] His argument is difficult to follow.
One feels either that it was meant as a joke or else that it is
simply fallacious. On the other hand, one's confidence in
Kahrstedt's accuracy is not enhanced when one finds him
speaking of the winter solstice as the winter 'equinox'—*Tag und
Nachtgleiche*. I shall therefore not enter into this highly technical
disputation; and fortunately there is no need to do so, for Livy
and Polybius provide a perfectly clear answer to it, at least as
far as this particular year was concerned.

Livy, as I have mentioned, tells us explicitly that Sempronius
was still consul when, after a period in winter quarters,[40] he
fought an indecisive engagement with Hannibal's forces 'at
the first dubious signs of spring'—*ad prima ac dubia signa veris*[41]—
before his successor, Flaminius, took over the command of his
army on the Ides of March;[42] and Polybius, though he does
not refer in so many words to a period in winter quarters, says
that the Roman forces 'were all collected in the towns' after
the battle of the Trebia. He describes the energetic measures
taken by the Senate when it realized the gravity of the situation,[43] which clearly implied an appreciable interval before
military operations were resumed 'when spring was coming in'
—ἐνισταμένης τῆς ἐαρινῆς ὥρας.[44] It is obvious that, whether
Sempronius continued for a short time in charge of the new
operations, as Livy said, or whether, as Polybius recorded, the
new consuls had taken over before they began, both writers
assumed a considerable fallow period between the battle of
the Trebia and the beginning of spring; and that for them, as
for us, 'the turn of the year' or 'the time of the shortest day'
meant, in that year at least, a calendar date in late December
or the beginning of January.

There can be no doubt about the fact that the consular year
at that period began on 15 March: it is attested by two other

[38] pp. 370–1.   [39] pp. 80–7.   [40] xxi. 56. 8 and 57. 5.
[41] xxi. 58. 2 and 59. 2.   [42] xxi. 63. 1.   [43] iii. 75. 3–4.   [44] iii. 77. 1.

references in Livy,[45] besides his explicit statement on this occasion that the new consul, Flaminius, took up his command on the Ides of March. The elections of the new consuls were held by the outgoing ones quite near the end of their own year of office, usually on their return from the season's campaign,[46] as happened on this occasion when Sempronius returned to Rome to hold them after the battle of the Trebia. It is not clear, therefore, why Hallward should have inferred that the battle of the Trebia 'cannot be later than December' from the fact that the election of Flaminius for 217 B.C. must have followed it[47] unless he was basing his argument on the theory that the calendar was some two months ahead of the seasons; but this reading of the calendar is disproved, as we have just seen, by the evidence of Polybius and Livy.

Livy, after all, only said that the time of *the elections*, not the date of the change of office, was near when the battle of the Trebia was fought; and if Hallward, like Kahrstedt, was influenced by Polybius' statement that this was the time for the change of office, neither of them should have been. The remark arose directly out of Scipio's advice to Sempronius, recorded by Polybius just before, that it would be better to wait 'until after the armies had *wintered*'—τὰ στρατόπεδα χειμασκήσαντα[48]— before accepting a pitched battle with Hannibal. Sempronius knew that to fight a battle before the troops retired to winter quarters was his only chance of winning a victory during his consulship, and this is what Polybius had in mind when he said this was the time for the change of office.

We may conclude, therefore—to sum up this long postscript to the story of Hannibal's march—that everything falls into place on a straightforward interpretation of the narrative of events after the march was over; that the change of consuls and the resumption of military operations in the early spring of 217 B.C. were preceded by a normal period of about two months in winter quarters; that 'the turn of the year' and 'the time of the shortest day' meant much the same to Polybius and Livy (though something not quite so precise) as they do to us; and that, whether the battle of the Trebia was in late December or early in January, the time that elapsed after Hannibal's

---

[45] XXII. 1. 4 and XXXI. 5. 2.   [46] Pauly-Wissowa, *Consul*, Col. 115.
[47] *CAH*, Vol. 8, p. 42.   [48] III. 70. 4.

crossing of the Alps early in November was 'neither too short nor too long'—to borrow De Sanctis's phrase—to cover the transfer of Sempronius' army from Lilybaeum and its junction with Scipio's army at Placentia shortly before the battle.

X

CONCLUSIONS ON CHRONOLOGY

I N the last chapter, about events after the march was over, I
cleared the thickets from the end of the runway and so
made sure that the touch-down could be accepted at any
time up to the middle of November. It remains to sum up the
results of our investigation.

We began by asking why it was that Hannibal seemed to
have waited so long before setting out on his dangerous march,
and the upshot of our review of all that had to happen before
the march began was that it was hard to see how he could have
started any earlier than he did. All the same, though I en-
deavoured to make realistic estimates of the time which the
various antecedent events must have taken, and though they
added up, on my reckoning, to a period from the fall of Saguntum in late December to a date near the middle of June, the
estimates were necessarily conjectural, and in point of fact only
the last event, the return of the messengers from Cisalpine
Gaul, was an effective determinant of the starting date of the
march. For, even if the previous episodes—the numbering of
the tribesmen, Hannibal's journey to Cadiz and back, the
trooping operations between Spain and North Africa, and the
arrival of the report from Carthage of the Roman declaration
of war—were contained within a shorter period of time than I
have assumed, Hannibal still waited for the return of the messengers before collecting his troops and announcing his plan
of invading Italy, and it was their arrival at Cartagena which
was the last and proximate cause of the start of the march.
This, therefore, is the critical point in our timetable for the
beginning of the march, and it behoves us to scrutinize it with
special care.

It may be objected that Hannibal need not have waited for
the fall of Saguntum before sending his messengers on their way,
and that in any case they would have made better speed on the
journey than I have reckoned, so that for either or both of these

reasons they would have got back to Cartagena well before my date near the end of May. Though it seems unlikely that Hannibal would have proceeded so far in his plan of invading Italy as to dispatch the messengers before he had extirpated the doughty Saguntines on his line of march from Cartagena, and though any faster estimate of their rate of progress would seem less realistic than mine, neither hypothesis can be dismissed out of hand. Let us, however, leave the question in the air for the time being and move to the other end of the timetable. Let us adopt at this point the procedure of all other constructors of timetables and work backwards from an assumed end-date of the march, and we will also allow ourselves here to suggest some hypothetical calendar dates to give precision to the argument.

Whatever date is taken to be the end-date of the march, it determines within narrow limits two previous dates in the course of the march: first, moving backwards in time, that of the battle between the Roman and the Carthaginian cavalry near Hannibal's camp on the left bank of the Rhône—for a period of 32 days on the march plus an unspecified halt at the 'Island' is itemized in Polybius' narrative between then and the end of the march; and secondly, the date of the start from Cartagena—for both Polybius and Livy say that the march lasted five months. The latter date is less precise than the former, for 'five months' may have been a round figure for anything between four and a half and five and a half months, while Appian's figure some 200 years later was six; but the tolerance for the date of the cavalry battle is no greater than the margin to be added for the halt at the 'Island', which I have assumed to have been 3 or 4 days, making a total of, say, 36 days for the whole of the rest of the march. The date of the cavalry battle, the point of intersection between any timetable of Hannibal's march and that of the concurrent events in Rome and Italy, determines in turn within equally narrow limits the date of a third significant event, Scipio's embarkation from Pisa, for the cavalry battle was not more than 2 or 3 days after his arrival at the mouth of the Rhône, and the voyage from Pisa had taken only 5 days.

It was close to the setting of the Pleiades when the army was on the final pass across the Alps, and I trust that the idea that this denoted a date in mid-September need no longer be entertained. I shall hope to have carried the reader with me if I now declare without more ado that 'the setting of the Pleiades' meant for Polybius and the Romans a date around 7 November, and that the only question calling for discussion is how close to that date was the closeness indicated by Polybius' expression διὰ τὸ συνάπτειν. Dunbabin thought that it might have been anything up to three weeks beforehand, and his own date was 19 October. I have given my reasons for thinking this too wide a margin, but I shall nevertheless stretch it still further to give every possible benefit of the doubt to an earlier timetable; I shall take the date to have been 16 October, that is, at the halfway line beyond which any reference to the time of year would have been expressed in terms of the autumnal equinox, and the setting of the Pleiades would not have been mentioned at all. On this basis, since the descent to the plains of the Po took 8 days, the march would have ended on 24 October—between a fortnight and three weeks earlier than my date near the middle of November. Let us now work backwards from there and check our results against this hypothetical time-table.

The cavalry battle, fought on the eve of Hannibal's departure for the last 36 days of the march, would have taken place, on this assumption, on 17 September, and if Scipio's sailing date from Pisa is put, say, 8 days before that, it would have been about 9 September, compared with my date near the end of that month. To advance the date still further, I shall assume (though the advocates of earlier timetables have scouted the suggestion themselves) that it took Scipio two and a half months, instead of the two which I previously assumed, to get his army ready for embarkation from the moment when the news of Hannibal's crossing the Ebro triggered off the revolt of the Boii; in other words, that the news was received in Italy about 26 June, in which case, if it took, say, a week to get there, Hannibal would have crossed the Ebro on about 19 June, compared with my date near the middle of July. Even so, since the march of 480 kilometres to the Ebro through open country under Carthaginian control cannot have taken more than the 24 days which I have allowed for it, Hannibal would not have started from Cartagena before 26 May, which is still, despite all the bisques I have conceded to earlier timetables, less than three weeks before my starting date in mid-June.

This means—to return now to the point at which we broke off to explore this hypothetical timetable—that, if we assume the same interval of about a fortnight as I previously allowed for the final preparations for the march after the return of Hannibal's messengers, they cannot on any hypothesis consistent with a tenable end-date of the march have got back to Cartagena before 12 May, and the difference between this and my date for their return near the end of the month is all the scope there is for variations of the timetable based on different views about the timing of their journey. Hannibal *may* have dispatched them to Cisalpine Gaul sooner than I said, they *may* have made better speed than I imagined; it will still not help to advance the starting date of the march by anything significantly more than the margin of error of all such estimates.

I certainly would not claim greater precision than a similar tolerance for my starting-date in mid-June: Hannibal may well have started somewhat earlier, as one would naturally have expected. The date is put forward in no dogmatic spirit: it is merely the end-result of the best estimates I could make of the previous time spans, and I may well have erred at one or more points in the compilation. All I would say about it is, that the method is the right one whether or not the execution has been faulty; and that, if any earlier date is to be established, it must be done by showing that the antecedent events which we have considered could have happened sooner than I have reckoned, not by crudely counting backwards five months from an arbitrarily chosen end-date, which is the method generally adopted.

I may, for instance, have been over-generous in allowing a fortnight for the final preparations for the march between Hannibal's address to the troops and the start of it; this and a dozen such adjustments of my guesswork could bring the starting-date forward to a date at the end of May without impairing the structure of the timetable, which I have never sought to specify in terms of dates in a month. A starting-date near the end of May would answer as well as mine to Polybius' description of the march from Cartagena to the Ebro 'at the beginning of summer'—perhaps even better, since it would not require us to presume such a long interval after 'the rising of the Pleiades' near the middle of the month. It would actually ease some problems too, for I have cut the timetable rather fine in allowing no more than a bare two months for Hannibal's subjugation of the tribes north of the Ebro and the subsequent pause for consolidation at the Pyrenees; and the same length of time is all I have been able to spare for all the commotions in Italy between the outbreak of the revolt of the Boii and Scipio's eventual embarkation from Pisa. Two and a half months rather than two would give more elbow room in both cases, and the resulting figure of five and a half months for the duration of the whole march (assuming the same end-date near the middle of November) would still not infringe Polybius' round figure of five: it would, indeed, go half-way to bridge the gap between his figure and Appian's.

Thus it may be felt on reflection that, if five and a half rather than five months can be granted for the whole march, Hannibal in northern Spain and Scipio in Italy stand more in need of the extra time than the messengers from Cisalpine Gaul, and I am quite content to leave this an open choice for the reader. The diary of events in Rome and the second embassy to Carthage up to the time of Hannibal's crossing the Ebro— or rather, up to the receipt of the news in Italy—can be adjusted to fit whatever date between the end of May and the middle of June is accepted for the start of the march, since the timing in this part of Polybius' and Livy's narrative is quite indeterminate. What is not indeterminate is the correlation between Hannibal's march and events in Italy *after* the crossing of the Ebro, for the two timetables in this period are linked by the same chain of causation, as I have shown. They are bound at the other end by a date for Hannibal's crossing of the pass which in my view cannot have been much before the end of October and was more probably early in November—for, if one thing is more certain than another, it is that this is what 'the setting of the Pleiades' meant—with the corollary that the end of the march on the plains of the Po was not much before the middle of November.

The claim I make for my timetable—which cannot be made for any other—is that it is consistent with the only two direct statements made by Polybius about the timing of the march, first, that it began at the beginning of summer, and, secondly, that it ended close to the setting of the Pleiades. It is equally consistent with the other indications of dating provided by him and Livy—except perhaps the much-discounted, though little-discussed, expression ὑπὸ τὴν ὡραίαν for Scipio's sailing date—if only these are read in a straightforward way without preconceived ideas of what the timetable *ought* to have been. Indeed, this long-drawn-out discussion would hardly have been necessary at all if the commentators had attended to the narrative of what took place instead of skimming over detailed facts without attempting to relate them to a time span, and twisting statements out of their natural sense to fit some schematic timetable. No question of source criticism arises here, for Polybius and Livy are in agreement on the main features of the timetable (in the few places where they are not, I have given my reasons for preferring one rather than the other). So the result of the whole discussion is simply to clear away the accretions which have grown up like a fungus on the original outline, and to show that the account of the timing of the march given by Polybius and Livy is truer to the facts than any of the glosses that have been put on it since.

PART II

GEOGRAPHY

I

POLYBIUS'
GEOGRAPHICAL DISTANCES

WHEN Polybius had brought Hannibal as far as the Pyrenees and described how he paused there for consolidation and regrouping of forces, he paused in his own narrative to give a dissertation on geography and a description of the countries of the western Mediterranean, and he ended it with a conspectus of the distances involved in Hannibal's march.[1] His notions of the geography were somewhat distorted, for he shared the usual conception of early cartographers that the countries on the north shore of the Mediterranean were arranged like spokes of a wheel radiating from a centre in Switzerland, so that he thought the Rhône flowed in a south-westerly direction from the Alps to the sea and spoke of Hannibal following it upstream towards the east and the centre of Europe;[2] but his figures for the distances, at least as far as the Rhône, are remarkably accurate. They are expressed in round hundreds of stades, which, since 100 stades was only about 18 kilometres, is a comparatively fine scale, the tolerance being only about 9 kilometres each way, irrespective of the distance measured.

From Cartagena to Ampurias at the foot of the Pyrenees he gives the distance as 4,200 stades, or 750 kilometres, compared with the actual distance of a little over 760 kilometres. From there to the Rhône-crossing at Beaucaire–Tarascon (begging the question for the moment whether this was *Hannibal's* crossing-place) his figure of 1,600 stades, or 286 kilometres, is almost exact; and either Polybius himself shortly before he died or an early editor of his text added a sentence to the effect that the figure was corroborated by the measured miles of the *Via Domitia* when the road was constructed along the same route around 120 B.C.[3]

---

[1] III. 39. 6–11.   [2] III. 47. 1–2.   [3] III. 39. 8.

Up to this point his figures are given as simple measurements of the distances between places, but from the Rhône onwards they are evidently intended to refer to the route taken by Hannibal, not the direct road to Italy, and since there is no agreement about what his route was, they cannot be checked conclusively against distances on the map. Polybius gives his first measurement after the Rhône-crossing as 1,400 stades, or 250 kilometres, 'following the river itself up-stream as far as the climb of the Alps into Italy',[4] which corresponds with his description later on of Hannibal following the Rhône up-stream after the crossing;[5] whereas Strabo says that the road to Italy left the Rhône at this point and either went by way of Cavaillon to the upper reaches of the Durance and over the Col de Montgenèvre (the shortest route) or else took a more southerly route through Aix and Antibes to the Ligurian coast road.[6] Strabo gives the distance by the shortest road as 63 Roman miles, or 93 kilometres, from the Rhône-crossing at Tarascon to 'the beginning of the ascent of the Alps'—almost the same expression as Polybius used for the end-point of his measurement—and the big disparity between the figures is enough to show that this cannot have been Hannibal's route.

Polybius' final measurement is 1,200 stades, or 214 kilometres, for 'the crossing of the Alps', which, he says, Hannibal 'had to cross to arrive on the plains of the Po in Italy',[7] and since this last expression is the only description he gives of the end-point of his measurement, its position cannot be pinpointed. Its location, and with it the age-long question of Hannibal's pass over the Alps, was already being disputed at the time of Livy and has been ever since. Later on in his narrative Polybius said that Hannibal 'descended into the plains of the Po *and the territory of the Insubres*',[8] who were settled round Milan, and this has led some later commentators to conclude that he must have crossed the Alps by the Little or Great St. Bernard and come down the long Valle d'Aosta to Ivrea;[9] but this would have brought him down into the territory of the

---

[4] III. 39. 9.   [5] III. 47. 1.   [6] Strabo IV. 1. 3 and 1. 12.
[7] III. 39. 10.   [8] III. 56. 3.
[9] e.g. Edward Gibbon, *Miscellaneous Works*, 2nd edn., Vol. 5, 1814, pp. 370–2; J. A. de Luc, *Histoire du Passage des Alpes par Annibal*, 1818, pp. 139–43; Th. Mommsen, *History of Rome*, 1862–75, tr. Dickson, Vol. 2, p. 106; W. W. Hyde, *Roman Alpine Routes*, 1935, p. 205.

Salassi, not the Insubres; from there he would have had to pass through the territory of two other tribes, the Laevi and the Libici, before he reached the latter; and even if these were subordinate tribes of the Insubres, as is sometimes said, Polybius himself had regarded them as sufficiently distinct to locate their territories, in an earlier conspectus of north Italian geography, between that of the Insubres and the sources of the Po [10]—in other words, between them and the western Alps.

The fact is that, whichever way Hannibal came, the territory of the Insubres cannot have been the scene of his arrival in Italy, and this must be written off as one of Polybius' carelessly misleading remarks. Livy, at any rate, would have none of it: he declared that it was 'agreed by all'—*cum inter omnes constet*— that Hannibal's touch-down in Italy was in the territory of the Taurini;[11] and Strabo quoted from Polybius himself a statement that Hannibal's pass led into their territory as distinct from the one that led into that of the Salassi,* though no such statement is to be found in the part of his *History* which has come down to us, but only in a later digest of one of the lost books.[12]

Everything else in Polybius' narrative bears this out. He relates how, on reaching the plain, Hannibal first camped and rested his men 'at the foot of the Alps'[13] and then, having made unavailing overtures to the Taurini, whom Polybius also describes as living 'near the foot of the mountains',[14] besieged and captured their chief town; and there is no mention of any intermediate march. The 'chief town' of the Taurini must have been at or near the modern Turin, and this fixes Hannibal's route across the Alps somewhere in the Cottian Alps, which form an arc at a radius of about 70 kilometres from Turin as the crow flies; for the Great and Little St. Bernard are much further to the north, and Turin could not have been his first objective if he had descended into Italy from either of them.

A consideration of the time span of the march points to the

[10] II. 17. 4.   [11] XXI. 38. 5–6.
[12] Strabo IV. 6. 12 and Polybius XXXIV. 10. 18.
[13] III. 60. 2.   [14] III. 60. 8.

---

* Though the words referring to Hannibal—ἦν Ἀννίβας διῆλθεν—do not occur in all the MSS., both De Sanctis (p. 65) and Walbank (*JRS*, p. 44) have accepted them as genuine.

same conclusion. According to Polybius' narrative, only 4 days were spent in actual movement from the top of the pass to the end of the march on the plains of the Po,[15] which puts a limit of about 70 kilometres on the distance, for the army, after all its privations in the mountains, can hardly have averaged more than 18 kilometres a day on a section which included the difficult first part of the descent; but it would have had to travel a much longer distance from either the Great or the Little St. Bernard down the Valle d'Aosta before it reached the 'plains of the Po'.

We shall consider the question of Hannibal's route over the Alps more fully later on; for the moment we are only concerned to fix an approximate end-point of the march. The actual routes from the passes over the Cottian Alps to Turin down the mountain valleys and through the foothills are naturally a good deal longer than the distance of 70 kilometres as the crow flies. Those from the Mont Cenis, the Montgenèvre, and the Col de la Traversette—to take these as a representative spread of the passes at about that radius from Turin—range between 80 and 100 kilometres. If, therefore, we take 70 kilometres as a working assumption for the distance travelled by the army from the summit of the pass before it camped on the plains of the Po, we might put the end-point of Polybius' measurement somewhere around 20 kilometres short of Turin, which fits reasonably well his account of the storming of the chief town of the Taurini directly after the halt in camp.

Strabo's route by the shortest road from Tarascon into Italy crossed the Alps by the Montgenèvre, and he took as its end-point the town of Ocelum,[16] which was also Julius Caesar's point of departure for the crossing of the Alps on his first expedition into Gaul.[17] Ocelum has not been certainly identified, but, since Strabo says that it was 28 Roman miles, or 41 kilometres, inside Italy,[16] it must have been somewhere between Susa and Turin. Strabo's figure for the total distance from Tarascon to Ocelum was 261 Roman miles, or 385 kilometres, which is almost exactly the distance by the modern roads over the same route to the village of Avigliana, 23 kilometres short of Turin on the Susa–Turin road, which some writers have

---

[15] III. 54. 4–7 and 56. 1.   [16] IV. 1. 3.   [17] *De Bello Gallico* I. 10. 4–5.

positively identified with Ocelum. Whether or not the two places were one and the same, Strabo's Ocelum must have been somewhere in that neighbourhood; and the fact that he made this the end-point of his measurement tallies with my suggestion that the end-point of Polybius' measurement might also be put at about that range from Turin. Polybius' figure for the total distance from the Rhône-crossing to the plains of the Po was 464 kilometres, and the difference between this and Strabo's figure of 385 kilometres by the shortest road is the measure of the diversion which Hannibal incurred when he followed the Rhône up-stream to avoid Scipio instead of taking the direct road to Italy.[18]

The total amount of his deviations would be more than doubled if some editors had their way. Polybius' figures for the separate sections do not add up to the total he gives for the whole march, 'about 9,000 stades':[19] they are 600 stades, or 107 kilometres, short; and a section of this length is sometimes inserted in modern editions on the ground that it must have dropped out of the text which has come down to us. The favourite place for such an insertion is between Ampurias and Narbonne. But this cannot be accepted, since it would falsify Polybius' figure for the distance from Ampurias to the Rhône, which, as we have seen, is remarkably accurate, as well as being corroborated by the milestones on the *Via Domitia*, and there is no reason to suppose that Hannibal deviated from the direct route on this part of the march. He must, indeed, have made many detours between the Ebro and the Pyrenees in the two months during which he was fighting his way through the Spanish tribes, but an insertion of 107 kilometres there would equally falsify Polybius' figure at a place where he was plainly recording geographical distances, not particulars of the actual march. Yet the missing 107 kilometres cannot have dropped out of the figures for the march from the Rhône-crossing onwards: for it is inconceivable that Hannibal should have gone the best part of 200 kilometres out of his way over a distance of 385 kilometres by the direct route, and no editor has suggested such an absurdity. The simplest explanation, as Walbank suggested,[20] is probably the best: that Polybius was giving a

---

[18] Polybius III. 47. 1 and Livy XXI. 31. 2.   [19] III. 39. 11.
[20] Note on Polybius III. 39.

round figure in thousands for the total (which he qualified as 'about'), just as he quoted the intermediate distances in round hundreds, and that he preferred rounding up to rounding down. This, at any rate, seems a safer conclusion than any tampering with the individual figures.

These, then, were the distances which Polybius gave in summary form to place the whole march in perspective for his readers before he embarked on the part of it in which he, like ourselves, was mainly interested—the march through southern France across the Rhône and then across the Alps to the plains of the Po. The picture they present of this part of the march is clear enough in outline: first a straight unimpeded transit of about 270 kilometres after the crossing of the Pyrenees along the regular route through Languedoc to the crossing of the Rhône; then a deviation away from the coast to avoid Scipio, involving a march of about 250 kilometres to a point which Polybius called the climb of the Alps into Italy; finally a section of about 214 kilometres over the Alps to a destination which we will assume to have been about 20 kilometres short of Turin. This is the broad framework provided by Polybius, but some more detailed (though not always very transparent) information about internal distances emerges in the course of the narrative, to which we shall now turn.

II

THE RHÔNE-CROSSING

ALL authorities, from Strabo onwards, have agreed that the main road from Spain to Provence, originally the ancient Iberian Way, later the Roman *Via Domitia*, crossed the Rhône at or near Beaucaire–Tarascon,[1] and I have assumed that this was Hannibal's crossing-place in the foregoing discussion of Polybius' geographical distances. But the prevailing view among modern historians is that he crossed the Rhône anything between 40 and 75 kilometres further upstream, somewhere on the stretch of river between Roquemaure and Pont St. Esprit, roughly straddling Orange on the opposite bank. This is because most writers, for reasons which I shall discuss in due course,[2] identify the 'Island', which the army reached after a 4-day march from the crossing-place,[3] with the confluence of the Rhône and the Isère a little way above Valence; and since it is deduced from certain of Polybius' measurements, which I shall also discuss later on,[4] that the crossing-place was about 107 kilometres from the 'Island', it is regarded as tethered by a string of that length to Pont de l'Isère in the junction of those two rivers. This view is upheld by those, like Marquion, who regard such a distance as a comfortable 4-day march for an army (or, at least, for one that is thought to have been hurrying to avoid Scipio), and it is supported by reference to Polybius' statement that the crossing-place was also about 4 days' march from the sea,[5] showing (it is said) that it must have been about half-way between Pont de l'Isère and the sea.

This body of opinion, among whose exponents are Kahr-

---

[1] e.g. Strabo IV. 1. 3 and 1. 12; G. de Manteyer, *La Voie fluviale du Rhône et ses chemins primitifs*, 1945, pp. 36–42; Camille Jullian, *Histoire de la Gaule*, Vol. 1, 1908, pp. 464–6; M. Cary, *The Geographical Background of Greek and Roman History*, 1949, p. 254.

[2] pp. 131–9, below.   [3] Polybius III. 49. 5 and Livy XXI. 31. 4.
[4] pp. 159–63, below.   [5] III. 42. 1.

stedt,[6] De Sanctis,[7] and Walbank,[8] as well as Marquion,[9] constitutes what may be called the 'long distance' school of
thought, for their views about the length of a 4-day march of an
army hang together with their basic premiss that the 'Island'
was in the confluence of the Rhône and the Isère; and their
various locations of the crossing-place are primarily the result
of deductions from the same basic premiss. We shall discuss
their views more fully when we come to the next stage of the
march, with which they are mainly concerned. For the present,
we have a more limited objective—to examine the evidence in
Polybius and Livy about the crossing itself, which few of those
who rely on these essentially arithmetical arguments to fix its
position have troubled to do. Only Walbank and Marquion
among them, in fact, have made any attempt to justify their
choice of a crossing-place higher up-stream than Beaucaire–
Tarascon by reference to considerations relating specifically
to this phase of the march.

Though their length of string obviously would not stretch
as far as Beaucaire–Tarascon, about 160 kilometres from Pont
de l'Isère (or anywhere appreciably beyond 100 kilometres),
Walbank and Marquion do nevertheless recognize that it is
necessary to explain why, according to them, Hannibal departed
from the direct route of the Iberian Way and went further afield
to a crossing-place over the Rhône some 100 kilometres inland.
Marquion admits that the shortest, easiest route into Italy
was up the valley of the Durance from a Rhône-crossing at
Beaucaire–Tarascon, but makes out that Hannibal was unaware of its existence,[10] though why he should have been left
in ignorance of the best-known route of all when he had sent
messengers ahead to reconnoitre, he does not explain. However,
Marquion soon drops this idea in favour of the theory, which
seems to be also Walbank's view, that Hannibal had always
reckoned with the possibility that the Romans might land an
army in southern Gaul, and had planned from the start to
cross the Rhône well away from the coast, lest his passage of
the river (one of the major obstacles on the march) should be
barred by a Roman army.[11] Marquion appends the rider that,
since the army moved in what he called 'approach formation'

[6] p. 378.   [7] p. 70.   [8] Note on Polybius III. 42. 1 and *JRS*, 1956, p. 42.
[9] p. 33.   [10] p. 79.   [11] pp. 75, 85, 95, and 109–10.

straddling a wide front, Hannibal was not restricted in his
choice of a route to the line of a road [12]—a dubious attraction,
one would have thought, for the foot-soldiers picking their way
across country— and he adds the engaging (but for his theory
necessary) detail that he must have instructed Magilus and the
Boian chieftains who were coming from Cisalpine Gaul to meet
him as to the route he intended to take and the place where they
were to wait for him on the Rhône.[13] Walbank, less confident
than Marquion, admits that 'the regular point for crossing
the Rhône in classical times was Beaucaire–Tarascon', and also
that 'there is nothing in Polybius to indicate that Hannibal
chose an unusual crossing'; but he makes the same conjecture
as Marquion that Hannibal had always planned to strike the
Rhône further north, and declares (as Marquion also does)[14]
that 'neither Polybius nor Livy contains any suggestion that
he changed his original route'.[15]

Now, all this is pure surmise: there is not a shred of evidence
for it in Polybius or Livy, and no unbiased reader of their
accounts of the crossing would derive any such impression from
them. Neither author gives any hint that Hannibal visualized
the possibility of a Roman army landing in France and planned
his route in advance to avoid an encounter; indeed, Livy de-
picts him as being in two minds whether or not to join battle
with Scipio when he heard of his arrival and only being dis-
suaded from doing so by the Boian chieftains[16]—though it is
true that he had negotiated the Rhône-crossing by then. The
Romans, for their part, had no plan of landing an army in
France: Scipio was under orders for Spain, and only anchored
off the mouth of the Rhône as a port of call until he decided to
disembark his troops on learning that Hannibal was already
crossing the Pyrenees;[17] and Hannibal only heard of his arrival
after he himself had crossed the Rhône.[18] He had no reason up
to that point for departing from the shortest, best-known route,
and he would scarcely have surprised Scipio by the speed with
which he covered the ground between the Pyrenees and the
Rhône, as Polybius says he did,[19] if he had taken some longer
route. There is therefore the strongest presumption that he

[12] pp. 84–5.   [13] pp. 80 and 120.   [14] p. 77.
[15] *JRS*, 1956, p. 41.   [16] XXI. 29. 6.   [17] Polybius III. 41. 5–6.
[18] Polybius III. 44. 3.   [19] III. 41. 8.

took the direct route of the Iberian Way as far as the normal
Rhône-crossing at Beaucaire–Tarascon, where the Boian chieftains, who had come by one of the regular routes from Italy,
were waiting for him.[20] Polybius himself evidently thought that
this was his route when he gave a measurement for this section
of the march which was corroborated by the milestones on the
Via Domitia;[21] and if it is asked why in that case did he not
give the name of this well-known crossing-place, the answer is
simply, as he himself explained, that he banished all local
place-names from his narrative on the ground that they would
convey nothing to his metropolitan readers.[22] Livy, writing
perhaps 120 years later, generally gave the names of tribes
rather than of places, and he located Hannibal's crossing-place
in the territory of the Volcae,[23] whose capital was Nîmes, the
last stage-point on the Via Domitia before Beaucaire.

Moreover, Polybius and Livy do contain very clear indications that Hannibal changed direction when he heard the news
of Scipio's arrival, and that he struck up river *after* the Rhône-
crossing to avoid him. Livy makes Hannibal chide his troops,
after the crossing, for keeping their spirits up as long as they
were moving from west to east, but losing heart at the prospect
of changing direction;[24] and he says that Hannibal altered
course after the crossing 'not because it was a more direct way
to the Alps, but because the further he departed from the sea,
the less likely he was to meet the Romans'.[25] Polybius puts the
same suggestion into the mouth of Scipio when he makes him
claim later on that Hannibal had taken fright after the encounter between the two cavalry forces (to which we shall come in a
moment) and retreated on a route through the Alps 'contrary
to his original plan'.[26] Most authorities, including Walbank
himself, agree that this is what Livy was referring to later on
when he spoke of Hannibal 'turning to the left' on leaving the
'Island',[27] and think that he had misplaced in his narrative an
extract from one of his sources which referred to a change of
direction made directly after the Rhône-crossing.[28]

[20] Polybius III. 44. 5 and Livy XXI. 29. 6.   [21] III. 39. 8.
[22] III. 36. 2–4.   [23] XXI. 26. 6.   [24] XXI. 30. 4.
[25] XXI. 31. 2.   [26] III. 64. 7.   [27] XXI. 31. 9.
[28] e.g. Colin p. 372; Kahrstedt, p. 149; De Sanctis, p. 72; Walbank, note on
III. 49. 5 to 56. 4. Devos reaches the same conclusion, though on different grounds,
pp. 77–9.

Polybius says that, when Hannibal was nearing the river, he made for a point where it was in a single stream, about 4 days' march for an army from the sea.[29] The first part of this obviously means a place above the point near Arles where the Rhône divided into several branches before reaching the sea; but the second part is susceptible of the wide differences of opinion about an army's speed of march which we discussed in Part I. These will become significant when we consider the next stage of the march between the crossing-place and the 'Island', but they are much less important, as we shall see, for settling the distance of the crossing-place from the coast. We shall continue, therefore, with our evaluation of the factors relating to the crossing itself and leave till later the more debatable question of the subsequent march to the 'Island'. Whatever may have been the rate of progress of Hannibal's army on that section of the march, we shall find that there are decisive reasons why his crossing-place cannot have been more than 50 to 60 kilometres from the sea.

Since Beaucaire–Tarascon is anything between 55 and 65 kilometres from the sea, according to the point one chooses on the ragged (and shifting) coastline of the Rhône delta, a crossing-place somewhere in that neighbourhood is upheld by those who adopt the shorter range for the distance of a 4-day march of an army, though most of them have their own variations as regards the exact point on the river, based usually on the evidence of the later Roman itineraries of Imperial times. Devos says that the actual crossing of the river by the regular route (and the place where Hannibal crossed) was not from Beaucaire to Tarascon, but 4 to 5 kilometres downstream opposite St. Gabriel, which, under its Latin name, Ernaginum, figures in the later itineraries as the next stage after Beaucaire (Ugernum) by one route, and the next after Arles (Arelatum) by another, whereas Tarascon (Tarusco) is not mentioned in any of them.[30] De Beer thinks Hannibal crossed further downstream between Fourques and Arles (just above the point where in those days the Rhône divided), relying more on the alternative route through Arles shown in some of the itineraries.[31] But both writers seem to overlook the fact that all the itineraries show Nîmes as the previous stage-point on either road when they make Hannibal approach the crossing-place along the western arm of the Rhône from the direction of Aigues–Mortes, which is a most improbable route. Even to this day, after all the modern works of drainage and canalization, it is marshy land on this side of the Rhône all the way from the sea up to Arles, and at that time it must have been quite unfit for the march of an army. The *Via Domitia* struck inland at Ambrussum near Lunel, to avoid the bad going round the Rhône delta, and went through Nîmes, just as the *Route Nationale 113* does now. From Nîmes the original road went straight on to Beaucaire and a Rhône-crossing near there: it was only after Marius had constructed a canal east of the silted-up channels at the mouth of the river to provide a navigable waterway for sea-going ships between Arles and the sea that the branch of the *Via Domitia* to a Rhône-crossing at Arles was opened.[32] But this was more than a hundred years after Hannibal's march, and he is much more likely to have followed the old Iberian Way through Nîmes to a crossing near Beaucaire–Tarascon.

However, these are all comparatively minor refinements. De Beer's crossing-place is only about 9 kilometres from that of Devos, and whether the actual crossing was at Beaucaire–Tarascon or just above Arles or somewhere between the two has no practical significance for the determination of the line of Hannibal's march from the Rhône onwards; they all belong to the same family, as distinct from any of the upstream crossing-places favoured by the other school of historians. I shall continue, therefore, *pace* Devos, to refer to this nexus of possible crossing-places as 'Beaucaire–Tarascon', not with any intention of excluding his more precise definition of the actual spot, but simply because this is the name by which it is generally known to other historians, and it seems more convenient to go on using it as a generic term for any crossing-place in that neighbourhood. Dunbabin sums up the situation when he declares that 'it is certain that the crossing-place could not have been much higher up the Rhone than Tarascon, for it was about four days' march from the sea for an army, i.e. about 40 Roman miles',[33]

---

[32] Strabo IV. 1. 8, and M. Cary, *Geographical Background of Greek and Roman History*, 1949, p. 254.   [33] *CR* 1931, p. 52.

and 40 Roman miles was 59 kilometres. His simple trust in Polybius' statement that the crossing-place was 4 days' march for an army from the sea was a little unguarded, as we shall see later;[34] but there are several other points in Polybius' description which confirm the truth of his conclusion, whatever may be thought of his reasons for it.

When Hannibal had arrived on the right bank of the Rhône and was collecting craft for the crossing, he found that (though he had to construct some rafts to make up the tally for his large army) there were plenty of boats to be had,[35] which shows that it must have been a main river-crossing where ferries were a normal feature; and the next main crossing-place above Beaucaire–Tarascon was over 130 kilometres up-stream at the confluence of the Eyrieux between Montélimar and Valence, with a minor intermediate one at Pont St. Esprit about 80 kilometres away.[36] We shall see in a moment that, when a detachment under Hanno went up-stream to a point some 36 kilometres from the crossing-place, they had to construct all their own rafts to cross the river.[37]

Polybius also says that many of the inhabitants at the crossing-place engaged in trade from the sea,[38] which suggests that it cannot have been very far from the coast; and he goes on to speak of Hannibal, after the crossing, first sending out a cavalry screen 'towards the sea',[39] and then following the main army up-stream himself 'away from the sea';[40] all of which, coupled with Livy's remark which I have mentioned that Hannibal 'retreated from the sea' to avoid the Romans,[41] builds up a strong impression that the sea was not very far away.

I have mentioned Magilus and the Boian chieftains who came from Cisalpine Gaul to meet Hannibal and guide him on his way into Italy, and this, unless one is to accept the fanciful suggestion of Marquion that Hannibal had concerted a meeting-place with them beforehand well away from any of the normal routes, is another circumstance which tells in favour of the crossing-place at Beaucaire–Tarascon. For Hannibal re-

[34] p. 120, below.   [35] Polybius III. 42. 2.
[36] de Manteyer, op. cit., pp. 33–6 and 42.
[37] Polybius III. 42. 8 and Livy XXI. 27. 6.   [38] III. 42. 2.
[39] III. 45. 5.   [40] III. 47. 1.   [41] XXI. 31. 2.

ceived the Boians at his camp on the one day which he spent on the left bank, after crossing the river, before moving upstream,[42] and it would have been an extraordinary coincidence if the Boians happened to arrive from Italy on that very day; obviously they had arrived before and were waiting for him at the river. The natural supposition is that they came by one of the well-known routes across the Alps, most probably by the Col de Montgenèvre and the valley of the Durance, but in any case converging on the regular Rhône-crossing at Beaucaire–Tarascon,[43] which, according to Livy,[44] though modern archaeologists deny it,[45] had been the routes of the original Celtic migrations into Italy nearly 400 years before. Be that as it may, both Polybius[46] and Livy[47] stress how familiar the Cisalpine Gauls were with these routes across the Alps, and it is most unlikely that the Boian chieftains would have accepted instructions from Hannibal to take some other route: they would have come to the crossing-place they knew best, which was Beaucaire–Tarascon.

However, we now have to deal with the account of an episode in the crossing itself which seems at first sight to tell in the opposite direction, for it appears, on the face of it, to contradict Dunbabin's assumption about the length of a day's march of an army and to confirm the much higher figures adopted by the other school of historians, though, strangely enough, it has rarely been quoted in support of their case. Its purport for our geographical purpose must remain doubtful; but it is necessary to deal with it (perhaps at greater length than it deserves) not only because its possible significance from this point of view has generally been overlooked, but also because the actual facts of the episode have been stated differently by different historians, and some discussion of the matter is inevitable. Polybius and Livy themselves, if their words are taken literally, are in agreement about the facts, and I shall first summarize their account of the episode and then discuss the implications.

[42] Polybius III. 44. 5 and Livy XXI. 29. 6.
[43] Strabo IV. 1. 3 and 1. 12, and Jullian, pp. 465 and 472.
[44] Livy, v. 34. 8.   [45] Hyde, pp. 133–6 and OCD^2, p. 242.
[46] III. 48. 6.   [47] XXI. 30. 8.

III

THE SORTIE OF HANNO

By the third day after Hannibal's arrival on the right bank
of the Rhône, while he was collecting boats for the
crossing, most of the tribesmen on that side of the river
had withdrawn to the other bank, where they were massing in
force, evidently intending to oppose the crossing, and Hannibal
judged that they were too strong for him to force one by a
frontal attack alone. He therefore detached part of his forces,
mostly Spaniards, under the command of Hanno and des-
patched them that night after sunset with some local guides to
go 'a day's march'[1] up-stream and cross the river there, so as
to return on the other side and take the enemy in the rear at
the same time as the main army crossed the river and attacked
from the front. Hanno's force went about 25 Roman miles
according to Livy,[2] or 200 stades according to Polybius,[3] up-
stream to a place where the river was divided into two branches
by a small island, under cover of which they were able to make
enough rafts from wood which they found there to carry men,
horses, and their loads across the river, while the Spaniards
among them swam. Having crossed the river without opposition, they camped at a strong point and rested for a day,[4]
preparing at the same time for the next stage of the operation,
and on the next night but one after they had set out they moved
down the river, arriving near the enemy camp just before dawn,[5]
gave notice of their presence to Hannibal by a pre-arranged
smoke signal, and fell upon the camp from the rear while
the tribesmen were lining the river-bank to repel the main
army crossing the river. The manœuvre was completely
successful; the tribesmen, after putting up some resistance on
the river-bank, broke and fled when they found themselves
attacked in the rear as well, and Hannibal was left master of

---

[1] Livy XXI. 27. 2.   [2] XXI. 27. 4.   [3] III. 42. 7.
[4] Polybius III. 42. 9 and Livy XXI. 27. 6.   [5] Polybius III. 43. 1. and Livy XXI. 27. 7.

the crossing. The main army crossed the river and camped that night on the left bank.[6]

Polybius' and Livy's figures for the distance of the night march up-stream are in close agreement—between 36 and 37 kilometres—and when I mentioned this in the chapter on the army's speed of march in Part I, I assumed that the force was 'a cavalry contingent, in any case a flying column of some sort, not a body of heavy troops';[7] but I was anticipating the conclusion on a matter which had not then been discussed, and we must now consider it more carefully, for the nature of the force is by no means certain. Obviously, if it was an ordinary mixed force of infantry and cavalry with the former pre-ponderating, Livy's description of the sortie as a day's march runs counter to all the accepted ideas of the performance of ancient armies on the march which we canvassed in our previous discussion; and it is even more extraordinary if a Roman historian, familiar with the strictly limited practice of Roman armies, applied such a description to a night march of a mixed force in unknown country and certainly not on good roads, and one which was repeated, moreover, by a second march of the same distance after only a day's interval. If this was the truth of the matter, it would open the door to the most extreme claims of the 'long distance' school of historians about the length of a day's march and, in particular, it would provide a further argument for pushing the place of the Rhône-crossing higher up-stream on the strength of Polybius' statement that it was about 4 days' march for an army from the sea.

It is therefore not surprising that Devos (who evidently took the point) should have grasped at the same solution which I have adopted, only unfortunately he justified it by declaring that Livy specified Hanno's detachment as consisting exclusively of cavalry,[8] when Livy said no such thing. Livy first said simply that Hannibal detached 'a part of his forces'—exactly the same expression as Polybius used[9]—under Hanno, remarking that it consisted mostly of Spaniards; he mentioned that they were equipped with the *caetra*,[10] which was a Spanish wicker shield lighter than the *scutum* of the Roman legionaries, but

---

[6] Polybius III. 43. 6 to 44. 1 and Livy XXI. 27. 7 to 28. 4.
[7] p. 26 above.   [8] p. 38.
[9] Livy XXI. 27. 2 and Polybius III. 42. 6.   [10] XXI. 27. 5.

which, according to Veith, was an *infantry* shield;[11] he referred
to the force as *exercitus*,[12] which normally meant just 'army';
and the words he used to describe the engagement at the enemy
camp, *ab tergo inprovisa premente acie*,[13] suggest an advance by an
army drawn up in line of battle rather than a cavalry charge.
The sole justification in the text of either historian for Devos's
statement that it was a cavalry contingent is the single word
equi in Livy's description of the crossing of the river on the rafts,[14]
but this by itself would not signify more than the presence of
some cavalry in a normally constituted mixed force; both
authors usually specified cavalry, ἱππεῖς or *equites*, when a
cavalry detachment was meant.[15]

Curiously enough, none of this seems to have been noticed
by the historians of the 'long distance' school, who might have
been expected to seize on it as evidence in support of their own
theories; there is a strange silence on the whole subject among
the commentators, most of whom content themselves with
some neutral expression to describe Hanno's force, such as a
'detachment' or (following Polybius and Livy) 'a part of the
forces', without discussing its composition (though Walbank
evidently takes it to have been a mixed force, for he remarks
that, according to Livy, it 'included' cavalry)[16] and without
offering any comments on Livy's description of the distance as
'a day's march'. Only Hallward (apart from Devos) commits
himself, without giving reasons, to a flat statement that it was a
cavalry force;[17] he must have felt , as Devos did, that the sheer
facts of the case admitted no other answer, and one is inclined
to infer from their silence on the subject that the other commentators agreed with him, though they did not say so.

Obviously the force was a flying column of some kind, not a
body of heavy troops, and this in itself takes some of the sting
out of Livy's reference to 'a day's march'. Some commentators
have spoken of its 'baggage' being carried across the river on
the rafts, but this is plainly a mistranslation of Livy's expression,
onera alia,[18] which clearly meant no more than the weapons
and packs of the men who swam the river; the Latin word for
'baggage' was *impedimenta*. It does seem, despite the rather odd

[11] p. 410   [12] XXI. 27. 6.   [13] XXI. 28. 3.   [14] XXI. 27. 5.
[15] e.g. Polybius III. 44. 3 and Livy XXI. 29. 1.   [16] Note on Polybius III. 42. 6.
[17] *CAH*, Vol. 8, p. 37.   [18] XXI. 27. 5.

way in which Polybius and Livy referred to it, that it must have been a cavalry force, as Hallward and Devos have said, and as most of the commentators may perhaps be assumed to have accepted by their silence; and, if so, everything falls into place. Livy's description of the distance as a 'day's march' is explained, and, though we have little information about Roman cavalry practice, the English equivalent of the distance, about 23 miles, falls precisely within the standard length of a day's march for cavalry laid down in the British Army's cavalry training manual after the South African War—20 to 25 miles.[19]

It remains to consider some details of time and place. In the above summary I have followed literally Polybius' statements about the sequence of days, as have De Sanctis[20] and Devos.[21] But his description of the sortie is far from a 'crystal stream', as Hallward elsewhere described his prose,[22] and other commentators, notably Kahrstedt,[23] Jullian,[24] and Walbank,[25] have interpreted his rather slipshod sentences as showing that he made a mistake in his timetable: they think that Hanno's men made the return march on the next night, not the next night but one, after the outward march, either marching all night for the second night in succession, or else starting on the way back just before daybreak (though why Hanno should have chosen the daylight hours in which to make the last and most exposed part of a march which was intended to take the enemy by surprise, is not explained), and arriving in the vicinity of the enemy camp during the afternoon; after which the fight with the tribesmen, the crossing of the river by the main army, and its encampment on the left bank after the crossing must all be supposed to have taken place before dusk on the same day.[26] Either alternative is contradicted by Livy's explicit statement that the men took a day's rest between the outward and the inward march[27] (for the day of the construction of the rafts, the crossing of the river, and the encampment at the strong point can have been no rest day), and both seem plainly contrary to the probabilities.

[19] *Cavalry Training*, 1912, p. 246.   [20] pp. 80–1.   [21] pp. 40–1.
[22] *CAH*, Vol. 8, p. 26.   [23] p. 380.   [24] pp. 467–8.
[25] Note on Polybius III. 43. 1.
[26] Polybius III. 43. 1 to 44. 2 and Livy XXI. 27. 7 to 28. 4.   [27] XXI. 27. 6.

However, it is not necessary to pronounce on this difference of interpretation; its only relevance to our purpose is that those who have compressed the whole sortie within a span of two nights and perhaps part of a second day must surely have been thinking (whether or not they admitted it and despite Walbank's apparent assumption to the contrary) in terms of a cavalry detachment, for their truncated timetable could not have been performed by infantry on any reckoning. So this strengthens the case for assuming that the commentators in general may be taken as accepting in silence the view of Hallward and Devos that it was indeed a cavalry force, which certainly seems the only sensible conclusion.

There is little to be gleaned about the location of the crossing-place from the topography of the sortie. If the main army crossed the Rhône at Beaucaire–Tarascon, the night march of some 36 kilometres up the right bank of the Rhône would have brought Hanno's force to the neighbourhood of Avignon, where there is indeed an island (though not a small one) at the present time, and since the river makes a big bend to the west between the two places, the return march on the opposite bank could have been considerably shortened by taking the direct route away from the river; but the course of the Rhône is constantly changing and it has been controlled in modern times by *levées*, so that no reliable conclusions about the topography described by Polybius and Livy can be based on the present configuration of the river. The force would have had to cross the Durance on the return match on the left bank if the crossing-place was at Beaucaire-Tarascon, which Polybius and Livy might have been expected to mention; but this would not have presented a very serious obstacle, for the Durance is at its lowest in late summer, flowing, in its lower reaches, in small streams over a wide stony bed, and in Hannibal's time the water would have been even lower, since, as Colin [28] and de Beer [29] have pointed out, the Durance at that time discharged its waters in three other branches in addition to the one which flows into the Rhône just below Avignon.

All in all, this episode of Hanno's sortie cannot be said to make any positive contribution to the problem of locating Hannibal's crossing-place; it has only seemed right to discuss

[28] pp. 33–7. [29] p. 30.

it in some detail because of the difficulties which it raises and the strange silence in which they have been shrouded. The best working assumption to adopt seems to be that of Hallward and Devos that Hanno's force *was* a cavalry detachment, in which case everything we are told about the sortie, including Livy's description of the distance as a day's march, is consistent with a Rhône-crossing at Beaucaire–Tarascon even if it does not provide any positive argument in favour of it.

IV

THE CAVALRY BATTLE AND SCIPIO'S
MARCH TO MEET HANNIBAL

HAVING routed the tribesmen, Hannibal brought the main body of the army (except the elephants) across the Rhône the same day and camped that night on the left bank. The next morning he heard for the first time that a Roman fleet had anchored at the mouth of the river and he sent out a detachment of 500 Numidian cavalry to reconnoitre.[1] Scipio too had just heard of Hannibal's arrival on the Rhône, and had sent out 300 of his best cavalry on a similar mission.[2] The two forces met before the Numidians had got very far from their camp and fought a battle.[3] Jullian infers from these facts alone that Hannibal's crossing-place cannot have been very far from the mouth of the river,[4] but this is a fallacy, for there is nothing so far to show that Scipio had not heard of Hannibal's arrival and sent his cavalry out a day or two before, in which case they could have been several days on their ride from the coast. However, the facts that follow do prove it, as we shall see.

While the cavalry were thus engaged, Hannibal received at his camp the party of Boian chieftains led by Magilus who had come from Cisalpine Gaul to guide him on his way into Italy.[5] According to Livy, Hannibal was in two minds, as I have mentioned, whether to fight the Romans there or to continue on his march to Italy; the Boians urged him not to be drawn into battle by Scipio, but to keep his forces intact for the invasion of Italy itself, and Hannibal accepted their advice;[6] this must have been the moment at which he decided to veer inland to avoid Scipio. He invited the chieftains to address the troops,

---

[1] Polybius III. 44. 3 and Livy XXI. 29. 1.
[2] Polybius III. 41. 9 and Livy XXI. 26. 5.
[3] Polybius III. 45. 2 and Livy XXI. 29. 2–3.
[4] p. 465.   [5] Polybius III. 44. 5 and Livy XXI. 29. 6.   [6] Livy XXI. 29. 6.

which they did through an interpreter; they promised to guide
them quickly, safely, and without undue hardships on the route
by which they would lead them into Italy, and painted a
glowing picture of the splendour of the country and the eager-
ness of the Gauls who lived there to join them in fighting the
Romans. The Boians then withdrew and Hannibal took over
the meeting; he delivered a general's harangue which met
with a resounding response, whereupon he told the troops to be
ready to start on the march the next day and dismissed them
to make their preparations.[7]

All this must have taken some time, and it was only after
the assembly had broken up that the remnants of the Numidian
cavalry, who, despite their superior numbers, had been worsted
in the battle, which had been a bloody one with heavy losses
on both sides, arrived back in headlong flight, pursued to
within sight of the camp by the Romans.[8] After this reverse
Hannibal was no doubt confirmed in his decision to avoid a
pitched battle. He sent the main army off at dawn the next
morning on their march up the Rhône, throwing out a cavalry
screen towards the sea, as we have noted, and remaining behind
himself, according to Polybius, to superintend the transport
of the elephants across the river,[9] for which large rafts covered
with earth had been prepared the day before. This having been
successfully accomplished, he called the cavalry in and followed
the main army up-stream with them and the elephants,
catching it up, no doubt, at the first camping-place that evening.[10] Livy's version is slightly different: he says the elephants
were brought across the river on the same day as the cavalry
battle, so that, according to him, the whole army started off
together the next morning;[11] but on either version the departure from the crossing-place occurred on the day after the
cavalry battle, which is the important point for the sequel.

Meanwhile, the Roman cavalry (or rather, the victorious
survivors), having pursued the Numidians to within sight of
their own camp, had hurried back to report to Scipio. Scipio,
when he heard the news, at once put the baggage on board the
ships and set out with his whole army to meet Hannibal, eager

---

[7] Polybius III. 44. 5–13 and Livy XXI. 30.   [8] Polybius III. 45. 1–3.
[9] III. 45. 5.   [10] Polybius III. 45. 5–6 and 47. 1.
[11] Livy XXI. 29. 1 and 31. 2.

to bring him to battle.[12] But when he arrived at the crossing-place, he found, to his amazement, that the Carthaginians had left 3 days before; so he decided to abandon the pursuit and returned to the coast with his army.[13]

Here at last are the facts which fix the position of the crossing-place within narrow limits, and the reader will no doubt have seen the broad argument in its simplicity. The crossing-place cannot have been more than a certain distance from the sea, for if it were, Scipio's cavalry, starting from within sight of the Carthaginian camp, would have taken that much longer to get back to base, Scipio's start would have been delayed that much later, and his army could not have covered the longer distance within 3 days after the Carthaginians had left. We shall now examine the matter more closely to see what these limits of distance were.

Let us first consider the statement that the Carthaginians had left the crossing-place 3 days before Scipio arrived there. Polybius says simply '3 days';[14] Livy says 'about 3 days' or 'nearly',[15] for the Latin word *fere* which he used cast its shadow on the hither, not the farther side. Since the Romans counted the first as well as the last day in reckoning intervals between dates (as the French still do), Livy must have meant that Scipio got there on the next day but one after the Carthaginians had left, and there is every reason to suppose that Polybius meant the same. R. M. Errington, in an interesting discussion of Polybius' methods of counting in Books I and II of his *History*,[16] has shown how, even in that introductory part of it, where he had to rely for his chronology of earlier times in terms of Olympiads on the diverse methods used by his various authorities, his own method, when he had occasion to use it, was that of inclusive counting; and at the beginning of Book III, where he began what he regarded as his *History* proper, from which point he had recourse to his own sources, Polybius gives the clearest possible indication that this was how he himself counted intervals: he refers back to Book I of his *History* as 'the third, counting backwards from this one'. It is a virtual certainty, therefore, that, when Polybius and Livy said that the Carthaginians had left 3, or nearly 3 days before Scipio arrived at the

---

[12] Polybius III. 45. 4.   [13] Polybius III. 49. 1–3 and Livy XXI. 32. 1–2.
[14] III. 49. 1.   [15] XXI. 32. 1.   [16] *JRS* 1967, pp. 107–8.

camp, both of them meant that Scipio got there on the next day but one. Since the Carthaginians left on the day after the cavalry battle, we can take nightfall on the third day (by our reckoning) after the battle as the outside limit for the time of Scipio's arrival at the crossing-place.

Scipio's camp was most probably at Fos, a little way to the east of the Rhône delta. Polybius and Livy say that he landed at the easternmost mouth of the Rhône (which at that time had several outlets),[17] and Devos has pointed out that the only practicable landing place was in the Gulf of Fos,[18] clear of the silted-up channels at the mouth of the river which Strabo later described.[19] But whether the camp was at Fos or at Port St. Louis at the mouth itself, as Jullian thought,[20] makes little difference for our present purpose; the distance is practically the same from either of them to any of the places up river—about 40 kilometres to Arles, a little under 60 to Tarascon, and about 80 to Avignon. The route from Fos first crosses the pebble-strewn plain of La Crau, which is like a vast inland beach, then threads its way through the marshes and pools round Arles, into which the Durance at that time, according to de Beer, discharged two of its branches;[21] that from Port St. Louis runs through the marshes which fringe the Rhône delta all the way to Arles. Either must have been a difficult route for an army, and perhaps even worse for cavalry.

Since Scipio's cavalry met Hannibal's (who had presumably started early in the day) before the latter had gone far from their camp,[22] they must have spent at least one night on the road; for wherever Hannibal's crossing-place was, it cannot have been lower down-stream than the point near Fourques where the river divided into several branches, and they could not have ridden 45 kilometres or more in less than half a day. If the battle took place during the morning, as therefore seems probable, it is likely to have been sometime after mid-day before they called off the pursuit of the Numidians within sight of Hannibal's camp;[23] which agrees well enough with the record that the colloquy with the Boians and the speeches to the troops in the assembly had finished and the assembly had broken up

---

[17] Polybius III. 41. 5 and Livy XXI. 26. 4.   [18] p. 30.   [19] IV. 1. 8.
[20] pp. 469–70.   [21] pp. 30–1.   [22] Polybius III. 45. 2.
[23] Polybius III. 45. 3.

before the Numidians got back. The first question we have to ask is, how long did it take Scipio's cavalry to get back to Fos, and when did they arrive? For this determines the time when Scipio and his army could start.

It is simplest at this point to take one of the crossing-places favoured by the 'long distance' school of historians to test as a hypothesis, and since Marquion has gone into the details of this particular part of the narrative more closely than anyone else, I shall take his crossing-place at Caderousse opposite Orange, about 106 kilometres from Fos according to the particulars he gives,[24] and see how it answers. Marquion agrees that, at this distance from their base, Scipio's cavalry must have bivouacked *two* nights on the way before they met the Numidians;[25] so that, by the time they called off the pursuit within sight of the Carthaginian camp sometime in the afternoon, men and horses had been the best part of 3 days on the road and fought a bloody battle, at which point they had a return ride of over 100 kilometres in front of them. Marquion evidently recognizes the impossibility of their getting back with a report in time for Scipio to set out first thing the next morning, so he postulates a series of dispatch riders with relays of fresh horses to carry the news to Scipio by nightfall the same day,[26] for which there is no authority in Polybius or Livy, both of whom refer to the cavalry returning in a body to report.[27] And if Scipio had had at his disposal a chain of posting stations and remounts all the way from Fos to Caderousse, he would scarcely have needed to send out a detachment of cavalry to ascertain Hannibal's whereabouts.

To save some more time in his timetable, Marquion makes out that Scipio did not wait for the return of his cavalry (or rather, on his version, the arrival of the dispatch riders) before putting the baggage on board the ships, but had done this while the cavalry were on their way,[28] although this too is contrary to what Polybius said.[29] By this combination of his own glosses on the narrative Marquion is able to retrieve 1 day in his timetable and sends Scipio off with his army at dawn the next day,[30] i.e. at the same time as Hannibal left the crossing-place; but

---

[24] pp. 110 and 123–4.   [25] pp. 117 and 119.   [26] p. 121.
[27] Polybius III. 45. 3 and Livy XXI. 29. 5.   [28] p. 120.
[29] III. 45. 4.   [30] p. 123.

even this is not enough, as he implicitly recognizes, for no Roman army could have kept up an average of 35 kilometres
a day for 3 days running, let alone be fit to fight a battle at the
end of it (as Scipio's army expected to do). So at this point
Marquion takes another bisque and borrows an extra day:
he allows Scipio 4 days on the march to the crossing-place [31]
and coolly announces at the end of it that he thus arrived 3 days
after Hannibal had left [32]—apparently quite unaware that this
was not how Polybius and the Romans counted.

In short, Marquion takes too many liberties in the attempt
to make his system work. He falls into other errors too. He
ignores Livy's information that Scipio's army (a normal consular army of two Roman legions and a larger number of
allied troops) numbered about 24,000,[33] the whole of which,
according to Polybius, went on the march,[34] and says that it
cannot have numbered more than 7,000 to 8,000, because this
was the most that the sixty ships assigned to Scipio could carry,
with horses and baggage,[35] not realizing that these were the
naval galleys (quinqueremes or *longae naves*) [36] which were
Scipio's fighting force for a war at sea, not the transports for his
army.*

But Marquion's most insidious misapprehension is one that
is shared by other commentators too, namely, his insistence that,
on the first 3 days at least, Scipio was making forced marches.[37]
A Roman army could perhaps have covered the distance of
just on 90 kilometres which Marquion ascribes to Scipio's
army in these 3 days [38] by forced marches, but Scipio had no
reason at that stage to do any such thing: he reckoned that he
was moving to meet an enemy in battle—he had put the baggage on board the ships for that very reason—not that he was
pursuing one who was trying to elude him; and he made his

[31] pp. 123–4.   [32] p. 124.   [33] XXI. 17. 8.   [34] III. 45. 4.
[35] p. 97.   [36] Livy XXI. 17. 8 and 26. 3.
[37] pp. 35 and 123.   [38] p. 123.

---

* Marquion seems to have derived his figure of 7,000 to 8,000 men (carried, as he
supposed, in sixty galleys) from Polybius' information elsewhere (I. 26. 7) that a
naval galley carried 120 marines (who were legionaries) in addition to its comple-
ment of 300 oarsmen (who were not); but a Roman expeditionary force required a
fleet of merchant ships (*onerariae* or *naves ornatae*) as well to carry the rest of the men,
the baggage train and the horses, as is clear from other references in Livy (e.g.
XXIV. 40. 5 or XLIII. 9. 5–6) and from Caesar's description of the invasion of Britain
(*BG* IV. 22. 3–4 and v. 8. 2–6).

dispositions accordingly, which were such as to preclude any
possibility of a forced march.

He was, as Spenser Wilkinson put it, 'marching to meet
the most dangerous enemy in the world',[39] while his own
troops, as Polybius later made Hannibal remark, were newly
recruited and untrained.[40] Livy explicitly says that he marched
in battle formation, *quadrato agmine*.[41] This was not a mere
façon de parler, but a technical term with a definite meaning.
It was more what we should call a diamond formation than a
square one; one division in fighting order formed the van with a
cavalry screen thrown out ahead, a strong division was deployed on either flank, and there was a strong rearguard.[42]
Veith gives some particulars of the amount of space taken up
by a consular army on the march which suggest that, when
moving *agmine quadrato*, it must have occupied a front of some
5 to 6 kilometres. He says that there was no *justum iter* for a
march in this formation, but remarks: 'One thing is certain:
this form of march, in which the majority of the troops had to
make their way across country, was extremely tiring and time-
consuming, and could only be kept up for short stretches.'[43]

This was the formation, according to Livy, in which Scipio's
army marched to meet Hannibal; and it must have been so,
for when Scipio supposed that Hannibal was similarly moving
towards himself, he would not have run the risk of meeting the
enemy with his army in column of route. We may be equally
sure that on an approach-march to meet the enemy he would
not have neglected the standard Roman practice of constructing a fortified camp each day, which meant that the day's
march finished at midday.[44] I have mentioned the difficulties
of the terrain through which the troops had to pick their way,
and the reader can judge for himself what the rate of progress
of an untrained army of some 24,000 men advancing on a front
of several kilometres in such conditions may have been; quite
obviously it cannot have been fast enough to cover a distance of
over 100 kilometres in 3 days, or even in the 4 days which
Marquion allows himself—still less in the *two* which is all that

---

[39] p. 16.   [40] III. 70. 10.   [41] XXI. 32. 1.
[42] J. E. Sandys, *Companion to Latin Studies*, 1921, p. 471.   [43] pp. 352–3.
[44] Veith, p. 354, and Sir Frank Adcock, *The Roman Art of War under the Republic*,
1940, pp. 13–14.

would have been left for the march if Scipio had to wait for the return of his cavalry, as Polybius and Livy both say he did, before setting out.

Marquion has no notion of any of this. He agrees that Scipio must have thought that Hannibal was likewise moving towards himself;[45] but he argues that, since his camp was over 100 kilometres from Fos, there was no danger of an encounter during the first part of the march and Scipio was therefore able to proceed by forced marches for the first 3 days.[46] (He still does not explain what reason he had for doing so, and one would have thought that, in any case, Scipio might have expected to meet Hannibal half-way and would have deployed into battle formation at latest by then.) Marquion ignores Livy's statement that the march was made *agmine quadrato*, and therefore shows no recognition of the limitations which this imposed on the army's speed of movement—or, for that matter, of the inflexible requirements of the Romans about the camp for each day's halt and the consequent rigid rule that the day's march ended at midday.

I have gone into some detail in discussing Marquion's hypothesis because he himself has been very explicit about it: he is, in fact, the only commentator of the 'long distance' school who has made any serious attempt to reconcile his view about the position of the crossing-place with the possible movements of Scipio's cavalry and the march of his army; and though his timetable is open to the objections which I have pointed out, it is to his credit that he should have constructed one at all, for no one else has taken the trouble to do so. He makes one point, moreover, in defence of his scheme to which there is no obvious answer, and this must now be mentioned: it is concerned with the transit of news, not of armies.

Hannibal spent 7 days in all at the Rhône crossing after his arrival on the right bank of the river, and the cavalry battle was on the sixth day: this is a fixed point in the timetable, quite clearly defined by Polybius;[47] Scipio's cavalry must therefore have started from Fos, if the crossing-place was in the neighbourhood of Beaucaire–Tarascon, some 50 to 60 kilometres from the coast, early on the fifth day, and if Scipio sent them out as soon as he heard of Hannibal's presence on the

[45] p. 123.   [46] Ibid.   [47] III. 43. 1 and 44. 3.

Rhône (as one would assume he did), the news must have reached him in the course of the fourth day; but this seems an inordinately long time for the news to take in travelling a mere 50 to 60 kilometres, especially in country within the zone of influence of Scipio's allies at Marseilles, where his 'bush tele- graph' should have been reasonably efficient. Marquion says that this shows that the crossing-place cannot have been as near the coast as Beaucaire–Tarascon, but must have been much further inland: he argues, indeed, that, if the crossing- place had been at Beaucaire–Tarascon, Scipio would not only have heard the news sooner, but would have had time to get there with his army to block the crossing, and the whole course of events would have been different.[48] There is no doubt that the facts about the news do fit together much better on Mar- quion's view that the crossing-place was some 100 kilometres from Fos, for in that case Scipio's cavalry would have been *two* full days on the road before they met the Numidians, as Marquion has quite rightly assumed,[49] and Scipio would have heard the news by the end of the *third* day after Hannibal's arrival on the Rhône, which is a much more reasonable transit time for the arrival of the news over a distance of some 100 kilometres.

It might be thought that a possible explanation would be that Scipio dallied a day or two at Fos before sending his cavalry out, but this, apart from being inherently unlikely, is excluded by the fact that Polybius and Livy make it clear that his troops had only just disembarked when he did so, for they both say that one of his reasons for sending the cavalry out in- stead of advancing at once with his whole army was to give the troops time to recover from the sea voyage,[50] which would not have been necessary if they had landed several days before.* On the other hand, the problem cannot be solved by supposing that, though the news had arrived earlier, Scipio himself only arrived later, for it is equally clear from the narrative of Poly-

---

[48] p. 97.   [49] p. 107 above.   [50] Polybius III. 41. 8 and Livy XXI. 26. 5.

* Marquion does, indeed, say that Scipio had arrived at Fos even before Hanni- bal reached the Rhône (p. 112), which cannot be the case, as I showed earlier (p. 58 in Part I); but the point is not material to his argument, which turns on the time when the news of Hannibal's arrival on the Rhône reached Fos, not on the time of Scipio's arrival there.

bius (and perhaps also, though less certainly, from that of Livy) [51] that the news arrived at Fos *after* Scipio's arrival there. The first report he heard on anchoring after his 5-day voyage from Pisa was that Hannibal was crossing the Pyrenees: this was the latest news at Fos when he got there, and on the strength of it he decided to disembark his army; the stop-press news that Hannibal had reached the Rhône arrived soon afterwards [52]—perhaps while the disembarkation was still in progress, but in any case after, not before, Scipio had arrived at Fos.

There is therefore no escape from the conclusion that Scipio only heard of Hannibal's arrival on the opposite bank of the Rhône about 3 days afterwards, and if, as all the other evidence goes to show, the crossing-place was somewhere in the neighbourhood of Beaucaire–Tarascon, it remains a mystery why the news should have taken that amount of time to reach Fos or Port St. Louis some 50 to 60 kilometres away. The crux must stand as a positive argument in favour of Marquion's scheme and an unexplained weakness in mine. The reader must decide for himself how much weight should be attached to this riddle of a message that flitted on the lips of men against the sheer plod of infantry on the march, for Marquion's views about the latter have neither authority nor common sense to commend them. He does everything he can to make Scipio's army more mobile: he reduces its size to less than a third of Livy's figure, he ignores the limitations of a march in battle formation and the daily halt at mid-day to make a fortified camp for the night, he insists that the army made pointless and impossible forced marches and credits it with a faster rate of progress than anyone else has done; even so, he has to allow that it could not have marched some 100 kilometres in 3 days, and ends by claiming an extra day for which there is no sound authority in Polybius or Livy. On his own view about the position of the crossing-place the time available for the march would have been, not 3 days, but 2, as he himself tacitly admits when he invents his chain of dispatch riders and fresh horses to carry the report to Scipio; for the cavalry themselves, setting out in the afternoon on a ride of 100 kilometres after the best part of 3 days on the road and a bitterly fought battle, could not possibly have struggled back to Fos in time for Scipio to set out first thing the

[51] XXI. 26. 4–5.   [52] Polybius III. 41. 5–6.

next morning: it would have been late the next day by the time they got there, after which, according to Polybius, the baggage had to be put on board the ships, which must have taken some time; and since no Roman army would have started on a march after midday, Scipio could not have moved before dawn the day after.

I have said enough to show that Marquion's location of the crossing-place at Caderousse near Orange cannot possibly be reconciled with the movements of Scipio's cavalry and the subsequent march of his army as described by Polybius and Livy; and the same objections apply, with only minor adjustments, to any of the other up-stream crossing-places favoured by the 'long distance' school of historians. Roquemaure, the nearest of them, is only 10 kilometres short of Caderousse; and the distance from Fos, about 96 kilometres, is almost as impossible. Pont St. Esprit, which I have taken as the other end of the 'long distance' range (though some historians have put the crossing-place still further up-stream), is over 130 kilometres from Fos.

Yet none of this seems to have occurred to those who locate the crossing-place at some such distance from the sea: not one of them has noticed how its position is fixed between the prongs of this Morton's fork. De Sanctis, for instance, assumes, like Marquion, that Scipio started at the same time as Hannibal on the morning after the cavalry battle, without even noticing, as Marquion at least had the grace to do, the impossibility of the cavalry riding back to base over a distance which he gives as about 100 kilometres (though in reality it is at least 120) from his crossing-place between St. Étienne-des-Sorts and Pont St. Esprit [53] in time for Scipio to start first thing the next morning. He then credits him with compressing Polybius' 4 days for the distance between the sea and the crossing-place into 3 days by dint of forced marches; [54] which, as I have said, would have been as pointless on Scipio's view of the situation as it was impossible of achievement for a Roman army in battle formation.

Other commentators have made the same assumption that the army was making forced marches, quoting in support of it Polybius' description of Scipio σπένδων συμμίξαι τοῖς ὑπεναντίοις, [55] which some have actually translated '*hurrying to meet* the

[53] p. 70.   [54] pp. 18 and 81.   [55] III. 45. 4.

enemy', whereas it simply meant that Scipio was *eager to come to grips* with the enemy, as is made clear both by Livy's version, *nullam dimicandi moram facturus*,[56] and by Polybius' use of the same word, σπεύδων in the passage to which I referred once before, to describe Scipio's state of mind when he was merely *waiting in camp* for Hannibal's descent from the mountains.[57] The implication of the phrase, in fact, is precisely the opposite of what these writers have supposed; for, if Scipio was hoping for an early encounter, he would not have risked meeting the enemy with his army in column of route, and a forced march in battle formation was an impossibility.

Colin, a soldier, seems to have been the first person to discern the implications of these military movements for the position of the crossing-place.[58] He was also the first person to locate it at Fourques, just above the point near Arles where the Rhône divided into several branches, as Spenser Wilkinson,[59] Hyde,[60] and de Beer[61] have done since. He rebutted the then nearly universal view that the crossing-place was somewhere much further up-stream, declaring that it was quite impossible for Scipios' cavalry to ride 110 kilometres back to Fos (the distance which he took as a sample assuming a crossing-place between Roquemaure and Pont St. Esprit) in less than 24 hours—which would have left Scipio only *two* days in which to arrive at the crossing-place with his army; and he added that even in 3 days the army could not have covered such a distance 'in proximity to the enemy', thereby clearly recognizing, as a soldier, the limitations of a march in battle formation.

Colin gave the distance from Fos to his crossing-place at Fourques as 56 kilometres, and Spenser Wilkinson and de Beer have both quoted similar distances for it, though on the map it appears to be not more than 45 at most. He seems to have fallen into the same trap as Marquion about the Roman method of counting, for he assumed, in his timetable of the march from Fos, that Scipio took *four* days to reach the crossing-place; but since he reckoned that the first day was only a part-day because the baggage had to be put on board the ships before the army started and that the last day was not a full one either, this does not materially affect his estimate of the average rate

[56] XXI. 32. 1.   [57] III. 56. 6.   [58] pp. 295–300.
[59] pp. 16–17.   [60] p. 207.   [61] p. 28.

of progress, which he reckoned at about 20 kilometres in a full day. This strikes one as too fast for a march in battle formation in the light of our previous discussion; and Colin does not seem to have allowed for the fact that a Roman army, especially in proximity to the enemy (as he himself had remarked), would have stopped marching at midday and spent the rest of the day constructing and fortifying a camp.

Spenser Wilkinson and de Beer both explicitly allowed for this, and the former also made the point that the army was marching in battle formation, which meant, he said, that it would not have covered more than 9 English miles, or $14\frac{1}{2}$ kilometres, in a day. De Beer allowed nearly the same as Colin's average of 20 kilometres a day, but he rightly specified the time taken as only *three* days, and his estimate of the rate of march seems to have been an arithmetical function of his estimate of the distance, which he puts at a little less than 60 kilometres[62]— though, as I have said, this seems a good deal too high. Credit is due to one other writer, Camille Jullian, for noting the significance of these military movements (as also many of the other points I have mentioned) in support of a Rhône-crossing at Beaucaire–Tarascon;[63] but neither he nor any of the other three worked out the details of times and distances as fully as Marquion did for his theory, mistaken though we have found it to be; and it behoves us now to show that his procedure can be applied, without his falsification, to a crossing-place in the neighbourhood of Beaucaire–Tarascon.

At Beaucaire–Tarascon the times and distances could just, but only just, be accommodated: Dunbabin, whatever may be thought of his reasons, was quite right in his conclusion that this was the outside limit from the sea of the possible crossing-places; and, of the various points in that neighbourhood which we have mentioned, the one nearest to the sea, namely the crossing-place at Fourques favoured by Colin, Spenser Wilkinson, Hyde, and de Beer, must, on this evidence, be accounted the most probable. Let us, however, take Devos's crossing-place opposite St. Gabriel, since this presents rather greater difficulty, and see how it answers to our criteria.

From St. Gabriel Scipio's cavalry would have had a ride of about 50 kilometres back to base (for Marquion's fantasy of

[62] pp. 26 and 28.   [63] p. 465.

the dispatch riders and the remounts cannot be taken seriously) when they called off the pursuit of the Numidians within sight of Hannibal's camp sometime in the early afternoon—that is, some 13 to 14 kilometres more than what Livy called a day's march for Hanno's contingent. It was therefore a tall order for them to get back to base, after all their exertions, in time for Scipio to set out with his army first thing the next morning. It was, however, just possible, which over a distance of 100 kilometres or more it would not have been. If Hanno's contingent could cover 36 to 37 kilometres in a night ride, Scipio's cavalry, ready to ride men and horses to the limit to get back quickly with their report, could somehow have managed to keep going during 4 to 5 hours of daylight and as far into the night as was needed to finish the ride back to Fos. The task would have been that much less difficult, as I have said, from a crossing-place at Fourques (which is certainly *not* more than 45 kilometres from Fos), but it could just be done from near St. Gabriel, 52 kilometres away, and on either assumption we may suppose that Scipio was able to set out on the march on the morning after the cavalry battle, i.e. at about the same time as Hannibal's army left the crossing-place, so that he had 3 full days in which to get there on the next day but one after the Carthaginians had left.

Even so, an average of 17 kilometres a day, kept up for 3 days running, seems a fast rate of progress for a full-sized consular army moving in battle formation under the conditions I have mentioned, and the average of 14 to 15 kilometres a day (Spenser Wilkinson's estimate) implied by a crossing-place at Fourques would be more credible, just as it would have been that much easier for Scipio's cavalry to get back in time from there. Be that as it may, it is certain that over any longer distance the thing would have been impossible; and what emerges from this examination of the movements of Scipio's cavalry and his own march to meet Hannibal is that, if Livy's and Polybius' accounts are to be believed—and the only difference between them is that one omits to mention that Scipio put the baggage on board the ships before he started, and the other that he marched in battle formation—Hannibal's crossing-place over the Rhône cannot possibly have been further from the sea than Beaucaire–Tarascon; so that these detailed facts embedded in the narrative confirm the conclusion which has already been strongly indicated on other grounds, and which was quite obviously what Polybius himself believed when he gave his geographical distance from the Pyrenees to the Rhône along the line afterwards taken by the *Via Domitia*.

V

RÉSUMÉ AT THE RHÔNE

I MAY seem to have laboured the arguments about the place of the Rhône-crossing longer than was needed to prove the point; but we have not yet examined the case for the opposition view, based on inferences from later stages of the march, and it seemed important to establish how strong is the direct evidence for a crossing-place in the neighbourhood of Beaucaire–Tarascon before we addressed ourselves to those more debatable questions. For we are entering now more difficult country: nothing will be as clear from now on as it has been hitherto. So far, the texts of Polybius and Livy have presented us with a straightforward account of the march on which they were substantially in agreement, and we have needed to do little more than follow their narrative in chronological order and draw out the implications as we went along. But when they leave the Rhône valley our two authors part company; they seem to be describing quite different routes on the next section of the march 'as far as the climb of the Alps into Italy'; and, even taken separately, neither account, as it stands, yields a clear, unmistakable route.

We shall have to alter our procedure, therefore. The discussion of the march from now on becomes an exercise in truth values—for Hannibal must have gone one way and not another: every statement has to be tested for truth or falsity against every other, and no part of the puzzle can be said to be completed until every other piece of evidence has either been fitted in or discarded. This means that we must abandon our simple progress along the line of march and be prepared to cast backwards and forwards over the whole distance from the Rhône-crossing to the Alps, fetching our data where we can find it and hoping that, if we refuse to accept anything as established until it has been tested against what comes after as well as what went before, we may eventually be

able to decide which of the evidence should be accepted and
which rejected.

Another change, too, is called for in our method. Around
the uncertainties of these later stages of the march a multiplicity
of different interpretations has grown up through the centuries
in the long attempt to unravel the difficulties, and some have
grown so thickly and taken root so firmly that we shall have to
find our way through them before we once again get an un-
obstructed view of the ancient texts. It will be necessary, therefore, to lift our gaze from Polybius and Livy and to consider
the history of the interpretations as well as their own history
of the march itself. Indeed 'it is very meet, right, and our boun-
den duty' so to do, for many devoted scholars and amateurs
have wrestled with the same problems which now confront us;
no new evidence has come to light to give a later opinion more
validity than an earlier one; it would be presumptuous folly
not to explore such paths through the thickets as have already
been cut.

But, before we proceed to this next, more complicated phase
of our enquiry, I shall rehearse the conclusions on the evidence
we have so far considered, and take stock of the position we
have reached. It may be summarized as follows: All authorities
agree that Beaucaire–Tarascon was the regular crossing-place
over the Rhône on the ancient Iberian Way from Spain to
Provence; Hannibal had no reason to depart from the normal
route until he had crossed the Rhône and learnt that a Roman
fleet was anchored at the mouth of the river; Polybius clearly
assumed that this was his route when he gave the distance from
the Pyrenees to the Rhône along the road which afterwards
became the *Via Domitia*; the Boian chieftains who came from
Cisalpine Gaul to meet Hannibal evidently made the same
assumption when they waited for him at the Rhône-crossing;
the plentiful supply of boats which Hannibal found at the
crossing-place suggests that it was a ferry-point on a regular
route, and Polybius' statement that the inhabitants engaged in
trade with the sea, coupled with the several references to the sea
in his own and Livy's narratives, shows that it was not very far
inland; finally, all these indications are clinched by the facts
which emerge from the Roman military movements, showing
that the crossing-place cannot have been more than about 55

kilometres from Fos or Port St. Louis, which locates it either at
Fourques just above Arles, as Colin, Spenser Wilkinson, Hyde,
and de Beer have thought, or at Devos's crossing-place opposite
St. Gabriel at the furthest—in either case in what I have called
for short the neighbourhood of Beaucaire–Tarascon.

The observant reader may have noticed that there is one
item which I have omitted in this catalogue of the evidence
about the position of the crossing-place—Polybius' statement
that it was about 4 days' march for an army from the sea.[1] I
have done so deliberately, for this calls for different treatment
from the rest of the evidence. All the rest is, on the one hand,
sound in its own right, but, on the other hand, must be held in
suspense until we have appraised any contrary evidence
drawn from later stages of the march. This statement, however,
is demonstrably *unsound* on the evidence we have considered,
and can be disposed of without any reference to what comes
after. It is not necessary here to enter into the question of what
was the length of a 4-day march of an army: the statement
stands self-condemned, whatever view one takes about that, for
Polybius himself has said enough to show, as Livy also confirmed, that Scipio's untrained army covered the distance, over
difficult, unknown country, in not more than *three* days, and Livy
added the significant detail, which must certainly be true, that
it did so deployed in battle formation.

The statement was a casual, inaccurate remark, quite un-
worthy of all the attention that has been paid to it by historians:
it should be banished, as Colin pointed out over sixty years
ago,[2] from the discussion of Hannibal's route in general and the
location of the Rhône-crossing in particular. With it, too, should
be banished the corollary, which has been accepted too readily
by both schools of thought about the length of a day's march,
that, because the next stage of the march, the section between
the Rhône-crossing and the 'Island', was also described by
Polybius and Livy as a 4-day march,[3] it follows that the crossing
place must have been about half-way between the sea and the
'Island'. This may well be true as a matter of fact, but not as a
deduction from a demonstrably unsound premiss.

A second conclusion which flows from the first is that not
even the prosy, painstaking Polybius was infallible, and this,

[1] III. 42. 1.   [2] pp. 299–300.   [3] Polybius III. 49. 5 and Livy XXI. 31. 4.

though it may sound flippant, is quite an important step in our argument; for while it is generally (though not universally) accepted that Livy's and Polybius' accounts of the section of the march between the Rhône-crossing and the Alps are mutually incompatible as they stand, it often seems to be assumed that Polybius' account is internally self-consistent and therefore reliable. The immediate relevance of this for our present purpose is that, if, in the course of our inquiry into the next stages of the march, we come upon evidence which conflicts with that which we have been considering about the position of the crossing-place, we must be prepared to make a choice between them, recognizing that even Polybius—quite apart from any discrepancies between himself and Livy—sometimes erred. All we can safely say at present is that the evidence for a Rhône-crossing in the neighbourhood of Beaucaire–Tarascon is very direct and very factual, and any contrary evidence will have to be extremely strong to be preferred to it.

VI

THE ISLAND
(1) THE NAME OF THE RIVER

I HAVE several times mentioned the place called the 'Island', formed by the confluence of the Rhône and another river, which the army reached in a 4-day march up the left bank of the Rhône after crossing the river,[1] and the part it has played in the formation of views about the position of the crossing-place. It can be admitted straight away that, if the currently prevailing view that the 'Island' was at the confluence of the Rhône and the Isère is correct, the crossing-places which we have been considering in the neighbourhood of Beaucaire–Tarascon, some 160 kilometres away, must be dismissed without further argument, strong though the evidence for them has been, for no such distance can be reconciled with Polybius' measurements or with the marching capacity of an ancient army. The 'Island' is thus a critically important pivot, and it is essential to determine its position before any final views can be formed about either the earlier or the later sections of the march.

Since Polybius and Livy departed for once from their accustomed reticence about place-names in Gaul by giving the name of the river which formed one side of the 'Island' at its confluence with the Rhône, one might have supposed that here was a fixed point in the geography of the march about which there need be no argument. But it has turned out quite otherwise: the name has undergone such extraordinary vicissitudes at the hands of editors, and these in turn have exerted so much influence on views about the geography of the march, that we shall hardly arrive at a proper understanding of the march itself without pausing to examine them. The fact is that all the modern conceptions, not only of the position of the 'Island' (and therefore of the crossing-place), but of the whole line of

[1] Polybius III. 49. 5 and Livy XXI. 31. 4.

march from the Rhône-crossing into Italy are deeply rooted in a series of emendations of the texts of Polybius and Livy [2] made by Renaissance scholars in the first 200 years of printed books; and since the story is not without interest for its own sake, and since it has been variously mis-stated, I propose to set it out in full.

In the extant MSS. of Polybius the name of the river appears in two forms—σκαρας in the majority; σκωρας in one and in two others which are derived from it.[3] In those of Livy it appears as *Arar* or *arar* in the majority, *sarar* in one, and *bisarar* in another (the last-named variant being apparently a corruption of the first words of the sentence, *Ibi arar* or *Ibi sarar*).[4] σκαρας or σκωρας conveyed nothing to any of the early editors, but *Arar* was well known, and well attested, as the Latin name of the Saône, which joins the Rhône at Lyon. When, therefore, a learned prelate, Andrea de Buxis, prepared the text for the first edition of Livy, printed by Sweynheym and Pannartz in Rome around 1469, it was quite natural that he should retain the reading *Arar*, and this continued to be the reading in all editions of Livy for the next 350 years.

The name in Polybius, however, had a more chequered history. Since Greek was much less accessible to the common reader than Latin, Polybius was first published in a Latin translation made by Nicholas Perotto in 1473, and Perotto adopted Livy's word *Arar* for his Latin version of the name of the river. It was nearly sixty years later before the Greek text of Polybius was printed for the first time—by Vincent Obsopoeus at Hagenau in 1530—and this was followed by an edition printed by Hervagius at Basle in 1549. Obsopoeus and Hervagius both printed the name of the river as σκωρας, but as they both also printed Nicholas Perotto's translation in the same book, the common acceptation still was that the river in question was the Saône. There was therefore nothing revolutionary about the suggestion made by the geographer Josias Simler in his book, *De Alpibus Commentarius*, published in 1574, that the reading σκόρας in the MSS. of Polybius (as he somewhat inaccurately wrote, for this spelling of the name does not occur in

---

[2] Polybius III. 49. 6 and Livy XXI. 31. 4.
[3] Schweighaeuser's edition of Polybius, Vol. 5, 1792, p. 594.
[4] Livy, ed. Conway and Walters (Oxford, 1914), note on XXI. 31. 4.

any MS., according to Schweighaeuser) [3] was probably a copyist's error for Ἄραρ.[5] Isaac Casaubon bowed to the prevailing view and printed Ἄραρος for the first time in his edition of Polybius in 1609, also retaining *Arar* in his own Latin translation, which he similarly printed with it.

Casaubon, however, working in Paris, did not know what had been happening at about the same time in Leyden, where a young law student from Danzig called Philip Cluver* was sitting at the feet of the great Joseph Scaliger, who had finally yielded to the entreaties of the university to accept the vacant chair of Lipsius and had moved from Paris to end his days at Leyden. Scaliger's interest, in his later years, had turned to the construction of a system of universal chronology for ancient history, and Cluver, under his influence, forsook the law and devoted himself to an analogous study of ancient geography under Scaliger's direction.

The fruits of the collaboration between master and pupil— those, at least, in which we are interested—were not seen until after they had both died, Scaliger in 1609, Cluver at the early age of 43 in 1623. When Scaliger's library was examined after his death, his copy of Hervagius' edition of Polybius was found to contain the marginal annotation "Ἰσάρας. male apud Livium *Arar*'; and on the strength of this he is credited with the authorship of the reading 'Ἰσάρας, meaning the Isère, in such of the modern editions of Polybius as mention the fact that this word in their printed text is an emendation at all. Cluver meanwhile, after a period of military service in Hungary and Bohemia, at the end of which he had a term of imprisonment, proceeded to fill out his geographical studies by extensive travel (including a visit to Oxford, where he married an English wife). He evidently paid particular attention to the march of Hannibal; for when his book, *Italia Antiqua*, was published in 1624, the year after his death, it included a long excursus on the march, and this contained, after a demonstration that the river which formed one side of the 'Island' could not possibly have been the Saône, the following sentence: 'Proinde corrupta ista duo amnis vocabula audacter ego emendo, apud Polybium

---

[5] W. A. B. Coolidge *Josias Simler et les origines de l'Alpinisme jusqu'en 1600*, 1904, p. 109.

---

* His German name, Philipp Klüwer, was variously latinized as *Cluverus* and *Cluverius*, and gallicized as *Cluvier*; so it seems natural to anglicize it as *Cluver*.

σκόρας in 'Ισάρας, apud Livium *Arar* in *Isara*.'[6] On the strength of this Cluver is credited with the authorship of the reading *Isara* in modern editions of Livy.

But the two emendations obviously hang together, and Cluver clearly regarded himself as the author of both of them. If he had owed one of them to his master, Scaliger, he would surely have acknowledged the fact; and Scaliger, if he *had* proposed the one in Polybius, would certainly have emended Livy too, as is plain from his own marginal annotation. It makes no sense to distribute the authorship of the two emendations between them. One can see clearly enough what happened: Cluver had put forward the emendation of both authors in the days when he was working under Scaliger's direction at Leyden; Scaliger approved it and carried it into his own copy of Polybius; but neither of them published it at the time. (Scaliger, though he continued to correct the text of Polybius to the end of his life, never published an edition either of him or of Livy.) The two emendations appeared for the first time in Cluver's *Italia Antiqua* the year after he died. Cluver should be recognized as the author of both of them, as he himself announced.

However, it was a long time before either of them percolated through to editors of the texts. J. F. Gronovius still printed *Arar* without comment in his edition of Livy in 1645, and his son, Jacob, continued to print Ἄραρος, following Casaubon, in the text of his edition of Polybius in 1670, though in a separate volume of notes he gave warm praise to the emendation 'Ισάρας —which he rightly attributed to Cluver, not Scaliger. It was not until Schweighaeuser's edition of 1789 that 'Ισάρας was actually adopted in a text of Polybius, and *Isara* only made its entry into a text of Livy in Kreyssig's edition of 1823—thereby completing the circular tour which began with Ἄραρος following Livy into the text of Polybius and ended with *Isara* following Polybius into the text of Livy.

Since then these two readings have swept the board to the exclusion of everything else. In the case of Polybius it is impossible to discover from any of the currently available editions that there were ever any alternatives. The Loeb editor (there is as yet no Oxford Polybius) prints 'Ισάρας and translates it

---

[6] *Italia Antiqua*, Vol. 1, 1624, p. 367.

'Isère' without qualification;[7] the Teubner editor more hein-ously—since he purports to provide an *apparatus criticus*—also prints 'Ισάρας and gives no indication that it is a conjectural emendation.[8] Livy has fared better at the hands of English editors: the Loeb editor records that *Isara* is Cluver's emendation and gives the MSS. readings as well;[9] and the editors of the Oxford Livy hoist two large danger signals in the text to give warning that it is an ill-starred passage, though they proceed to discuss the possible readings in a long, rambling note which can only be described as polite, high-table gossip.[10] But the German editor of the Teubner Livy is as culpable as his Poly-bian colleague, for he too prints *Isara* in the text and remains silent about it in his *apparatus criticus*.[11] It is not surprising, therefore, that almost every modern school edition of Livy's Book XXI—a very popular school text—adopts the same reading and expounds Hannibal's route accordingly.

Thus Cluver's emendation has become the standard version of the text, and it has passed into the common stock of ideas about Hannibal's march. Almost any textbook or work of reference will record that the 'Island' where Hannibal arrived after a 4-day march up the Rhône and from which he started on his approach march to the Alps was at the confluence of the Isère just above Valence, and the same conception has bitten deeply into local folklore. There are restaurants and cafés along the *Route Nationale 7* between Montélimar and Valence bearing names such as *Relais d'Hannibal*, though few of their patrons can have any notion that the tradition to which they owe their names was shaped by a young German geographer working with his professor in a quiet library at Leyden in the time of Henri IV.

Such is the bibliographical history of the name of the river in the texts of Polybius and Livy, and, despite the convolutions which occurred, it is essentially a simple story of the transition from a universal acceptance of Livy's authority for identifying the river with the Saône to an equally universal assumption that

---

[7] W. R. Paton, 1922.

[8] The current Teubner edition is a reprint of the edition of Buettner-Wobst of 1882–1904 and 1905.

[9] B. D. Foster, 1929.   [10] Conway and Walters, 1914.

[11] M. Mueller, 1900–8.

it was the Isère. Though the early editors of Polybius retained the reading Σκωρας from certain of the MSS., it is clear from the fact that they continued to publish Perotto's Latin translation *Arar* in the same book that they did so from motives of editorial probity, not because they thought it signified any other river than the Saône; and when Isaac Casaubon actually incorporated the reading Ἄραρος in the Greek text, he was doing no more than accord diplomatic recognition to what had all along been the *de facto* régime. However, as tends to be the fate of all such actions, it came too late and became a façade; for the wind of change was already blowing, and, though Jacob Gronovius and other editors continued to keep up appearances by printing Ἄραρος in their texts, it was ultimately dethroned, and the authority of Livy's *Arar* collapsed with it. *Isara*, ᾽Ισάρας, and the Isère took over, and now the very idea that people once thought that Hannibal's 'Island' was near Lyon at the confluence of the Rhône and the Saône is only a half-forgotten absurdity.

But we have not yet reached the end of our textual story. When Cluver rejected the Saône and came to the conclusion that the river in question must be the Isère, he did so for purely geographical reasons—which I shall discuss in the next chapter—and it probably never occurred to him, any more than it did to the editors who eventually adopted his emendation, that, once the link with Livy's *Arar* was broken, there was no logical reason for stopping short at the Isère, which to him had seemed a sufficiently bold departure from pre-existing ideas. But a handful of writers in modern times have located the 'Island' some 100 kilometres further down the Rhône at the confluence of the Aygues, and the latest of them, de Beer [12] and Devos, [13] have dealt at least as effectively with the textual problems involved as any of the earlier scholars.

Fortia D'Urban in 1808 seems to have been the first person to break with the view, by then universally accepted, that the 'Island' was at the confluence of the Rhône and the Isère and to locate it at that of the Aygues, [14] but he did not enter at all deeply into the textual problem. He contented himself with the surmise that the reading Σκωρας (as he correctly wrote it,

[12] pp. 14–24.   [13] pp. 53–6.
[14] *Antiquités et monuments du département de Vaucluse*, 1808, p. 188.

unlike most of his predecessors who had written Σκορας) in one or two of the MSS. of Polybius and the variant *Bisarar* in one of those of Livy might have been respectively the names of the two branches into which the Aygues divided in those days just above Orange.[15] No one seems to have followed his lead about the location of the 'Island' for nearly a hundred years, when first Colin in 1904[16] and then Spenser Wilkinson in 1911[17] placed it still further down-stream, at the confluence of the Sorgues, and in 1931 Dunbabin reverted for the first time (though without acknowledgement) to Fortia D'Urban's location at that of the Aygues.[18] Colin and Spenser Wilkinson only touched on the textual problem, and Dunbabin, while accepting Cluver's emendation, 'Ισάρας and *Isara*, proffered merely the somewhat lame suggestion that this might have been the name of the Aygues as well as of the Isère. It has been left to the two most recent writers, de Beer and Devos, to go more deeply into the history of the text.

Their view about it is precisely the opposite of the prevailing view that Σκαρας or Σκωρας in the MSS. of Polybius was a corruption of 'Ισάρας, meaning the Isère: they hold that, on the contrary, Σκαρας is sound, being the Greek transliteration of the ancient Gaulish name of the Aygues, and either that *Arar* and its variants in the MSS. of Livy were corruptions of the Latin name *Iscara*, as Devos thinks, or else, as de Beer rather less convincingly supposes, that *Arar* was the name of the Aygues as well as of the Saône. To one who is unversed either in palaeography or in etymology they seem to have the best of the argument.

Jacob Gronovius, in his note in praise of Cluver's emendation, had applauded a suggestion of Cluver's friend and pupil, Holsten, who had accompanied him on his travels in Italy and left some notes on *Italia Antiqua* which were published after his death,[19] that the reading in the MSS. of Polybius might have arisen from a palaeographic confusion in uncials between *OICAPAC* and *CKOPAC*; and Schweighaeuser endorsed the compliment, with the addition that the reading σκορας did not in fact exist in any of the MSS. and that the resemblance between the two words would have been even closer if Holsten

---

[15] op. cit., p. 204.   [16] p. 348.   [17] p. 19.   [18] pp. 53–5.
[19] *Adnotationes . . . in Italiam Antiquam Cluverii*, 1666, p. 16.

and Gronovius had quoted the true reading, *CKAPAC*.[20] This is very pretty, and such a confusion might indeed have occurred in the *reverse* direction; but Ἰσάρας in Greek and *Isara* in Latin were well-known names of the Isère in ancient authors from Cicero onwards,[21] and it is most unlikely that the copyists of half a dozen MSS. (for they did not all have a common archetype) should have made the same mistake and converted a name which was perfectly familiar into one that meant nothing to them. If, however, *Iscara* was the original reading in Livy, as Devos thinks, the unfamiliar word might well have been changed into the well-known name *Arar*, and the variants *sarar* and *bisarar* may have been stepping-stones on the way.

De Beer and Devos both give a list of a dozen Latin names of the Aygues found in medieval documents, mostly trisyllables beginning with a vowel, and they are doubtless philologically correct in pointing out that it was a Gallic tendency (which has persisted in modern French) to prefix a vowel to words beginning with *s* followed by a consonant, so that such names would have been equivalent to the dissyllable Σκαρας in Greek; and some of their names are sufficiently close to *Iscara* on the one hand and the modern 'Aygues' or 'Eygues' on the other to justify Devos's contention that there was a chain of etymological changes connecting the two—though one of them, *Araus*, is also close to the Latin *Arar*, which de Beer thinks was the name of the Aygues as well as of the Saône.

It is, however, the more surprising that de Beer should have preferred this latter explanation, in that he himself mentions the fact that Georges de Manteyer marked the river Aygues as *Iscarus* in one of his maps of the ancient routes of southern Gaul,[22] which one would have thought supported Devos's view rather than his own; and de Beer is certainly mistaken in arguing that the occurrence of *Arar* in Silius Italicus' poem *Punica*,[23] authenticated as it is by the metre, proves that this was the reading in Livy in his time. As Walbank has pointed out,[24] Silius was here giving a general account of the Rhône, not a narrative of the march of Hannibal, and it is perfectly clear

[20] *Polybius*, Vol. 5, 1792, p. 594.
[21] *Epistolae ad Familiares*, x. 15. 18 and 21 and xi. 13.
[22] *La Voie fluviale du Rhône et ses chemins primitifs*, 1945.
[23] *Punica*, III. 447–54.   [24] Note on Polybius III. 49. 5.

from his description of the tributary in question that he was referring to the Saône, not the Aygues. It certainly seems that, on balance, Devos's view is to be preferred, that *Iscara*, or some such word, being the Latin equivalent of *Σκαρας* as the name of the Aygues, was the original reading in Livy.

However, this is a subsidiary matter compared with the main point on which they are both agreed, that the reading *Σκαρας*, signifying the Aygues, in the MSS. of Polybius was sound, and I look forward to the day when it will be restored in the text of an edition. Neither de Beer nor Devos is a professional editor of classical texts any more than Cluver was. It took the best part of 200 years before his emendation was adopted by editors; but the pace of events has quickened, and perhaps we shall not have to wait quite so long this time.

THE ISLAND
(2) THE HISTORIANS

THE reader will have gathered that I am going to agree with de Beer and Devos in locating Hannibal's 'Island' at the confluence of the Rhône and the Aygues; but we have a long way still to go before we arrive at that simple conclusion, and we must pause before we set out on the journey and survey the scene at the start. Cluver himself attached no significance to his relocation of the 'Island' as a sign-post to Hannibal's route; but it became for later writers the starting-point of a deviation which led far from the line of march as he and all his predecessors conceived it, and we shall not be able to make a proper appraisal of the modern interpretations unless we spend a little time examining the commonly accepted view at the time when Cluver made his emendation and his reasons for making it.

Polybius and Livy described the Rhône and the other river in question (whichever it was) as running close together before they joined, and they said that the tract of land between them was called the 'Island'. This is the sum total of explicit information on the subject common to both of them; but each of them added further details of his own, and Cluver based his emendation of the name of the river on a somewhat arbitrary selection from their supplementary statements about it. Livy added that the two rivers rose on either side of the Alps, and that the Allobroges, whom he described as second to none among the Gallic tribes in wealth and prestige, lived near the 'Island'. Polybius supplied the details that the two rivers met at a sharp point and that the 'Island' was rich, well-populated cornland, and added, as a travelled man who had visited Egypt as well as Gaul, that it resembled the delta of the Nile both in shape and in size, except that, whereas the base of the triangle was formed in the one case by the sea, in the other it was a range of mountains 'difficult to approach or penetrate and almost, one might say, inaccessible'.[1]

Cluver gave three reasons for rejecting the Saône as the river in question: first, that it did not rise in the Alps, but in the Vosges;* secondly, that there was no mountain range forming the base of a triangle between it and the Rhône; thirdly, that the Allobroges were settled between the Rhône and the Isère not between the Rhône and the Saône. It will be seen that the first and third were derived from Livy. They were evidently the ones that weighed with him most; for when he came to defend his own location of the 'Island' in the confluence of the Rhône and the Isère, he took exception to Polybius' figure of a triangle on the ground that the area enclosed by the Rhône and the Isère was more like a quadrilateral with a short eastern side, and he did not trouble to name the range of mountains at the base of the supposed triangle; so that, in effect, he dropped any pretence of relying on Polybius to support his own solution. He fastened chiefly on Livy's statement that the Allobroges lived near the 'Island'—so much so that he refers to it afterwards as 'the Island of the Allobroges'; thus relying mainly on Livy to refute Livy's own apparent statement that the river in question —the *Arar*—was the Saône.[2]

A glance at a map will show that all Cluver's geographical statements were perfectly correct, and so, without question, was his statement about the position of the Allobroges; but it does not follow that his location of the 'Island' was also correct, for he leant too heavily on this last indication without noticing that Livy only said that the Allobroges lived *near* the 'Island'; and the narrative of the next stage of the march points strongly to the conclusion, as we shall see, that its inhabitants were not the Allobroges, but some other tribe. This, however, is to anticipate a later part of the story, and for the moment we must continue with our appraisal of Cluver's arguments and the pre-existing ideas from which they arose.

As long as it continued to be accepted without question that Livy's *Arar* meant the Saône, the natural interpretation of the

[1] Polybius III. 49. 5–7 and Livy XXI. 31. 4–5.   [2] p. 367.

---

* Strabo, however, said that it did rise in the Alps (IV. 1. 11), and if Livy (his contemporary) thought so too, this particular reason for rejecting the Saône was not necessarily valid.

ancient texts was that Hannibal marched up the left bank of the Rhône to Lyon and continued to follow the river from there, where its course, going up-stream, turns sharply eastwards towards the Alps. It never occurred to Cluver, though he had replaced the Saône by the Isère as the river which formed one side of the 'Island', to suggest any departure from such a route. Neither he nor any of his predecessors seems to have made any serious attempt to check their route against the times and distances recorded by Polybius, such as the 4-day march between the crossing-place and the 'Island' or the next 10-day march of 143 kilometres 'along the river'; nor did they take the obvious point, which J. A. de Luc made later,[3] that the river which formed one side of the 'Island' cannot possibly have been a *right*-bank tributary of the Rhône like the Saône, for, if it had been, Hannibal would have had to cross back to the right bank of the Rhône to enter the 'Island' and then to cross the river a third time to continue on his way to the Alps. Polybius and Livy, who both devoted pages to his difficulties in making the first crossing, would certainly not have passed over such supererogatory manœuvres in silence.

Cluver's one concession to facts and figures in Polybius was patently erroneous. He made Hannibal continue up the Rhône as far as Seyssel, a little under 40 kilometres south-west of Geneva, and traverse the mountains from there round the north flank of the Mont Blanc massif to descend into Italy by the Great St. Bernard;[4] and he sought to justify his choice of Seyssel as the point of departure from the Rhône by claiming that the distance to it from Tarascon (which he accepted as the place where Hannibal had crossed the Rhône)[5] was exactly Polybius' figure of 250 kilometres from the Rhône-crossing 'as far as the climb of the Alps into Italy'. But it is a good 250 kilometres from Tarascon to Lyon alone and 133 kilometres from there along the Rhône to Seyssel, so Cluver's computation of the distance was seriously at fault. He would have been involved in a similar falsity if he had attempted to correlate his new 'Island' at the confluence of the Isère with Polybius' 143 kilometres 'along the river', for it is just 225 kilometres up the Rhône from there to Seyssel.

To us it seems obvious that Hannibal cannot have continued

on a course due north up the Rhône as far as Lyon before turning towards the Alps; but Cluver had another reason, apart from the old identification of Livy's *Arar* with the Saône, for believing that he did, and it is one to which some modern writers would have done well to pay more attention. Polybius twice prefaced his account of the march from the Rhône-crossing onwards by statements to the effect that it followed the river up-stream—once when he gave the measurement of 250 kilometres 'travelling along the river itself in the direction of its source as far as the climb of the Alps into Italy',[6] and again when he recorded that after the crossing Hannibal 'marched along the river away from the sea towards the midlands of Europe' and then described the structure of the mountains over which he crossed into Italy 'from the region of the Rhône'[7] —all of which seemed to imply that the whole of the approach march to the Alps before the actual crossing of the mountains was along the Rhône. Livy evidently had a similar idea of the line of march when he said that Hannibal set off up-stream after the crossing and 'made for the midlands of Gaul'.[8] Polybius, moreover, in four other places in the course of his narrative of events before and after the crossing referred to movements 'along the river' where the context shows that he meant the Rhône;[9] and there can be no reasonable doubt, as four French writers have effectively pointed out in the last 150 years,[10] that when he used the same expression 'along the river' to describe the 10-day march of 143 kilometres which followed the halt at the 'Island',[11] he still meant the Rhône and not some other river.

When, therefore, Cluver continued to make Hannibal follow the Rhône up to Lyon and beyond despite his relocation of the 'Island' at the confluence of the Isère, he was simply adhering to a plain reading of the text of Polybius (and, to a lesser extent, of Livy too), and it did not occur to him that any alteration in the line of march was called for as a result of shifting a particular stage-point from one river-confluence to another. But such simple trust in the words of the text was forgotten when people realized the full possibilities of his new location of the

---

[6] III. 39. 9.   [7] III. 47. 1–5.   [8] XXI. 31. 2.
[9] III. 42. 7, 43. 1, 44. 2, and 45. 4.
[10] de Luc, p. 75; Perrin, p. 106; Colin, pp. 337–9; Marquion, pp. 40–1.
[11] III. 50. 1.

'Island', and it was nearly 200 years before anyone remembered them again. His own pupil, Lukas Holsten, was the first to break away from the old conception. He founded the heresy which has been the orthodox view ever since—that Hannibal branched off from the Rhône at the 'Island' and that, if his approach march to the Alps was along a river at all, it was some other river than the Rhône, usually the one that joined it at the 'Island'.

Holsten, in his notes on *Italia Antiqua*, which were published in 1666 five years after his death, accepted Cluver's identification of the 'Island' with the confluence of the Rhône and the Isère, but made Hannibal leave the Rhône there and travel back in a south-easterly direction to join the valley of the Drôme and follow it on a route connecting with the valley of the Durance between Gap and Embrun and so to a crossing of the main ridge of the Alps by the Col de Montgenèvre;[12] and one or other of the various routes joining an 'Island' at the confluence of the Rhône and the Isère with the upper valley of the Durance and the Col de Montgenèvre became the standard version of Hannibal's march for the next 150 years. All these routes, like that of Holsten himself, were dominated by respect for the authority of Livy, who said that the army crossed the Druentia (Durance) on its way from the 'Island' to the main ridge of the Alps,[13] which, coupled with his positive asseveration that Hannibal descended from the Alps into the territory of the Taurini,[14] seemed to point clearly to a route to the upper reaches of the Durance and over the Col de Montgenèvre, whereas Cluver had poured scorn on Livy's geographical indications of this part of the march.[15]

However, as is normal in any transition from one system to another, there was a period of overlapping, and two or three English writers, perhaps constitutionally more conservative than their contemporaries on the Continent, clung to the old route up to Lyon and beyond. James Hampton did so quite gratuitously in his translation of Polybius published in 1756, when, having given the name of the other river at the 'Island' as 'Isara' in his English translation, he chose to render Polybius' words 'along the river' for the march which followed 'along the Rhône'.[16] Edward Gibbon studied Cluver's *Italia Antiqua*

---

[12] pp. 16–23.   [13] XXI. 31. 9–12.   [14] XXI. 38. 5–9.   [15] p. 373.
[16] *The General History of Polybius*, 1756, p. 242.

in the autumn of 1763 during his second stay at Lausanne, and recorded his reflections on it in his *Journal*. He perpended at some length between Livy's and Polybius' accounts of Hannibal's march, which he said were so different that a choice had to be made between them. He gave due weight to Cluver's emendation of *Arar* and *Scaras* (as he wrote it) into *Isara*, which he allowed was 'extremely probable', but in his final conclusion he discounted it and came down in favour of what he regarded as Polybius' version of the march in its traditional form, namely that the 'Island' was at the confluence of the Rhône and the Saône, and that Hannibal crossed the Alps into Italy by the Great St. Bernard.* John Whitaker still agreed with him on both points in 1794,[17] but he was the last person to do so: by then the new shoots that budded from Cluver's emendation, which he himself had kept tightly furled round the old stem, had sprouted in quite different directions, and no one has ever again entertained the once universal assumption that the 'Island' was at Lyon in the confluence of the Rhône and the Saône and that Hannibal continued from there up the Rhône round the north flank of the Mont Blanc massif to descend into Italy from the Great St. Bernard.

The fact is that Cluver's retraction of the 'Island' some 100 kilometres down-stream had paved the way for what was regarded as Livy's route along the upper reaches of the Durance to the Col de Montgenèvre, which could not conceivably have been approached from an 'Island' at Lyon; and the French writers of the eighteenth century seized on this newfound freedom to extol Livy at the expense of Polybius. Mandajors,[18] de Folard,[19] D'Anville,[20] Saint-Simon,[21] and Denina[22] all brought Hannibal by one route or another across the Dau-

[17] *The Course of Hannibal over the Alps Ascertained*, 1794, pp. 41, 293, and 298.
[18] *Acta Academiae Parisinae*, Vol. 3, 1725, pp. 93 ff. and Vol. 5, pp. 198ff.
[19] *Histoire de Polybe*, Vol. 4, 1728, pp. 88–90.
[20] *Notice de l'ancienne Gaule*, 1760, pp. 59, 386, and 388.
[21] *Histoire de la Guerre des Alpes*, *1744*, 1770, pp. xiv–xvii and xxiv–xxxiv.
[22] *Tableau historique, statistique et moral de la haute Italie*, 1805, pp. 360–3 and 380.

---

* *Miscellaneous Works of Edward Gibbon*, 2nd edn., Vol. 5, 1814, pp. 370–81. Both de Beer (p. 108) and Devos (p. 160) record Gibbon as locating the 'Island' at the confluence of the Isère, and the crossing of the Alps at the Col de Montgenèvre, and it is true that at one point (p. 378) he appears to accept the former and that he allowed high probability to the latter; but his final conclusion, clearly stated on p. 380 and confirmed in his notes on *Nomina Gentesque Antiquae Italiae* (Vol. 4, pp. 172–3), was as quoted in the text above.

phiné from Cluver's 'Island' near Valence to join the Durance and cross the main ridge of the Alps by the Montgenèvre or a more southerly pass, untrammelled by any scruples about reconciling such a route with Polybius' march 'along the river'. But by the end of the eighteenth century the writing was on the wall for the overthrow of this conception of the route in its turn.

In 1789—fateful year—the Alsatian scholar, Schweighaeuser, began the publication of his new edition of Polybius, in which, as I have mentioned, he printed the name of the other river at the 'Island' as Ἰσάρας for the first time in a published text. This helped to fix attention once again on Polybius—for it was more than another thirty years before the corresponding reading *Isara* was incorporated in an edition of Livy—and reminded people that, according to him, the approach march to the Alps had been 'along the river'; only this time the river in question was taken to be, not the Rhône itself, but the other river, authenticated, it now seemed, as the Isère, which joined it at the 'Island'. So at last there dawned the idea which had not occurred to Cluver or to any of his successors till then, that one possible line for Hannibal's onward march from Cluver's 'Island' at the confluence of the Rhône and the Isère was neither to continue up the Rhône nor to break away across the Dauphiné to the upper valley of the Durance and the Col de Montgenèvre, but to follow the Isère itself, either all the way in its own gently sloping valley to the Little St. Bernard, or up the valley of its tributary, the Arc, to the Mont Cenis or its variant, the Col du Clapier; and these have been the most popular routes for Hannibal's crossing of the Alps ever since.

The Mont Cenis had indeed been sponsored by Josias Simler together with the Montgenèvre as early as 1574, on the grounds that from either of them the army could have had a view of the plain of the Po, as Polybius and Livy described—a point we shall consider more fully later—and that both these passes answered to Livy's affirmation that Hannibal descended from the Alps into the territory of the Taurini.[23] Indeed even before that Dominico Maccaneo in 1525[24] and Paolo Giovio in 1553[25] had

[23] W. A. B. Coolidge *Josias Simler et les origines de l'Alpinisme jusqu'en 1600*, 1904, pp. 108–10.

[24] Commentary on the *Lives* of Aurelius Victor attributed to Cornelius Nepos *c.* 1525, ch. XLII.

[25] *P. Jovii historiarum sui temporis libri*, Book 15, 1553, p. 168.

proposed the Mont Cenis as Hannibal's pass, on the mistaken ground that it belonged to the 'Pennine' or 'Jovian' group of Alps. But all three of these writers had accepted the traditional identification of the river at the 'Island' with the Saône (Simler, in fact, had proposed emending Polybius' text to bring it into line with Livy's name *Arar*), whereas no realistic approach route to the Montgenèvre or the Mont Cenis could have been sustained from an 'Island' near Lyon: it was only after Cluver had shifted the scene of the 'Island' from the confluence of the Saône to that of the Isère that either of those passes, or the Little St. Bernard, could seriously be entertained as a candidate for Hannibal's pass.

We shall consider the Little St. Bernard later and concentrate for the moment on the Mont Cenis (of which the Col du Clapier is a variant introduced more recently). When the Mont Cenis did emerge as a serious candidate, it made its entry almost by stealth. In a book published anonymously in 1764 under the curious title *Nouveaux Mémoires ou observations sur l'Italie par deux gentilshommes suédois* its author, P. J. Grosley, after a careful analysis of the possible alternative routes for Hannibal's march, arrived at the conclusion that one of Simler's two proposals was sound and that Hannibal's pass must have been the Mont Cenis.[26] The book had not been published when Gibbon was reading *Italia Antiqua* and recording his reflexions on Hannibal's pass in his *Journal*, and at that time he took no cognizance of the Mont Cenis as one of the alternatives to be considered. He did read the book later, however, and commented: 'the pretensions of mount Cenis are supported in a specious, not to say a convincing, manner by M. Grosley'.[27] The book was evidently a success, for it went into three editions in French and one in an English translation within ten years, and it must have sown the seed for acceptance of the Mont Cenis as Hannibal's pass even before Schweighaeuser's edition of Polybius brought such a route into the foreground as a possible interpretation of Polybius' march 'along the river'.

Grosley, however, has rarely been given the credit for this,

[26] I have not been able to inspect the first or second editions of this book. The reference in the third edition, published in 1774 under the different title, *Observations sur l'Italie . . . données en 1764 sous les noms de deux gentilshommes suédois*, is Vol. 1, pp. 44–51.

[27] *Decline and Fall*, edition of 1825, Vol. 2, p. 81.

and the person generally regarded as the author of the Mont Cenis route is Napoleon. In 1823 General de Montholon, who had accompanied him in exile at St. Helena, published a long account of his conversations there, and among them he recorded some ill-tempered and ill-considered sentences in which Napoleon had contemptuously dismissed the whole problem of Hannibal's march as the simple journey of a traveller and delivered himself of various pronouncements about its route.[28] He first said that, having crossed the Rhône near Orange, Hannibal marched in a straight line towards Turin—oblivious both of the explicit statements of Polybius and Livy that Hannibal did *not* take the direct road to Italy, but marched inland up the Rhône to avoid the Romans, and of his own quite different route which he proceeded to give. He located the 'Island' either at the confluence of the Rhône and the Isère or at that of the Isère and the Drac near Grenoble, both of which, he said, 'satisfied equally the text of Polybius and Livy' —though how a confluence which they both said was that of the Rhône and another river could have been that of the Isère and the Drac, or how a 4-day march from the Rhône-crossing could have brought Hannibal equally to a point near Valence and to one nearly 100 kilometres further on, he did not explain. However, he said that on either assumption Hannibal marched up the Isère from the 'Island' and crossed the Alps into Italy by the Mont Cenis; and this is the route which, with its variant, the Col du Clapier, has been the most popular solution ever since.

The idea that the 'Island' could have been near Grenoble was an aberration which is best forgotten, as it has been; but Napoleon's route up the Isère from an 'Island' at its confluence with the Rhône near Valence has been adopted by the great majority of all subsequent writers in one variation or another. It has come to be regarded as the Polybian route *par excellence*, and, though it flouts his plain meaning that the march from the 'Island' continued up the Rhône itself, there is much to be said for it, as we shall see when we come to examine the narrative of this part of the march. We shall consider this, and the facts of geography implied, in the next chapter.

[28] *Mémoires à Sainte-Hélène*, Vol. 4, 1905 edn., pp. 277–81.

VIII

THE ISLAND
(3) GEOGRAPHY

W E need not waste time trying to reconcile an 'Island' at the confluence of the Rhône and the Isère with Polybius' figure of a triangle and his comparison with the delta of the Nile. Cluver was wise in his generation in not worrying too much about this, for Polybius' geometry falls hopelessly awry, however one looks at it. If the area enclosed by the two rivers and a range of mountains is to be regarded as a triangle at all, it is more like a triangle with a north–south base along the Rhône between Lyon and Valence and a sawn-off eastern apex than one with its apex at Valence, for the two rivers converge just west of Chambéry and are not much more than 30 kilometres apart at that point. But in fact, as Cluver said, the shape is more like an irregular quadrilateral with a short eastern side. Nor will the chain of the Mont du Chat, Montagne de l'Épine, and Grande Chartreuse, which is commonly taken as the base of Polybius' triangle by those who adopt this location of the 'Island', fit his statement that it resembled the delta of the Nile in size as well as shape, for these mountains are less than 100 kilometres from the supposed apex near Valence, whereas the Nile delta is about 150 kilometres deep; and since they are only some 1,300 to 1,400 metres above sea level, they were hardly an 'almost inaccessible' barrier compared with the main range of the Alps which Hannibal was later to cross. However, none of this need seriously be reckoned an objection to an 'Island' at the confluence of the Rhône and the Isère, for the truth is that Polybius' comparison with the delta of the Nile was like the flourish of a would-be stylish batsman who fails to keep his eye on the ball, and, as a piece of information, it is on a par with the rogue item in a schoolboy's riddle which is put in 'to make it more difficult'.

The case is very different with his description of the march

'along the river' through the territory of the Allobroges
which followed the halt at the 'Island'; for the Allobroges
were certainly settled along the Isère, and the Isère is the only
river which fits his description of the march proceeding 'in
the flat country', given the assumption that it was not along
the Rhône itself. There is no other river except the Durance
(which Hannibal had left far behind by that time) which
stretches like a long finger into the heart of the mountains and
can be followed at a gentle gradient in a broad, level valley
up to a point which could be called the beginning of the climb
to the Alps. The Isère can, in fact, be followed in its own valley
up to the very foot of the Little St. Bernard just beyond Bourg–
St. Maurice; and for this reason de Luc,[1] Mommsen [2] and many
other nineteenth-century writers, and more recently Hyde,[3]
have thought that this was Hannibal's route across the Alps.
Both Mommsen [4] and Hyde[5] say that long before Hannibal's
time the Little St. Bernard had been one of the main routes
used by the Gauls to enter Italy, which may well be true
(though neither of them quotes his authority for the statement);
but the Little St. Bernard led into the territory of the Salassi,
and, as such, it was differentiated by Polybius himself, in his
list of Alpine passes to which I referred earlier,[6] from the pass
which led into the territory of the Taurini, and which either
Polybius himself or a later editor of his text identified as Hannibal's pass. Varro similarly quoted Hannibals' pass as a different
one from the Little St. Bernard in his own list of Alpine passes,[7]
which we shall consider more fully later. I shall adopt, therefore,
as Devos has done,[8] the robust conclusion of Livy that 'it is
agreed by all'—*cum inter omnes constet*—that Hannibal descended
from the Alps into the territory of the Taurini,[9] in which case
he could not have come by the Little St. Bernard; and I shall
exclude the latter as plainly contrary to the testimony of the
ancient authors.

A few writers, wishing to marry Polybius' march 'along the
river' with what they take to be Livy's route by the Durance
and the Col de Montgenèvre or a neighbouring pass (a view
which we shall consider later), have made Hannibal strike

[1] pp. 139–43.   [2] *History of Rome*, 1862–75, tr. Dickson, Vol. 2, p. 106.
[3] p. 198.   [4] op. cit., p. 106.   [5] p. 207.   [6] p. 85 above.
[7] Servius *ad Aeneidem* x. 13.   [8] pp. 99–100.   [9] xxi. 38. 5–6.

off from the Isère near Grenoble and cross the Dauphiné Alps
to join the upper Durance valley, either, as De Sanctis [10] and
apparently also Kahrstedt [11] think, by the valley of the Drac
and the Col Bayard, or more directly, according to de Folard, [12]
up the Romanche and over the Col du Lautaret to join the
Montgenèvre route at Briançon. But the great majority of
modern writers have adopted Napoleon's route up the Isère
as far as its confluence with the Arc and then up the latter
river to the Mont Cenis or the Col du Clapier, [13] and I shall
take this as the representative modern conception of Hannibal's
route, based essentially on Polybius.

It ignores, as I have said—or at least heavily discounts—
Polybius' plain meaning that the march from the 'Island'
continued along the Rhône itself, though few of its advocates
have allowed themselves to be worried on that score. Walbank,
to his credit, seems to have felt some uneasiness on the point,
and he offers a slightly mysterious explanation. Having asserted,
of Polybius' description of the confluence which formed the
'Island', 'undoubtedly, whatever name stood in the original
source common to Polybius and Livy, the river indicated is the
Isère', he writes a little later:

παρὰ τὸν ποταμόν: which river? To Polybius clearly the Rhone...
But the reason is his false picture of the Rhone's direction and rela-
tion to the Alps, which would make Hannibal follow its bank up to
the point when he turns right and begins the ascent of the Alps.
In reality Hannibal must have left the Island up the valley of the
Isère...[14]

Walbank's diagnosis of Polybius' picture of the geography
is undoubtedly correct; and if all he means is that Polybius
thought that, on leaving the 'Island', Hannibal continued to
march up the left bank of the Rhône, he is only saying what I
have been stressing, though in that case his assertion that

---

[10] pp. 22–3 and 70–2.   [11] pp. 187 and 381.

[12] *Observations*, in Dom V. Thuillier, *Histoire de Polybe nouvellement traduite du grec*,
1728, Vol. 4, pp. 89–90.

[13] e.g. Larauza, *Histoire critique du passage des Alpes par Annibal*, 1826; Macé,
Description du Dauphiné, 1852, p. 340; J. Maissiat, *Annibal en Gaule*, 1874, pp. 210–11;
Perrin, p. 145; Colin, pp. 317–18; Jullian, p. 485; Osiander, *Der Hannibalweg*,
1900; Spenser Wilkinson, pp. 9–11 and 32–3; Dunbabin, p. 53; Walbank, *JRS*
1956, p. 45; Marquion, pp. 56–8.

[14] Notes on Polybius III. 49. 5(4) and 50. 1(5).

Hannibal branched off up the Isère is contradicted by Polybius. What he seems to be suggesting is that Polybius agreed with him about the route but confused the two rivers; and this would be an absurdity, since Polybius cannot have mistaken one river for the other just after he had named them both and given an elaborate description of the confluence. And if he *had* meant that Hannibal branched off up the tributary, he would surely have repeated the name, not used the same expression which he had consistently used before for the Rhône.

There is another objection to this supposed route up the Isère from an 'Island' at its confluence with the Rhône which has scarcely ever been pointed out. If this is where the 'Island' was, Hannibal's army had to cross the Isère to enter it, and so would have begun the approach march to the Alps along the *right* bank of that river. But the routes to all the passes except the Little St. Bernard lead off from the *left* bank of the Isère, so that the army would have had to cross the river a second time somewhere up-stream, yet there is no mention of any such double crossing of a river in Polybius or Livy. Livy did describe a crossing of the Druentia (Durance) on the march from the 'Island' to the Alps, in a vexed passage which we shall examine in due course.[15] But, though various interpretations have been put on the passage, no one has suggested that the river in question was really the Isère; nor could it have been, for Livy describes it as flowing in a number of shallow streams over a wide, stony bed, as the Durance does in its lower reaches, whereas the Isère is contained between banks in a single deep channel.

To transport the army across the Isère would have required a fleet of boats and rafts, and to do this twice on a march towards the Alps in late autumn strikes one as a needlessly difficult and time-consuming operation which one would have expected Polybius or Livy to mention. Napoleon did recognize that a second crossing of the Isère was required on his route, but offered no comment on the fact.[16] Nor did Marquion, who also made Hannibal recross the Isère at about the same place as Napoleon: he had pointed to the absence of any authority in Polybius for a second crossing of the river as a mote in someone

---

[15] XXI. 31.9–12. See pp. 171–4 below.
[16] *Mémoires . . . à Sainte-Hélène*, 1905 edn., Vol. 4, pp. 280–1.

else's eye, but did not notice the beam in his own when he came
to describe his own route.[17]

But the difficulties which arise in the 'Island' itself militate
still more strongly against the orthodox view that it was in the
territory of the Allobroges between the Rhône and the Isère.
I have mentioned before that the historians of the 'long distance' school reckon that the 'Island' was about 107 kilometres
from the place where Hannibal had crossed the Rhône, and
that this, according to them, was the distance covered in the
4-day march between the two. I have given my reasons, in the
chapter on the army's speed of march in Part I, for thinking
this too much, but I shall accept it here as an outside limit for
the present purpose. It means that the army cannot have
penetrated further inside the 'Island' than just beyond the
confluence of the two rivers when it halted at the end of the
4-day march, for the village of Pont de l'Isère, 3 or 4 kilometres
above the confluence, is already 117 kilometres from Roquemaure (the most popular crossing-place among the historians
of the 'long-distance' school), and the army certainly could
not have got any further in the time. But the capital of the
Allobroges was at Vienne 64 kilometres further on,[18] and the
events described by Polybius and Livy during the halt at the
'Island' were such as can only have taken place in the capital.

Both authors tell how, when Hannibal arrived at the 'Island',
he was called in to settle a dispute between two brothers over the
throne of the ruling tribe, and how he settled it—by arbitration
according to Livy, by a *coup d'état* according to Polybius—in
favour of Brancus,* the elder brother; and, as though this were
not enough to show that Hannibal must have been on the spot
to settle a dispute which can only have taken place in the capital
itself, Livy adds the interesting detail that he was guided in his
decision by the opinion of the Senate and local leaders, which
shows that he consulted them, and he must have been in the
capital to do so. The difficulty cannot be avoided by supposing
that Hannibal left the army behind at the camping-place and

[17] pp. 38 and 49.
[18] Strabo, IV. 1. 11; Pomponius Mela, *Chorographia*, II. 5; Pliny, *HN* III. 4. 36;
Ptolemy, *Geographica*, II. 10. 7.

* I have adopted this version of the name, since this is how it is printed in most
modern editions, though in the MSS. of Livy it is *Braneus*.

went on by himself to Vienne to handle the affair; for both
Polybius and Livy relate how the grateful Brancus rewarded
him for his decision by a supply of provisions for his army and a
comprehensive refitting of its clothing and equipment, and the
re-equipment of an army of nearly 50,000 men was another
operation which could only have been carried out in or near the
capital.[19]

These practical necessities of the narrative are enough in
themselves to refute the orthodox view that Hannibal's 'Island'
was in the territory of the Allobroges, for the events described
by Polybius and Livy during the halt cannot possibly have
taken place at a range of some 60 kilometres from the capital
of the tribe in question; and their account of the events that
followed reinforces the same conclusion when carefully analysed.
But Livy, it must be admitted at once, contradicts it, for he
refers to the dispute about the throne as 'the disputes of the
Allobroges',[20] and Cluver relied on this, as others have done
since,[21] to describe the 'Island' flatly as the 'Island of the Allobroges'. Yet, a little while before, Livy had said merely that
the Allobroges lived *near* it,[22] and Polybius did not mention
them at all in connection with the 'Island': he only brought
them in on the next stage of the march.

Both authors, as I have said, described how Hannibal settled
the dispute between the two brothers and how the grateful
king whom he had re-established on the throne rewarded him
by re-equipping his army; and it was at this point that Livy
spoke of the dispute about the throne as 'the disputes of the
Allobroges', Polybius not mentioning the name of the tribe.
But the greatest service, according to Polybius, which the
victorious elder brother rendered to Hannibal was that he
promised to escort him with a rearguard of his own forces—τῆς
σφετέρας δυνάμεως—on the march through the territory of 'the
Gauls called Allobroges'—διὰ τῶν Ἀλλοβρίγων καλουμένων
Γαλατῶν—about which Hannibal had been uneasy, and so
ensured a safe passage for the army until it neared the crossing
of the Alps.[23] It is hard to believe that Polybius would have
introduced the name 'Allobroges' for the first time in such a
way, or drawn such a distinction between them and the king's

---

[19] Polybius III. 49. 8–12 and Livy XXI. 31. 6–8.   [20] XXI. 31. 9.
[21] e.g. Hyde, p. 201.   [22] XXI. 31. 5.   [23] III. 49. 13.

forces, if he had thought that Brancus was their king and that
they were the ruling tribe in the 'Island' as well as the inhabitants of the country on the next stage of the march; yet
this is the assumption that is commonly made.

The explanation usually offered is that the people whom
Polybius described as 'the local chiefs of the Allobroges'— οἱ
κατὰ μέρος ἡγεμόνες τῶν Ἀλλοβρίγων [24]—on the next stage of the
march, who did in fact shadow the army on its march from the
'Island' along the river and attacked at the end of it, were outlying chieftains under the suzerainty of the king, perhaps dissi-
dent supporters of the unsuccessful claimant to the throne, and
that Brancus undertook to quell them with his superior authority.[25] But nothing in the subsequent narrative bears out such an
interpretation. Polybius describes how the chieftains kept their
distance as long as the army was in the flat country, from fear
partly of the Carthaginian cavalry, but also of 'the escorting
barbarians'—not quite the description one would expect of
troops acting under orders from their king, if this is what Polybius meant—and how, as soon as the escorting force had departed and the army began the difficult climb into the mountains,
they collected their forces, seized the commanding heights
between which it would have to pass, and prepared to contest
the passage.[26] From that point on Polybius and Livy give
practically the same account of the bloody battle which ensued
and the way in which Hannibal eventually forced his way
through: the only difference between them is that, whereas
Polybius referred to the enemy throughout as Allobroges,[27]
Livy called them simply *montani*—highlanders.[28] If the Allobroges or *montani* were subjects of the king at the 'Island', why
in the world should the escorting force sent out by the grateful
Brancus have abandoned the Carthaginians at such a moment
to the mercies of their fellow-tribesmen—and this without a
world of comment or reproach from Polybius? No explanation
is vouchsafed by those who take this view: the difficulty is not
even noticed.

Livy did not mention the escorting force: he only took up the
narrative at the point where the climb into the mountains
began; but there is nothing in his account either to suggest that

[24] III. 50. 2.   [25] e.g. Jullian, p. 477 or Walbank, note on III. 49. 8.
[26] III. 50. 2–3.   [27] Ibid. and 51. 9.   [28] XXI. 32 and 33 *passim*.

he identified the hostile tribesmen with the ruling tribe at the 'Island'. Both authors describe how, after a night operation reminiscent of Gideon's operation against the hosts of Midian and a desperate struggle on the pass the next day, the Carthaginians eventually routed the tribesmen, forced their way across the pass, and occupied a town on the other side, where they paused to consolidate and collected enough corn and cattle for 3 days' rations.[29] The town (or *castellum* as Livy called it) must therefore have been a substantial centre of local agriculture. Livy said that it was 'the capital of that region' and that it was only after a further 3 days' marching that the Carthaginians passed into the territory of 'another, though still highland, tribe';[30] all of which may well have been a true description of an outlying settlement of the Allobroges on the borders of their territory. But he never made any connection between them and the ruling tribe in the 'Island'. He had mentioned the Allobroges twice by name in his account of events there: he would surely have made *some* reference to them in his subsequent narrative, some mention of the relationship between the *montani* and the kingdom of the Allobroges, if he had thought that they belonged to the same tribe.

It seems plain that one thing on which Polybius and Livy both agreed was that the tribesmen who attacked the army on its first entry into the mountains (and who, according to Polybius, had been shadowing it on the approach march) did *not* belong to the tribe whose throne was in dispute at the 'Island'. Polybius calls the former consistently Allobroges, but does not name the latter: Livy calls the latter Allobroges and the former *montani*: neither of them, if his words are read attentively, can be credited with a belief that it was the same tribe in both cases. If, then, their evidence is to be respected, it is necessary to choose between them and not, as is commonly done, to confound the march 'along the river' and the halt at the 'Island' with one and the same tribe, the Allobroges. Which of them was right? Did the 'Island' belong to the Allobroges as Livy thought, in which case it certainly was in the confluence of the Rhône and the Isère, or was Polybius right in making the Allobroges the tribesmen who shadowed the army on the

---

[29] Polybius III. 50. 4 to 51. 12, and Livy XXI. 32. 9 to 33. 11.
[30] XXI. 33. 11 to 34.1.

march 'along the river' and eventually attacked at the end of it, in which case the river in question was certainly the Isère?

The answer is not a new one. It is a safe assertion that no solution of any one problem in the march of Hannibal that is offered now after two thousand years of speculation is being suggested for the first time: it will invariably be found that someone else has proposed it before, though it may not have been combined in quite the same way with other parts of the data. In this case it seems that only one person has previously put forward precisely the same solution as the one which I now propose—though he did not follow through its implications to the same extent—and he was R. L. Dunbabin, whom the reader may remember as the other writer who came closest to my reconstruction of the timetable of the march in Part 1. He adopted as his location of the 'Island' the confluence of the Rhône and the Aygues, about 100 kilometres down-stream from Pont de l'Isère, which Fortia D' Urban had first proposed in 1808 and which de Beer and Devos have recently revived. But, whereas all three of them made Hannibal branch off from the Rhône at or near the 'Island' on a route to the Col de Montgenèvre or a more southerly pass without going anywhere near the Isère, Dunbabin made him follow the left bank of the Rhône as far as the confluence and then continue up the left bank of the Isère on his approach march to the Alps;[31] and this is precisely the route which I shall adopt.

Dunbabin proffered his route as a modification of that proposed by Spenser Wilkinson, whom he regarded as its main author, the only difference being that he located the 'Island' at the confluence of the Aygues, as I have said, whereas Spenser Wilkinson had put it at the confluence of the Sorgues, about 16 kilometres down-stream. But Spenser Wilkinson, as he himself handsomely acknowledged more than once,[32] was following in the footsteps of the French soldier, Captain Colin, and Colin was the true founder of the scheme which I shall now expound.[33] I shall not follow him, any more than Dunbabin did, in locating the 'Island' at the confluence of the Sorgues: I agree with Dunbabin, de Beer, and Devos, as I have said before, that it was in the confluence of the Rhône and the Aygues; but, substantially, my conception of the march from the 'Island' to the

[31] p. 53.   [32] pp. 15–17, 19 and 26.   [33] pp. 317–67.

first battle at the beginning of the climb into the mountains, and many of the arguments on which it relies, are those of Captain Colin.

Colin prefaced his examination of Hannibal's route with a long discussion of the geography of the ancient Gallic tribes, our authorities for which—mainly Strabo, Pliny, and Ptolemy—range between 200 and 350 years later; he concluded that, though the zones of influence of the different tribes no doubt fluctuated on the borders, they occupied in 218 B.C. substantially the same territories as those attributed to them by the later writers,[34] and I shall follow him in accepting their indications as valid for all practical purposes in the time of Hannibal. Though Livy singled out the Allobroges for mention as 'second to none among the Gallic tribes in wealth and prestige',[35] their southern neighbours—the Cavares in the west next to the Rhône, and the Vocontii to the east in the highlands of the Vercors—were of comparable importance. The Cavares occupied the whole length of the country on the east side of the Rhône between Cavaillon on the Durance and the confluence of the Rhône and the Isère just above Valence,[36] the Isère in its lower reaches being the frontier between them and the Allobroges. They embraced within their suzerainty a number of subordinate tribes, including the Memini at Carpentras, the Tricastini in the modern Tricastin round St. Paul-Trois-Châteaux,* and the Segovellauni (or Seggalauni) at Valence,[37] all of which are mentioned as towns within their territory by Pliny[36] or Ptolemy[37] or both; but the central towns of Avignon and Orange are assigned, not to any subordinate tribe, but to the Cavares themselves.

If, therefore, the 'Island' was near Orange in the confluence of the Rhône and the Aygues, it was in the heart of their country; the scene of the dispute over the throne which Hannibal was asked to settle must have been somewhere near, and the principal supply centre for the re-quipment of his army cannot have been far away. The Cavares, a major tribe of some consequence,

---

[34] pp. 104–40. [35] XXI. 31. 5.
[36] Strabo IV. 1. 11 and Pliny *HN* III. 4. 36–7.
[37] Strabo IV. 1. 12; Ptolemy, *Geographica*, II. 10. 7; and Holsten, p. 18.

---

* This location of the Tricastini, which has been disputed, will be discussed more fully later—pp. 166–9.

11—H.M.I.H.

would have been equal to the task, and they would have been strong enough to send an escorting force with Hannibal to quell the frontiersmen of their neighbours, the Allobroges, on his march up the Isère. The conclusion is irresistible that the 'Island' was in the territory of the Cavares, not of the Allobroges, and to Colin in 1904 belongs the credit of being the first person to pronounce it.[38]

Two points, however, may have worried the reader in this reconstruction of the picture. If the Isère was the frontier between the Cavares and the Allobroges, and if Hannibal was marching up the *left* bank of that river, and began the climb into the mountains from there, how can the resistance which he encountered have come from the Allobroges as Polybius said? Alternatively, if the Allobroges *were* the enemy, was it not an act of war on the part of the Cavares, of which there is no mention in Polybius or Livy, to send an armed force into the territory of their powerful neighbours, the Allobroges? The answer to both questions must be the same. Though the frontier of the two tribes was indeed the Isère in the settled country of the Rhône valley between Valence and Vienne, it was much more indeterminate further up-stream where the river flowed between the mountains of the Grande Chartreuse on the north and those of the Vercors on the south, and in this area the Allobroges certainly spread across the Isère into the northern extremity of the Vercors. Cularo, the ancient Gaulish town on or near the site of Grenoble, was on the *left* bank of the Isère, as Grenoble still is, and it was mentioned in Cicero's time as a town of the Allobroges near their border;[39] and Strabo says explicitly that the Vocontii, who occupied the upland country behind the Cavares and their subordinate tribes along the Rhône valley, and whose main axis was the river Drôme, extended as far as the Allobroges in this mountainous area to the north.[40] This part of the country, which is still a wild, secret region—it was one of the lairs of the French resistance in the last war—must have been an ill-defined hinterland over which no one tribe could positively claim sovereignty.

The escorting force of the Cavares was strictly within its own territory while it was covering the army along the left bank of the Isère across the comparatively narrow strip of

[38] p. 350.   [39] Cicero, *Epistolae ad Fam.*, x. 23.   [40] IV. 6. 4.

plain occupied by their subordinate tribe, the Segovellauni, but
when the mountains began to close in on the river, they were in
a kind of no-man's-land. As long as they hugged the river
bank, they might still claim to be marching along their own
frontier, but the Allobroges were shadowing the army now, not
merely from across the river, but from the heights above on the
left bank, just as Polybius described, and they were indeed, as
Livy called them, *montani*. They were, as Polybius and Livy both
indicated in their different ways, outlying tribesmen on the
indeterminate frontiers of the main tribe, the Allobroges, but
not, as the commentators make out, of the tribe that ruled at
the 'Island'. So the escorting force of the Cavares continued
to cover the army, without any overt breach of sovereignty, as
long as it hugged the river bank, but left it to its own devices
when it began the ascent into the mountains. From the point of
view of the Cavares, who had already come, according to
Polybius, some 140 kilometres from their base into potentially
hostile country, this was reasonable enough, and there was no
call for any comment from Polybius, whereas he would surely
have expressed his disapproval if troops sent out by the king of
the Allobroges himself had left them in the lurch at such a
moment.

Everything, therefore, points to a location of the 'Island'
somewhere short of the Allobroges in the territory of the Cavares except the two references to the Allobroges in Livy, and
these, one would have thought, might have appeared a little
suspect in themselves under a cool look, for it does not seem very
natural to attribute a dispute over a throne and a comprehensive re-equipment of Hannibal's army, both of which Livy
describes as taking place *in* the 'Island', to a tribe which only
lived *near* it. Something must have gone wrong here, one feels,
and this alone might have sapped some of the confidence in the
two statements. Livy's reference to the Allobroges as the ruling
tribe of the 'Island' must certainly be reckoned a mistake. His
statement that they lived near it might perhaps just pass
muster, though it seems a strange way of alluding to a tribe
whose frontier, if the 'Island' was where I take it to be, was
some 90 to 100 kilometres away. Probably neither Livy nor
his source had any very distinct idea of the geography of the
Gallic tribes, and perhaps they simply lifted their gaze at this

point from the Cavares to the next major tribe along the line of march.

All the rest of the evidence shows that the march 'along the river' did indeed proceed along the Isère, as the great majority of modern commentators hold, but that this cannot be combined with an 'Island' in the confluence of that river and the Rhône. The disregard of Polybius' plain meaning that the march from the 'Island' at least began along the Rhône itself, the necessity for a double crossing of the Isère not mentioned by him or Livy, the impracticability of Hannibal's intervention in the dispute over the throne and the subsequent refitting of his army at a distance of over 60 kilometres from the capital, and the distinction clearly present in the minds of both Polybius and Livy between the ruling tribe in the 'Island' and the tribesmen who attacked the army on its first climb into the mountains all go to show that, if the march 'along the river' was along the Isère in the territory of the Allobroges, the 'Island' cannot also have been in their territory. On the other hand, the physical character of the Isère valley, answering as no other river valley does to Polybius' description of the march 'in the flat country', and the fact that it was unquestionably in the territory of the Allobroges as he said, prove equally conclusively that this was the scene of the march 'along the river'.

How, then, does the confluence of the Rhône and the Aygues answer to the description of the 'Island' in Polybius and Livy? At least as well as that of the Rhône and the Isère, and some would say better. De Beer, for instance, claims that it is the *only* confluence of the Rhône and a tributary which fits the description.[41] The Aygues, though a much shorter river than the Isère, rises in the Alps, as Livy said; it meets the Rhône at a sharp point, with a tract of rich agricultural land between them, just as Polybius described. The one stumbling block, as usual, is his comparison with the delta of the Nile. The *shape*, indeed, is more amenable to his figure of a triangle than that of Cluver's 'Island' at the confluence of the Isère; but the resemblance in size to the delta of the Nile is minimal, since the mountains of the Baronnies and their north-western outliers, which de Beer[41] and Devos[42] take to be the base of the triangle, are only some 40 kilometres from the confluence. Moreover, since only at one

[41] p. 22.   [42] p. 65.

point do they rise as high as 1,300 metres above sea level, they cannot be said to answer to Polybius' description of an 'almost inaccessible' barrier.

However, we should not be deterred by Polybius' *jeu d'esprit*, any more than Cluver was, from accepting a location of the 'Island' which fits the facts in every other respect. All the rest of the evidence confirms the conclusion of de Beer and Devos that this was the scene of Hannibal's 'Island', and in the next chapter we shall trace the progress of the march 'along the river' from its starting-point there.

IX

THE MARCH ALONG THE RIVER

THE first thing to be said about Hannibal's march 'along the river' from an 'Island' located at the confluence of the Rhône and the Aygues is that it began, as Polybius clearly meant, by continuing up the Rhône itself, and, as such, it is immune from the heresy that he branched off from the Rhône at the 'Island', which has become the orthodox doctrine associated with an 'Island' at the confluence of the Isère and has even infected some of those who locate it at that of the Aygues.* Once past the narrows at Donzère, Hannibal would have proceeded comfortably with plenty of room for his army 'in the flat country' of the Rhône valley as Polybius described. A little way above Valence, after marching some 90 to 100 kilometres, he would have met the Isère, which joins the Rhône from the north-east at an angle of about thirty degrees; he would have continued along the left bank of the Isère—no unrecorded crossing of that river has to be assumed—heading now for the first time since he had crossed the Rhône towards the Alps.

Polybius thought he was still following the Rhône, and this is understandable, for, though it makes nonsense of his intellectual processes to suppose that he could have confused the Rhône with its tributary at the 'Island', this is by no means the case if Hannibal continued for 90 to 100 kilometres up the Rhône before leaving it. If Polybius made the journey up the Rhône himself, he may have cut across country just before the

---

* Devos, for instance, makes Hannibal branch off up the Ouvèze. Marquion, who accepts the orthodox location of the 'Island' at the confluence of the Isère, does give full value to Polybius' plain meaning that the march 'along the river' at least began along the Rhône itself, and he dutifully makes Hannibal continue up the Rhône for about 60 kilometres to a point near Vienne (pp. 40–1); but he then makes him turn sharply to the right on a course to the Col de l'Épine (his location of the first entry into the mountains), and the second half of his unnatural dog-leg route, across an open plain, bears no resemblance to a march 'along the river'.

junction of the two rivers and thought, when he joined the Isère, that he had rejoined the Rhône, as Dunbabin suggested;[1] or, even if he followed the Rhône right up to the confluence, he may still have thought that the left-bank river was the Rhône, which he could not possibly have thought at the 'Island', where he had just given it a different name. Indeed, such a misconception harmonizes perfectly with his earlier description of the Rhône as flowing from north–east to south–west;[2] for this is precisely the general direction of the Isère over the main part of its course from Albertville to Valence, whereas the Rhône flows almost due north to south all the way from Lyon to the sea. It is true that, as I mentioned earlier, the points of the compass were tilted askew in Polybius' orientation of Gaul, and that he had what Walbank called a 'false picture of the Rhone's direction'; but this may have been precisely for the reason I have just suggested—that he mistook the Isère for the Rhône in this part of its course.

In its lower reaches the Isère flows across a plain—still 'in the flat country'—but about 50 kilometres above the confluence, on the stretch of river between St. Marcellin on the right bank and the village of Rovon on the left, the steep slopes of the Vercors begin to close in on the left bank, and the floor of the valley shifts to the other side. It is also about here that the course of the river, going up-stream, begins to form a kink in its general north-easterly direction before straightening out again at Grenoble, and the shortest (though not the easiest) route to Grenoble is to leave the river and cut off the corner. The apex of the corner—the extreme northernmost tip of the Vercors—is the cliff of the Bec de l'Échaillon, towering to a peak some 800 metres above the river and rising another 600 metres or more to the heights of the range behind. For some 25 kilometres down-stream from the Bec de l'Échaillon the river washes the foot of the mountains all the way, and before the modern *corniche* road was engineered the left bank of the Isère on this reach must have been practically impassable for an army the size of Hannibal's. Somewhere on this stretch of the river Hannibal must have been faced with a decision whether to make a second difficult river-crossing and transfer the army and all its animals on a fleet of boats and rafts to the opposite bank,

[1] p. 55.   [2] III. 47. 2.

and then to follow the outside of the big bend to Grenoble, or to take to the mountains and cut across the corner. Obviously he chose the latter, and it must have been about here that the march 'along the river' ended and the climb into the mountains began.

Colin,[3] Spenser Wilkinson,[4] and Dunbabin,[5] my three predecessors in this conception of the march, marked the spot as St. Quentin, just short of the Bec de l'Échaillon itself. This is some 160 kilometres from an 'Island' in the confluence of the Rhône and the Aygues, which would have been two steps up in Polybius' scale of measurement in round hundreds of stades, making the figure for the march 'along the river' 1,000, not 800, stades. So although one should not press Polybius' measurements too precisely, it seems more probable both for this and other reasons that Hannibal left the river somewhere short of St. Quentin. His difficulties in proceeding along the left bank of the river would have begun a good deal earlier than that, and, once he had got as far as St. Quentin, he would only have had to negotiate the Bec de l'Échaillon to have a level valley floor on his own side of the river once again for the rest of the way.

But there is no need to be dogmatic about the precise spot. Along the river for some 20 kilometres down-stream from St. Quentin there are twisting gullies and ravines debouching on the left bank from the recesses of the mountains; any one of these may have been the one up which the army began its climb, and any of them will answer to Livy's graphic description of the scene. The gullies grow narrower as they go up and end in an impassable mountain wall; the paths that lead across the range climb the slopes at one side and thread their way precipitously through the heights above; and this is just how Livy described the one by which Hannibal's army made its entry into the mountains. He transposed it in his narrative to a different stage of the march, but his description tallies so closely with that of Polybius that they must both have been describing the same episode.

Livy tells how, after sending out Gaulish scouts to reconnoitre, Hannibal pitched camp amidst steep jagged crags in the widest available part of the valley—'castra inter confragosa omnia praeruptaque quam extentissima potest valle locat';[6] how, when he heard from the scouts that the enemy only occupied the commanding heights above the pass during the day and retired to a town on the other side of the range for the night, he emerged from the narrows—'angustias evadit'[7]—and took possession of the heights with a picked force during the night; and how the next day, when the main army, with its horses, pack animals, and elephants, was strung out along the narrow winding path as it painfully made its way up the slopes— δυσχερῶς ἐκμηρυομένους καὶ μακρῶς τὰς δυσχωρίας—as Polybius here describes it,[8] the enemy tribesmen bore down on it from the pass which they had reoccupied, and many men and horses were hurled in the press over sheer precipices into the chasm below—'multosque turba, cum praecipites deruptaeque utrimque angustiae essent, in immensum altitudinis dejecit.'[9] Polybius similarly spoke of Hannibal making his way through the narrows—διῆλθε τὰ στενά[10]—to gain the heights above, and described the way up to the pass as not only rough and narrow, but also precipitous—οὔσης γὰρ οὐ μόνον στενῆς καὶ τραχείας τῆς προσβολῆς, ἀλλὰ καὶ κρημνώδους.[11]

Hannibal saved the situation by swooping down with his picked men from the heights above the pass, though only after a desperate mêlée, in which his own army suffered heavy losses of men and animals from the sheer weight of the struggle bearing down on them from above.[12] The tribesmen were put to flight and evacuated the town on the other side of the range which had been their operational base; Hannibal occupied it, finding there enough corn and cattle for 3 days' rations of his army, and rested there for a day before proceeding any further.[13] It was evidently a place of some substance in an agricultural setting, to which Hannibal descended after the difficult crossing of the Vercors—αἱ δυσχωρίαι, as Polybius repeatedly called the region[14]—and it must have been the Gaulish town of Cularo on or near the site of the modern Grenoble, the capital, as Livy called it, of the local settlement—some 15 to 20 kilometres as the crow flies from the point where the army had left the river.

---

[6] XXI. 32. 9.   [7] XXI. 32. 13.   [8] Polybius III. 51. 2.   [9] XXI. 33. 7.
[10] III. 50. 9.   [11] III. 51. 4.   [12] Polybius III. 51. 7–8 and Livy XXI. 33. 9.
[13] Polybius III. 51. 11–12 and Livy XXI. 33. 11.
[14] III. 50. 3 and 8, and 51. 2, 5 and 9.

Here Hannibal was poised, after this first taste of the mountains, for the attack on the Alps themselves, and here, for the moment, we shall leave him.

A postscript may be added for its own sake, though it does not contribute to solving the problem of Hannibal's route. Livy says that the Gaulish scouts who reported the fact that the enemy tribesmen retired to their town every night were able to gain the information in conversation with the *montani* because their language was not very different from their own.[15] The scouts could conceivably have been men from the escorting force which accompanied the army from the 'Island' if some of them stayed with Hannibal after the others had gone back, but there is nothing in Polybius' account to suggest that this is what happened, and it seems unlikely. They cannot have been local inhabitants picked up on the way from the 'Island', for in that case, apart from the fact that the local inhabitants on this part of the march were hostile, they would have spoken the *same* language as the *montani*. Polybius describes them as some of Hannibal's Gaulish *guides*,[16] and his use of this word suggests that they belonged to the party of Boians who had come to meet him at the Rhône to guide him on his way into Italy.[17] But the Boii had been settled round Bologna for 200 years, and, according to modern archaeologists, they had come into Italy over the Brenner, not from France.[18] If, therefore, the guides on this occasion were indeed Boians, it is an interesting example of the spread and persistence of a generic language that they were able to make themselves understood in conversation with a different Gallic tribe which had been settled for at least as long in the Dauphiné.

[15] XXI. 32. 10.   [16] III. 50. 6.   [17] III. 44. 9.
[18] Hyde, pp. 133–6 and *OCD*², p. 242.

X

THE MARCH FROM THE RHÔNE-CROSSING TO THE ISLAND

AFTER this excursion up the Rhône and the Isère we are at last in a position to return to the question of the Rhône-crossing. We saw how all the direct evidence about the crossing itself pointed unmistakably to a location in the neighbourhood of Beaucaire–Tarascon, but we reserved our conclusion until we had examined the contrary view that its position was fixed at a range of some 100 kilometres from the 'Island' by a calculation about the distance between the two places, and that the 'Island' was in the confluence of the Rhône and the Isère. Now we have found that the 'Island' itself was nearly that distance further south, and the calculation about the position of the crossing-place is left hanging in the air. But it was never, in fact, a sound one, and we shall now examine it.

The essential argument was a simple subtraction sum. In his preliminary geographical conspectus Polybius had given the distance from the Rhône-crossing 'as far as the climb of the Alps into Italy'—ἕως πρὸς τὴν ἀναβολὴν τῶν Ἄλπεων τὴν εἰς Ἰταλίαν[1]—as 250 kilometres. Later, in the course of his narrative of the march itself, he gave the figure of 143 kilometres which I have several times mentioned for the march 'along the river' from the 'Island' to the point where the army 'began the climb to the Alps'—ἤρξατο τῆς πρὸς τὰς Ἄλπεις ἀναβολῆς.[2] Therefore, it is inferred, the distance from the crossing-place to the 'Island' must have been the difference between the two—about 107 kilometres—and this is taken as the length of the piece of string by which the crossing-place is tethered; so that if one end of it is regarded as fastened to an 'Island' in the confluence of the Rhône and the Isère, the crossing-place is fixed somewhere on the stretch of river between, say, Roquemaure and Pont St. Esprit—the locations favoured

[1] III. 39. 9. [2] III. 50. 1.

by what I have called the 'long distance' school of historians.[3]

The first comment one might make on this form of reasoning is that in principle it is a comparison of two larger totals to arrive at a smaller balancing figure, a method which every statistician knows to be wide open to error; and in this case one of the totals is picked from a different part of Polybius' *History* where he was giving a geographical conspectus, not an account of the march itself, so that the comparison is not exactly one of like with like. It referred, moreover, to a part of the journey in which Hannibal had left the direct road to Italy far behind and in which it cannot have been so easy to gauge the true distances. It is not even certain that Polybius himself knew what this part of the route was. Although he claimed to have made the crossing of the Alps to see the country for himself, he did not explicitly say that he travelled the same route as Hannibal.[4] The method itself, therefore, is dubious, even if the data were sound, which in fact they are not.

For should it, after all, be taken for granted that Polybius meant one and the same place by the two phrases which I have quoted? On *a priori* grounds alone it might be doubted whether he carried in his memory the words which he had used ten chapters earlier when he came to describe the end of the march 'along the river' and intended to identify the two places; and, in point of fact, the words are *not* the same. In the first place he spoke of the climb *of* the Alps into Italy, in the second the beginning of the climb *to* the Alps; and we have just seen how well the latter expression fits the army's first experience of the mountains on its climb from the Isère across the northern extremity of the Vercors before it embarked on the ascent of the main range of the Alps into Italy. So it is not merely pedantic to peg down Polybius to such a rigid interpretation of his words, but it actually falsifies their meaning; and, if the two phrases are to be brought into juxtaposition at all, the natural interpretation is that there was an unspecified interval between the two places, which means that there is a missing term in the subtraction sum.

Yet most of the modern writers upholding the orthodox view

---

[3] e.g. de Luc, pp. 56–7; De Sanctis, p. 70; Walbank, *JRS*, p. 42; Marquion, p. 33.

[4] III. 48. 12.

of Hannibal's route have assumed that the two places were the
same and have done their sum on that basis.[5] Freshfield is an
honourable exception to the extent that he did see the necessity
to argue the point; but his exposition, though it seems to have
satisfied Walbank,[6] is so confused, adducing arguments about
the *starting-point* to demonstrate the identity of the end-points,
that it cannot be said to carry conviction.[7] Here, as elsewhere,
Colin saw the truth and recognized that there must have been
a gap between the end of the march 'along the river' and the
point which Polybius called 'the climb of the Alps into Italy';[8]
and Perrin before him,[9] and de Beer [10] and Devos [11] since, have
all constructed their itineraries on the same assumption, though
they have not explicitly discussed the point.

But there was still another objection which should have given
pause to the others before they committed themselves to their
arithmetical conclusion—the speed of march required to cover
a distance of some 107 kilometres between the crossing-place
and the 'Island' in 4 days. This, indeed, is their distinguishing
characteristic, and it is why I have dubbed them the 'long
distance' school of historians. The reader may remember how
we found their estimates of 26 kilometres and upwards for the
length of a day's march on this particular section quite out of
line with the norm when we considered the army's probable
rate of progress in Part i. Cluver [12] and his pupil, Holsten,[13]
who both accepted Beaucaire–Tarascon as the place of the
Rhône-crossing, had taken no stock in the subtraction sum, but
neither did they trouble to reconcile their location of the 'Island' at the confluence of the Rhône and the Isère, nearly 160
kilometres away, with the explicit statement of both Polybius [14]
and Livy [15] that the distance between the two was covered in 4
days. Camille Jullian, who also made the same identification
of the two points without troubling about the subtraction sum,
and did not blench from the inference that the army must have
travelled at a speed which he put at 37 kilometres a day [16]
(though in fact it would have been rather more), must be regarded in this instance as a joker in the pack.

[5] e.g. de Luc, p. 74; De Sanctis, p. 70; Marquion, p. 33.   [6] *JRS*, p. 42.
[7] *Hannibal Once More*, 1914, p. 34.   [8] pp. 337–9.
[9] pp. 106–14 and 119–27.   [10] p. 39.   [11] pp. 91–6.   [12] p. 373.
[13] pp. 22–3.   [14] iii. 49. 5.   [15] xxi. 31. 4.   [16] p. 474.

De Luc in 1818 seems to have been the first writer to introduce the subtraction sum. He accepted the conventional identification of the 'Island' with the confluence of the Rhône and the Isère, and deduced from it that the Rhône-crossing was at Roquemaure,[17] about half-way up the stretch of the Rhône between Avignon and Orange, which has since become the typical crossing-place of the 'long-distance' school. De Sanctis[18] Walbank,[19] and Marquion[20] have all made the same calculation, though their answers differ. De Sanctis had some difficulty with his, for he thought the crossing-place was at Pont St. Esprit or St. Étienne-des-Sorts, which are only some 85 or 90 kilometres from the Isère, not 95 or 100 as he said, and therefore fall rather short of the required distance of 107 kilometres—quite apart from the fact that, as we have seen, either of them is far beyond the extreme limit of possibility for the movements of Scipio's forces from his camp at Fos. De Sanctis, however, writes up the distance to $106\frac{1}{2}$ kilometres when he comes to his subtraction sum, though he does not explain how a 4-day march of that length is to be reconciled with his own estimate of Hannibal's average speed of march, given a few pages later, at 20 kilometres a day.[21]

Walbank, following De Sanctis in the subtraction sum and locating the crossing-place further down-stream to suit it, grasped the nettle more firmly, and justified the resulting average of $26\frac{1}{2}$ kilometres a day on the ground that it was 'by no means impossible, since Hannibal was in a hurry to leave Scipio behind';[22] and Marquion offered the same justification of his still faster rate of just on 30 kilometres a day over the last 3 days of the march.[23] But this is pure surmise on their part: there is nothing in the text of Livy or Polybius to suggest that Hannibal was forcing the pace unless the neutral word ἑξῆς [24]— 'straight on'—is to be so interpreted; and such a speed would have been well beyond the capacity of his army to keep up for 4 days running.

But the gravest defect of these writers is their failure to take account of Polybius' information (accepted by them in its

---

[17] pp. 51–62.   [18] p. 70.
[19] Note on Polybius III. 49. 5 and *JRS*, 1956, p. 42.
[20] p. 33.   [21] p. 80.   [22] *JRS* 1956, p. 42.
[23] p. 125.   [24] III. 49. 5.

context) about the 10-day march of 143 kilometres 'along the river', which must have been performed in very similar conditions. Whether that march was wholly along the Isère, as they think, or partly along the Rhône, partly along the Isère, as I maintain, it proceeded up a wide, gently sloping river valley—'in the flat country', as Polybius called it—and there is no obvious reason why the length of a day's march along another stretch of the Rhône should have been widely different. If Hannibal is thought to have been forcing the pace between the crossing-place and the 'Island' to get away from Scipio, he can equally be presumed to have made all the speed he could in the march from the 'Island' onwards; for his army had just been rested and refitted; the autumn was closing in on him and he was on the last lap before the mountains; he must have wanted to make sure of crossing the Alps before it was too late. There is no rational ground for supposing that he could conjure up an extra 10 kilometres a day from his army—well over 50 per cent above the daily average 'along the river'—and keep it up for 4 days running on the march between the crossing-place and the 'Island'.

De Beer [25] and Devos [26] were much nearer the mark in adopting the evidence of the march 'along the river' as the criterion of the speed of march on the preceding section, as Colin had done before them;[27] and although, as we saw in Part I, they probably underestimated the distance covered in a day on a march which Polybius says was made 'straight on'—that is, without a rest day—the adjusted rate of 16 to 17 kilometres a day, after allowing for one rest day on the 10-day march,* is a much more probable estimate of the speed of march between the crossing-place and the 'Island' than any of the figures postulated by the 'long distance' school of historians. De Beer and Devos therefore put the distance between the two, from their slightly different crossing-places in the neighbourhood of Beaucaire–Tarascon, at about 60 kilometres.[28] There is no

---

[25] p. 25.   [26] p. 24.   [27] pp. 336–7.
[28] de Beer, p. 26; Devos, p. 50.

---

* The upper limit of 17 kilometres allows for the possibility that Polybius' '800 stades' (which is equivalent to 143 kilometres) was a round number for anything up to 850 stades or 152 kilometres, and on my view of the route the actual distance is likely to have been near the top end of the range.

need to alter their figure upwards for the adjustment in the length of a day's march, for the march did not necessarily consist of four full marching days: indeed the probability is that the first day was a short one if, as Polybius says, Hannibal waited behind at the crossing-place to bring the elephants across the river [29] and had to catch up with the army at the first camping-place that evening; and the last day need not have been a full one either.

So, starting from a position of the Rhône-crossing in the neighbourhood of Beaucaire–Tarascon, firmly established, as we have seen it to be, by all the direct evidence surrounding the operation itself and no longer tied by any valid chain of reasoning to an 'Island' in the confluence of the Rhône and the Isère, de Beer and Devos, following Fortia D'Urban over a century before and Dunbabin more recently, have located the 'Island' in the confluence of the Rhône and the Aygues about 60 kilometres away. They have demonstrated that the textual authority for the Aygues as the name of the river at the 'Island' is at least as sound as that of the conjectural emendation 'Isère', if not sounder; the topography of that confluence fits the description of the 'Island' equally well; it is at the right distance for a 4-day march from the Rhône-crossing: no exaggerated estimate of the army's speed of march has to be made, and there is no longer any need to inflate the distance to satisfy a spurious subtraction sum; an 'Island' in the territory of the Cavares is immune from all the difficulties to which a location in the kingdom of the Allobroges gives rise; the onward march from it began along the Rhône, as Polybius clearly meant; no unrecorded crossing and recrossing of the Isère has to be postulated; and the march continued for the right distance of 140 to 150 kilometres up to the point where the first climb into the mountains began. There cannot be any further doubt that de Beer and Devos are right in locating the 'Island' here; and, with this conclusion, we can confirm too once and for all that they were also right in locating the place of the Rhône-crossing somewhere in the neighbourhood of Beaucaire–Tarascon.

[29] III. 45. 6 and 47. 1.

XI

LIVY'S ROUTE

WE have concentrated mainly up to now on Polybius' evidence for Hannibal's route between the 'Island' and the first climb into the mountains; but Livy gave a different account which has generally been held to denote quite a different route, and to this we must now turn. I have mentioned once or twice before that he described a crossing of the *Druentia* (Durance) by the army on this section of the march. He introduced it by a short passage which Jullian [1] and Cluver before him [2] said had bedevilled the discussion of Hannibal's route ever since and ought to be ignored, and I have done so up to now; but now we must come to grips with it, and in doing so we shall regretfully have to part company with de Beer and Devos, who have for so long been the Dioscuri of our navigation.

Livy says that, having settled the disputes of the Allobroges (as he called them), Hannibal, 'though he was now on his way to the Alps, did not take the direct route, but turned to the left into the territory of the Tricastini; from there he made for the territory of the Tricorii along the far frontier of the Vocontii, and nowhere met with any hindrance until he reached the river Durance'. [3] No sense can be made of this as it stands; for, no matter where the 'Island' was, or where exactly these tribes lived in the country between the Rhône and the Alps, Hannibal could not have moved towards any of them by turning to the left when he was travelling northwards up the Rhône. There was, in fact, only one place in the whole of the march from Cartagena to north Italy at which he could have turned to the left at all (apart from deviations to subdue the tribes in northern Spain) and that was directly after he had crossed the Rhône when he turned northwards up the river to keep away from the Romans; and it is quite obvious that Livy had lifted from one

---

[1] pp. 475–6.　　[2] p. 373.　　[3] XXI. 31. 9.

of his sources a passage referring to that stage of the march, and that either he or his source put it in the wrong place in the narrative. One can almost hear the echo of the muddle in Livy's words. Describing the turn to the left after the Rhône-crossing (which, as the reader may remember, he made Hannibal explicitly mention in his address to the troops at the time),[4] he explained that Hannibal took the new direction in order to avoid the Romans, not because it was a more direct way to the Alps—'non quia rectior ad Alpes via esset'[5]—and then, when he came to the alleged turn to the left into the territory of the Tricastini on leaving the 'Island', he used the very similar words which I have just translated—'cum jam Alpes peteret, non recta regione iter instituit.'[6]

Colin seems to have been the first person to divine that this is what happened,[7] but Kahrstedt,[8] de Sanctis,[9] and Walbank[10] all saw it clearly enough too; and Devos has reached the same conclusion by dint of a somewhat strained argument to the effect that Livy intended to mark the phasing of the movements described by using different tenses of the verbs in the same sentence.[11] In fact, it can be taken as certain that this was a sheer mistake on the part of Livy or his source, and that the famous turn to the left occurred directly after the Rhône-crossing, not on the departure from the 'Island'. On leaving the 'Island', Hannibal must have continued straight on up the Rhône. He passed first, according to Livy, into the territory of the Tricastini, and we must now make sure where this was.

Livy had mentioned the Tricastini earlier in his *History*, when he described them as facing the Alps—'Alpes inde oppositae erant'—and related that the Gaulish king, Bellovesus, made the first mass crossing of the Alps from their territory into that of the Taurini in the reign of Tarquinius Priscus about 600 B.C.[12] Though the story itself is discredited by modern archaeologists, as I have previously mentioned, it does not necessarily follow that Livy was wrong about the position of the Tricastini at that time; but it seems more likely that this was another of his mistakes, and that he (or his source) had muddled them up

[4] XXI. 30. 4.　　　[5] XXI. 31. 2.　　　[6] XXI. 31. 9.
[7] p. 372.　　　[8] p. 149.　　　[9] p. 72.
[10] Note on Polybius III. 49. 5 to 56. 4, and *JRS* 1956, p. 40.
[11] pp. 77–9.　　　[12] v. 34. 1–8.

with the *Tricorii*, who were much nearer to the Alps, as we shall see in a moment. In any case, Livy himself must have located the Tricastini in quite a different position in the present passage when he named them as the first of the three tribes through whose territory Hannibal passed on his way to the Alps, and they were certainly settled much further to the west in Imperial times, from which all our other authorities for them date.

Ptolemy defined their position very precisely as lying to the east of the Seggalauni (located by him at Valence) between the Allobroges in the north and the Vocontii in the south[13]— in other words, in the uplands of the Vercors which I have previously described as the frontier region between the last two tribes; and since this is the only explicit statement about the geographical position of the Tricastini that has come down to us from an ancient author, it is perhaps not surprising that it should have misled some later commentators from Cluver onwards. But in fact it was quite erroneous. Ptolemy himself virtually contradicted it in the same sentence when he said that the capital of the Tricastini was Noiomagus, for Noiomagus was the modern Nyons—the same word was one of the Latin names of Nyon in Switzerland[14]—and Nyons is over 40 kilometres *south* of the river Drôme, on which one of the two capitals of the Vocontii, Lucus Augusti (either the modern Die or Lucen-Diois), was situated.[15] But Strabo had already put Ptolemy's location of the Tricastini to the north of the Vocontii out of court when he described how the Vocontii themselves occupied the mountainous region of the Vercors and said explicitly that they extended to the north as far as the Allobroges.[16] Thus no third tribe could have come in between them. Pliny had similarly bracketed the Vocontii with the Segovellauni (a variant form of Ptolemy's 'Seggalauni') as the two tribes next before the Allobroges, going north.[17]

Pliny also said, however, that the capital of the Tricastini was called Augusta,[15] which Walbank—not implausibly—has identified with the modern Aouste-en-Diois, a village near Crest on the Drôme about 25 kilometres above its confluence with the Rhône; and in a passage criticizing de Beer's location

---

[13] *Geographica*, II. 10. 7–8.   [14] Graesse, *Orbis Latinus*, 1909, under *Neodunum*.
[15] Pomponius Mela, *Chorographia*, II. 5 and Pliny, *HN* III. 4. 36.
[16] IV. 6. 4.   [17] *HN* III. 4. 34.

of the Tricastini a good way to the south along the left bank of the Rhône he appears to regard this as evidence in support of Ptolemy's location,[18] though he does not explain how siting the capital of the Tricastini on the Drôme to the west of one of the two capitals of the Vocontii helps to demonstrate a location in the uplands to the north between them and the Allobroges. Walbank suggests that Ptolemy's Noiomagus may have been the same as Pliny's Augusta, and certainly the latter, which in its various modern forms is a name that is sprinkled all over the lands of the Roman Empire, may well have displaced an earlier Gallic name of the same town; but Walbank seems to have been unaware of the identity of Noiomagus with the modern Nyons, which, according to the French geographer, D'Anville,[19] was first pointed out by Joseph Scaliger. If this is true (D'Anville gives no reference), Scaliger's pupil, Cluver, should have known better than to accept, as he did, Ptolemy's mistaken location of the Tricastini, for which his own pupil, Holsten, rightly rebuked him in these words; 'In hisce Tricastinorum et Vocontiorum sedibus constituendis Cluverius mirum in modum hallucinatur, dum Ptolemaeum non satis expensum sequitur, qui suo more omnia turbat.'[20]

But, though Noiomagus or Nyons is nearer to the borders of the Tricastini than Aouste-en-Diois, Holsten did not agree that it was their capital, for he pointed out that it was in the territory of the Vocontii, being situated a little to the north of their second capital of Vaison-la-Romaine,[15] whereas he located the Tricastini on the left bank of the Rhône between the Seggalauni to the north and the Cavares to the south, flanked by the Vocontii on the east, and he cited the cathedral town of St. Paul-Trois-Châteaux as their ancient capital.[20] This is precisely where de Beer located the Tricastini, along the left bank of the Rhône between Bollène and Montélimar,[21] in the passage to which Walbank took exception. And here we shall leave the confused and discordant references to the tribe in ancient authors and turn to the far more solid evidence on which de Beer relied—the sheer weight of a continuous local tradition.

[18] *JRS* 1956, p. 39.
[19] *Notice de L'ancienne Gaule tirée des monuments Romains*, 1760, p. 120.
[20] p. 17.   [21] pp. 35–6.

When Holsten mentioned the 'cathedral town' of St. Paul-Trois-Châteaux—Fanum D. Pauli—he might have added that the mere fact that it *was* a cathedral town (which Nyons and Aouste-en-Diois were not) was in itself evidence that it had been the capital of an ancient tribe: for, as de Beer pointed out, the territories of the Gallic tribes were preserved by the Romans as the *civitates* of their province, and these in turn were taken over by the early Christian Church as dioceses, and St. Paul-Trois-Châteaux was the bishopric of the small diocese covering the district which is known to this day as the *Tricastin*. Both D'Anville in the eighteenth century [22] and de Manteyer more recently [23] reached the same conclusion as Holsten and de Beer that this must have been the territory of the Tricastini, and the very name, St. Paul-Trois-Châteaux, is evidence of its truth, for the town never had three châteaux: it is a back-formation from the Latin *Tricastini*. This is the accepted location of the Tricastini, to be found in any guide-book and recently granted the accolade of a sign on the new motorway up the Rhône valley, and it is quite absurd to question it. It should not have been necessary to discuss the matter at all.

We will take it, therefore, as a certainty that the territory of the Tricastini was the district still called the *Tricastin* along the left bank of the Rhône between Bollène and Montélimar, and it was, as Livy said, the first territory into which Hannibal moved on leaving the 'Island' in the confluence of the Rhône and the Aygues, though no 'turn to the left' was required at that point to enter it.

Next, according to Livy, Hannibal 'made for the territory of the Tricorii along the far frontier of the Vocontii'. The Vocontii, as I have several times mentioned already, occupied the whole of the upland country between the Cavares in the south and the Allobroges in the north, to the east of the smaller tribes along the left bank of the Rhône, their main east-to west axis being the river Drôme. [24] Their physical frontiers were the Isère in the north and the barrier of Mont Ventoux and its eastward continuation, the Montagne de Lure, in the south; and there can be no reasonable doubt that when Livy spoke of

[22] op cit., p. 655.   [23] *La Traversée des Alpes par Hannibal,* 1944, pp. 7–19.
[24] Strabo, IV. 1. 11 and 6. 4; Pliny, *HN* III. 4. 36–7; Holsten, p. 17; and de Manteyer, *La Traversée des Alpes par Hannibal,* 1944, pp. 7–19.

their 'far frontier'—per extremam oram Vocontiorum agri—he meant, as D'Anville long ago pointed out,[25] their northern frontier. In the same way Strabo proceeded from south to north in his description of their territory as lying between the Cavares in the south and the Allobroges in the north,[24] for this was the natural geographical direction to a Roman looking out from the centre of the known world in the Mediterranean towards an outlying territory on its northern shore. Devos, to suit his own theory that Hannibal marched up the Ouvèze, which skirts the northern flank of Mont Ventoux, professes to think that he meant the southern frontier;[26] but he is a good enough Latinist to know better, for, if Livy had meant the southern one, he would have written *proximam*, not *extremam*, *oram*.

Thus Livy's description of Hannibal's route so far, once the 'turn to the left' is brought forward to its proper place directly after the Rhône-crossing, turns out to be perfectly in accord with the route which we ourselves have followed, beginning with a march from the 'Island' near Orange along the Rhône through the territory of the Tricastini and continuing up the Isère and then across the northern extremity of the Vercors along the far frontier of the Vocontii; and his mention of the Tricorii as the next objective also fits such a route, for, though their position is less clearly attested than those of the other tribes, Strabo and Pliny agree in placing them nearer to the high Alps than the Vocontii,[27] so that an ascent to the main range of the Alps beginning near Grenoble would naturally have passed through their territory.*

[25] op. cit., p. 657.   [26] pp. 85–6.
[27] Strabo IV. 1. 11 and 6. 5, and Pliny, *HN* III. 4. 34.

---

* de Beer (p. 71) quotes Appian ('Εκ Τῆς Κελτικῆς, Frags. 1. 8 and 15. 1–3) to the effect that Julius Caesar defeated the Tricorii on his way from Ocelum on the Italian side of Mont Genèvre to the frontier of the Vocontii, which would certainly harmonize with Strabo's and Pliny's location of the tribe; but Caesar himself makes no mention of the Tricorii in his own quite detailed account of this campaign (*BG* I. 10)—in fact, he does not mention the Tricorii anywhere in his *Commentaries*—and Appian's testimony two centuries later must be regarded as suspect, particularly as he calls the tribe in question *Tigurii*, not Tricorii. Appian, moreover, makes no mention of the Vocontii in either passage: he links the *Tigurii* in both of them with the Helvetii, which suggests that he meant a different tribe much further to the north and a different campaign of Caesar's.

But Livy's reference to a crossing of the *Druentia* (Durance), which follows next in his account, is quite incompatible, as it stands, with such a route, and it was this which drew the French writers of the eighteenth century, as it has drawn de Beer and Devos more recently, to plot a much more southerly course for Hannibal's march. Livy says that the *Druentia* was far the most difficult of all the rivers of Gaul to cross, for the reason that, though it carried an immense head of water, it swirled down a number of constantly shifting channels unconfined by banks, which were too shallow and too treacherous for boats; and he proceeds to give a graphic description of the army floundering on slippery rocks as it picked its way on foot across the rushing waters swollen by recent rain.[28] Everyone has agreed that it is not easy to recognize the upper reaches of the Durance in this description,[29] and the writers of the 'long distance' school have not been under any temptation to do so, for, according to them, Hannibal never went near the Durance anywhere in the march.

The solution generally adopted by them is that Livy was drawing here on a different source from Polybius, that a choice has to be made between two conflicting traditions, and that, if, as they think, that of Polybius is to be preferred, Livy's account should be altogether rejected.[30] This certainly cuts the knot, but it is rather a cavalier way of disposing of a highly circum-stantial account of an incident in the march, and one cannot help feeling that, whatever the origin of the account, there cannot have been so much smoke without fire. Others have taken refuge in the suggestion that Livy (or his source) confused the Durance with the Drac, which joins the Isère at Grenoble and which (they say) Hannibal had to cross on his march up the Isère;[31] but these writers overlook the fact that Hannibal, starting, according to them, from an 'Island' in the confluence of the Rhône and the Isère, would have been marching up the *right* bank of the Isère, and that, since the Drac flows into it on the left bank, he would not, on their view of the route, have had to cross that river at all.

For those, like de Beer and Devos, who have more respect

---

[28] XXI. 31. 10–12.
[29] e.g. Walbank, note on Polybius III. 49. 5–56. 4 or Devos, p. 101.
[30] e.g. Walbank, *JRS* 1956, pp. 44–5.
[31] e.g. A. Macé, *Description du Dauphiné*, 1852, pp. 338–40 or Jullian, p. 478.

for Livy's evidence, and think that Hannibal must have crossed the Durance somewhere in his march between the 'Island' and the main range of the Alps, the problem is not so easy. Any route to the Alps from an 'Island' on the Rhône in the neighbourhood of Orange must strike the Durance somewhere above Sisteron, but the Durance does not spread out into a number of separate streams over a wide stony bed such as Livy described before it is joined by the Bléone 20 kilometres *below* Sisteron: over the whole of its course above Sisteron it is deeply encased between banks, as is testified by several writers from the beginning of the nineteenth century onwards,[32] and there is no suggestion that the river had been artificially canalized. Devos recognizes the difficulty and attempts to meet it by making Hannibal cross the Durance at Monêtier-Allemont, where, as he says, it is already wide;[33] but it is still in a single stream contained between banks and bears little resemblance to Livy's description.

De Beer brings Hannibal down to the Durance valley near La Bâtie-Montsaléon, more or less level with the same point on the river. He says that he had 4 good days' marching up the valley before he reached the point at Montdauphin, above Embrun, where the road forked, and that here he took the branch up the valley of the Guil on the opposite bank of the Durance;[34] from which one assumes that he means that this was the point at which Hannibal crossed the river.* But the Durance here is quite narrow and flows between walls of rock—quite unlike Livy's description. De Beer offers a series of graphs to show that the flow of water in this part of the Durance would have been at a seasonal peak at that time of year, and so to explain the army's difficulties in crossing it; but he ignores the main point in Livy's description—the wide, open river-bed traversed by a number of separate streams—and the flow of water is subject at any season to rapid fluctuations after rain, as Livy says was the case on this occasion.

Cluver had long ago taken the point that the nature of the Durance above Embrun was incompatible with Livy's description,[35] and he went on to make the further point, as others

[32] e.g. de Luc, p. 214; Macé, op. cit., pp. 338–40; Jullian, p. 476.
[33] pp. 102–3.   [34] pp. 61–2.   [35] p. 374.

---

* He has since confirmed in *Hannibal's March*, 1967, p. 95, that this is what he does mean.

have done since, that nowhere after a crossing of the Durance
in this part of its course could the army have enjoyed a march
'mainly in the plain'—*campestri maxime itinere*—as Livy said it
did;[36] for, whichever route it took, it must have been in the
heart of the mountains here. But de Beer and Devos remain
silent about this too. Lastly, it may be added, there is no obvious
reason why Hannibal should have crossed the Durance at all
in this part of the march, when he could have followed the
right bank of the river all the way up to Briançon and gone on
from there to the easy Col de Montgenèvre. In short, the whole
of Livy's description of the crossing and the subsequent march
contradicts his statement that the crossing took place somewhere in the section between the 'Island' and the main range
of the Alps, which has dictated the routes adopted by de Beer
and Devos and the French writers of the eighteenth century.

The explanation is the perfectly simple one, as Cluver also
saw,[37] that Hannibal's crossing of the Durance took place soon
after he had crossed the Rhône when he was on his way up the
left bank of the Rhône to the 'Island', and that either Livy or
his source misplaced the incident in their account of the march,
just as they did the 'turn to the left'; and the only reason why
Cluver's solution has been so largely ignored is that the great
majority of all subsequent writers, who have placed the crossing
of the Rhône somewhere *above* its junction with the Durance,
have had no interest in accepting it. If, however, the crossing
of the Rhône was in the neighbourhood of Beaucaire–Tarascon,
as we can now feel sure that it was, the army certainly had to
cross the Durance not far above its confluence with the Rhône
near Avignon on the march up the left bank of the Rhône to the
'Island'. The Durance near there is a fordable river flowing
in separate streams over a wide stony bed just as Livy described;
and the crossing was followed by a march 'mainly in the plain'
as he said.

The river would not have been a major obstacle in early
autumn (especially as in those days, as I mentioned earlier,
the Durance discharged its waters in three other branches as
well),[38] and this may be why Polybius did not think it worth
while to mention the crossing in his account of the march; but
all the rivers in that part of the country rise at a phenomenal

[36] XXI. 32. 6.   [37] p. 373.   [38] p. 101 above.

rate after a storm, and if it was swollen by recent rain as Livy says, it could easily have been awkward enough for a crossing on foot to be mentioned by a chronicler and so to present Livy with an opportunity for a purple passage. It seems obvious that this is where the episode occurred, as Cluver said, and that someone made a muddle about its placing in the narrative. It may have been Livy's muddle or it may have been that of his source, but a muddle it was, not a rival version of the route from the 'Island' onwards, for no chronicler could have registered such a vivid impression of the Durance at a place where it bore no resemblance to his description. There is therefore no reason to infer that the discrepancy in Livy's text reflects an independent tradition in conflict with that of Polybius; and we can conclude, not only that his reference to the crossing of the Durance should be discarded as a sort of lodestone of the approach march to the Alps, but that it can now be claimed as further circumstantial evidence that Hannibal crossed the Rhône below its confluence with the Durance, in other words in the region of Beaucaire–Tarascon.

It remains to consider in a little more detail the routes of de Beer and Devos, and we shall have to scrutinize them from the point of view of Polybius rather than Livy; for, though basically their routes are founded on Livy's reference to the crossing of the Durance in its accepted connotation, both writers have attempted to show that they can also be harmonized with the account of Polybius. They have both, therefore, been at pains to plot their routes up river valleys to match Polybius' march 'along the river'. Starting from the 'Island' in the confluence of the Rhône and the Aygues on which they both agree, Devos makes Hannibal branch off from the Rhône at the 'Island' itself up the valley of the Ouvèze [39] (which he thinks joined the Aygues in those days a little way above its confluence with the Rhône) [40] to the village of Ruissas at the foot of the Col de Perty, which he takes as the end of the march 'along the river', [41] and proceed from there to a crossing of the Durance at Monê-tier-Allemont. De Beer splits the march 'along the river' half and half between the Rhône itself and the Drôme, which flows into it at right angles near Loriol some 70 kilometres up-stream from the 'Island'; and he takes Châtillon-en-Diois, some 70 kilometres up the Drôme, as its end-point,[42] from which he brings Hannibal over the Col de Grimone to near the same point as Devos in the valley of the Durance.

Neither of these routes can be regarded as a natural interpretation of Polybius' march 'along the river'. Devos's route obviously offends against Polybius' plain meaning, as I have repeatedly stressed, that the first part, at least, of the onward march from the 'Island' was along the Rhône itself, not along a tributary. His route includes a length amounting to nearly half the distance along the Rhône itself, as de Beer's does, but in his case it is measured backwards to the place of the Rhône-crossing (near St. Gabriel according to him), because this was the only way in which he could make up the required distance of some 140 kilometres to match Polybius' figure. Since his end-point up the Ouvèze at Ruissas is less than 80 kilometres from the 'Island', he had to include the preceding section of some 60 kilometres along the Rhône as well, though it is obvious that Polybius meant his measurement of 143 kilometres 'along the river' to start from the 'Island'.[43]

De Beer manages his arithmetic more deftly, for his two sections, first up the Rhône from the 'Island' to Loriol and then up the Drôme to Châtillon-en-Diois, do add up to the required total of about 140 kilometres; but a march in two halves along two rivers at right angles to each other seems no more like a march 'along the river' than that of Devos. It is a very different picture from the combination of the Rhône and the Isère which I have suggested. The Isère is a much bigger river than the Drôme, and it meets the Rhône at an easy angle, so that Polybius might have been uncertain which was which, whereas he could not possibly have mistaken the Drôme for the main river; and the Drôme would not have answered, as the Isère does, to his description of the *Rhône* as rising in the heart of the high Alps and flowing generally from north-east to south-west.[44]

These difficulties of de Beer and Devos in reconciling their measurements of the march 'along the river' with Polybius spring directly from the fact that their routes from an 'Island' in the confluence of the Rhône and the Aygues to the upper valley of the Durance have to cross a watershed which runs continuously at a height of 1,300 to 1,400 metres above sea level

[42] pp. 38–9.   [43] III. 50. 1.   [44] III. 47. 2.

between the valley of the Isère in the north and that of the Durance in the south, and the rivers that drain from the watershed into the Rhône are only about 80 kilometres long over their whole course. The character of these rivers, moreover, is no less fatal to a reconciliation with Polybius than their deficiency of distance, for they begin as mountain torrents falling steeply through gorges and narrow defiles in rugged, inaccessible country, and only in their lower reaches do they approximate to anything that could be said to resemble his march 'in the flat country'. Devos's route up the Ouvèze is a fairly steep climb of about 1 in 100 in a continually narrowing valley which contracts at several places into defiles or gorges, and it must have been nearly impassable for an army before the modern road was engineered. De Beer's route up the lower reaches of the Drôme is not so steep (about 1 in 145), but neither of them can compare as a march 'in the flat country' with the average gradient of 1 in 1,000 up the Rhône and the Isère.

De Beer and Devos are perfectly justified in making the point, as they both do, that the crossing of any of the passes over the watershed constitutes the entry into 'the Alps'. De Beer says: 'it is clear that the place described [by Polybius] as 'the ascent towards the Alps' must be the first pass, leading out of the Rhône valley';[45] and Devos fairly reflects the impressions of any traveller over the Col de Perty, his own route across the watershed, when he says: 'Having crossed the pass, where does one arrive? Quite simply, in the Alps.'[46] This, indeed, corresponds with the official nomenclature of the modern *départements*, roughly divided by the ridge of the watershed between the Vaucluse and the Drôme on the west and the Basses Alpes and Hautes Alpes on the east; and Strabo had the same conception when he marked 'the beginning of the ascent of the Alps'— almost the same expression as Polybius used—in his description of the shortest road from the Rhône valley into Italy, at a point only 93 kilometres from Tarascon.[47]

But this very fact, as Cluver was the first to point out,[48] destroys any possibility of harmonizing such a route with Polybius' account of Hannibal's route, for Polybius' figure for Hannibal's distance from the Rhône-crossing to the beginning of 'the climb to the Alps' was over twice as great—say 60 kilo-

[45] p. 34.   [46] p. 93.   [47] IV. I. 3.   [48] pp. 382–3.

metres between the crossing-place and the 'Island' plus 143 kilometres 'along the river'—while his figure for the longer distance from the Rhône-crossing 'as far as the climb of the Alps into Italy' was 250 kilometres.[49] Both de Beer and Devos make the tacit assumption, which in my view is correct (though neither of them discusses the point),* that there was an interval between the end of the march 'along the river' and the end-point of the longer distance—de Beer by moving forward some 24 kilometres from Châtillon-en-Diois to the Col de Grimone, which he takes as the beginning of 'the climb of the Alps into Italy',[50] Devos by moving forward some 50 kilometres from Ruissas to his different location of the same point at Monêtier-Allemont.[51] But de Beer, at a distance of about 224 kilometres by his route, is still left some way short of Polybius' figure of 250 kilometres from the Rhône-crossing; and Devos can only make up the required distance on his much shorter route by taking the measurement from Aigues-Mortes, which could never have been a crossing-place over the Rhône and certainly was not Hannibal's, as he himself agreed. (He had located Hannibal's crossing-place at St. Gabriel near Beaucaire–Tarascon; and he had actually named Aigues-Mortes in that context as the place on the coast from which Polybius estimated the distance of a 4-day march between the crossing-place and the sea.)[52]

Such are the shifts to which anyone is reduced who makes Hannibal march up one of the rivers which descend from the watershed into the Rhône and tries at the same time to harmonize his route with Polybius' account. Yet those of de Beer and Devos do not fit Livy's indications either, despite their adherence to a crossing of the Durance based on his text. We have already noticed that Devos's route up the Ouvèze offends against the Latin by making Hannibal follow the near instead of the far frontier of the Vocontii, and de Beer's route up the Drôme is in conflict with the same indication, for it takes him across the very middle of their territory. Neither of them,

[49] III. 39. 9.   [50] p. 39.   [51] pp. 96 and 118.   [52] p. 31.

---

* de Beer does discuss the placing of Polybius' 143 kilometres 'along the river' in the revised edition of his book (*Hannibal's March*, p. 60), but he does so in terms of its starting-point: he still does not discuss the question whether the *end-point* was the same as that of the 250 kilometres.

moreover, takes him anywhere near the territory of the Allobroges, who for both Livy and Polybius played an important
part in the events of the march in one role or another. One
senses that both writers were uneasily aware of this as a weakness in their case; for, though they could not avoid some
mention of the Allobroges, they seem to slide past the awkward
place, saying as little as possible about them, and even a cursory
reader of either book is left with a feeling that something is
amiss here.[53]

To sum up, then, on this examination of Livy's route and its
most recent exponents: we must convict de Beer and Devos of
failing to satisfy either Polybius' or Livy's indications of the
route between the 'Island' and the main range of the Alps; and
Livy's route, once his obvious mistakes are corrected, turns out
to be no different from that of Polybius. This is a surprising
conclusion which runs counter to the generally accepted view
of the two accounts, and we shall consider it more fully in the
next chapter.

[53] de Beer, pp. 36–7 and 60; Devos, pp. 55, 74, and 85.

XII

LIVY OR POLYBIUS?

IT has been a recurrent theme in all the writing about the
march of Hannibal down the centuries that the accounts of
the route in Polybius and Livy are hopelessly at odds with
each other and cannot be reconciled. This was Gibbon's view,
as I have mentioned,[1] and Marquion is its latest and perhaps
most emphatic exponent.[2] They both shared the orthodox view
of Livy's route, that it led to the upper reaches of the Durance
and the Col de Montgenèvre, while ascribing to Polybius a
much more northerly route—along the valley of the Isère and
that of its confluent, the Arc, to the Col du Clapier according
to Marquion;[3] round the north flank of the Mont Blanc massif
to the Great St. Bernard according to Gibbon,[4] who kept to
the old pre-Cluver concept of an 'Island' at the confluence of
the Rhône and the Saône. Both of them, in common with all
the writers who have found a similar opposition between the
two authors, came down on the side of Polybius.

Gibbon's reason for thinking the two accounts irreconcilable
was a curious one that has now dropped out of the picture. He
said that Livy's assertion that Hannibal descended from the
Alps into the territory of the Taurini[5]—and this rather than
the reference to the Durance was his reason for holding that
Livy's route implied a crossing of the Alps by the Col de
Montgenèvre—was quite incompatible with Polybius' statement that Hannibal descended into 'the plains of the Po and
the territory of the Insubres',[6] which he took to imply a route
over the Great St. Bernard and down the Valle d'Aosta a long
way to the north;[7] and in the last resort he thought more weight
should be attached to Polybius. Gibbon, at the time when he
was going into the matter in 1763, took no cognizance either
of the Little St. Bernard (which, since it also leads into the

---

[1] p. 136 above.   [2] p. 65.   [3] pp. 56–8.
[4] *Journal* for October 1763, in *Miscellaneous Works*, Vol. 5, 1814, p. 370.
[5] XXI. 38. 5–9.   [6] III. 56. 3.   [7] op. cit., pp. 370–2.

Valle d'Aosta, would have been an equally Polybian route on his criterion) or of the Mont Cenis (which by the same token would have been a Livian one, since it leads, like the Mont-genèvre, to Susa and Turin). He seems to have dropped his objection to a 'Livian' route later on, for he commented favourably on Grosley's advocacy of the Mont Cenis after he had read his book.[8] But the Mont Cenis is now regarded, with its variant, the Col du Clapier, as the Polybian route *par excellence*, and it is common ground between all the modern schools of thought that, whatever Polybius may have meant by his reference to the Insubres, Hannibal must have descended from the Alps somewhere near Turin—the conclusion which I adopted in my initial discussion of Polybius' geographical measurements.[9] This, therefore, is no longer an issue between a Polybian and a Livian route.

The supposed antithesis between the two is based on the much-vexed passage in Livy we have been discussing. This is held to imply, as Marquion in common with de Beer and Devos has assumed,[10] that his route must have led to the upper valley of the Durance and therefore to the Col de Montgenèvre, if not, as de Beer thinks, to an even more southerly pass such as the Col de la Traversette; and the difference between what is thought to be Livy's route and the route described by Polybius has actually been magnified by the efforts of writers like de Beer and Devos to reconcile them when they claim that Poly-bius' account of the march 'along the river' can be made to fit their routes across the watershed: with such effect that Walbank, in an otherwise admirable summary of the issue, has unguardedly accepted their delineation of Livy's route and relied on it to show that it cannot be reconciled with Polybius' account. 'Attempts have been made', he says, 'to reconcile the two routes (in favour of the Mont Genèvre); but they always run up against the difficulty that Polybius has no knowledge of a march over high land from the 'Island' to the Durance. . . . According to him Hannibal, after leaving the 'Island', marched for 10 days along a river, and then begins the 'ascent' of the Alps'.[11]

But Livy, once his crossing of the Durance is adjusted to

[8] p. 138 above.   [9] pp. 85–7 above.
[10] pp. 27 and 65.   [11] *JRS* 1956, pp. 38–41.

become an incident in the march up the left bank of the Rhône to the 'Island', has no more 'knowledge of a march over high land' than Polybius. Walbank may well be right in saying, as he does, that Livy turned to a second source for the crossing of the Durance just as he did for the 'turn to the left',[12] but it does not follow that the second source is to be rejected as false. The two items occur next door to each other in Livy's text, and both of them must have been part of the same muddle, whether on Livy's part or on that of his source. Walbank might have recognized that the simple explanation which he accepted for the one, that the episode was wrongly placed in Livy's narrative, applied also to the other, instead of branding the second source in this case as an 'irreconcilable' tradition with which Livy 'contaminated' a Polybian one.[13] It seems that what prevented him from seeing this was the irreconcilability of *any* crossing of the Durance, not with Polybius, but with his own view that Hannibal crossed the Rhône above its confluence with the Durance and never afterwards went near the latter river. That, however, was not the fault of the ancient authorities.

If, then, the 'turn to the left' and the crossing of the Durance are both brought forward to their proper place in the narrative, all that remains of those indications of Livy which are supposed to be in conflict with Polybius' account is his description of the march 'into the territory of the Tricastini and along the far frontier of the Vocontii to the territory of the Tricorii'; but this, as we have seen, so far from conflicting with Polybius, describes precisely his route up the Rhône and then along the Isère and across the northern extremity of the Vercors in the borderland between the Vocontii and the Allobroges. De Beer and Devos should have contented themselves with pointing out how well Livy's indications of the route agree with those of Polybius instead of making an impossible attempt to force Polybius' description of the march 'along the river' into harmony with their own routes across the watershed; for the truth is that no such route, and no 'march over high land', is indicated by Livy at all.

When we turn to the 'Polybian' routes as commonly conceived, the position is even more paradoxical. The identification

[12] Note on Polybius III. 49. 5 to 56. 4 and *JRS* 1956, p. 40.
[13] *JRS* 1956, pp. 44–5.

13—H.M.I.H.

of the 'Island' with the confluence of the Rhône and the Isère
(their central hypothesis) turns out, as we have seen, to rest on a
single phrase of Livy, not on Polybius at all, and Cluver, its
author, relied entirely on Livy's evidence for its justification.
The route along the Isère through the country of the Allobroges certainly is Polybian, but to make Hannibal branch off
from the Rhône at the 'Island'—the heresy introduced by
Cluver's pupil, Holsten, and now the orthodox doctrine for
most of those who uphold Polybius against Livy—is plainly
contrary to what Polybius himself thought. Devos has had to
espouse the same heresy—indeed, he takes it for granted—to
justify his route up the Ouvèze; de Beer may perhaps be said
to have avoided it by making Hannibal continue for some 70
kilometres up the Rhône before branching off up the Drôme;
but both of them have felt obliged to accommodate the Polybian march 'along the river'—unlike the French writers of
the eighteenth century, who had no such scruples about their
'Livian' routes to the upper Durance—and we have seen the
difficulties they encountered in the attempt to do so.

So the unexpected result of this analysis—for it was no part
of my original intention to effect a reconciliation between
Polybius and Livy—is that there is at least as much of Livy as
of Polybius in the so-called Polybian route, and that there is no
separate 'Livian' route at all: both accounts coalesce, once they
are properly understood and Livy's obvious mistakes corrected,
into the route which I had deduced before we embarked on
this examination of the so-called Livian route and the aberra-
tions of its modern exponents. And since I may seem to have
found fault for one reason or another with most of the writers I
have mentioned, I shall close this chapter by recapitulating
my conclusions in terms of their agreement with other writers.

I agree with de Beer and Devos and their twentieth-century
predecessors, Dunbabin, Spenser Wilkinson, Jullian, Hyde, and
Colin, that Hannibal's crossing-place over the Rhône was at
what I have called, following Jullian, Beaucaire–Tarascon, but
which is more likely to have been at one or other of the places a
little further down-stream adopted by de Beer, Devos, Spenser
Wilkinson, Hyde, and Colin. To find any earlier exponents of
the same view one has to go all the way back to our first commentators, Cluver and Holsten; and the weight of authority

is not as overwhelming as it should be for a conclusion which seems to me to be proved up to the hilt by the direct evidence about the Rhône-crossing itself and now no longer threatened by inferences drawn from later stages of the march, but actually corroborated by them.

For the 'Island' at the confluence of the Rhône and the Aygues I gratefully acknowledge my debt to de Beer and Devos, who have made this their own Tom Tiddler's ground. They have beaten the editors of classical texts at their own game, and used hard facts provided by Polybius about the army's speed of march rather than spurious arithmetic to demonstrate the distance of the 'Island' from the crossing-place. Fortia D'Urban and Dunbabin had hit on the same location of the 'Island' before them, but pride of place among their predecessors should be given to Colin; for, though he strangely located it at the confluence of the Sorgues a few kilometres away (as Spenser Wilkinson did later), he was the first to seize the principle that the 'Island' could not have been in the territory of the Allobroges, as the majority of historians and commentators from Cluver onwards have assumed, but must have been in that of the Cavares.

For the march 'along the river' the only supporters I can claim for the route up the Rhône from the confluence of the Aygues to that of the Isère and then up that river to a point somewhere short of the Bec de l'Échaillon are Dunbabin, Spenser Wilkinson, and Colin, its originator; but plenty of others who located the 'Island' at a different confluence on the Rhône, and have therefore had a different starting-point for this section of the march, have been equally positive that it must have begun along the Rhône itself and not branched off along the tributary at the 'Island'. Cluver, Gibbon, Hampton, Whitaker, de Luc, Perrin and Marquion are all of this company, as well as the three who adopted the same route as I have. On the other hand, in so far as part of my route runs up the Isère, it is in agreement with that proclaimed by Napoleon and adopted by all the later writers who have followed him in making the whole of the march 'along the river' proceed along the Isère from an 'Island' at its confluence with the Rhône, including Larauza, Macé, Jullian, and Walbank.

Finally, for the conclusion that the army proceeded some way after its first entry into the mountains at the end of the march 'along the river' before it began what Polybius called 'the climb of the Alps into Italy', i.e. that there is a missing term in the subtraction sum, I have the support of Whitaker, Perrin, Colin, de Beer, and Devos.

The catalogue may strike the reader as an unprincipled, eclectic farrago. I can only say, and ask him to believe, that each of my conclusions was first arrived at by ratiocination on the texts (coupled with some knowledge of the country); and that, if the first reaction on discovering that I had been fore-stalled by someone else was a pang of disappointment, this was quickly replaced by a new sense of confidence in the conclusion on finding that I had not been alone in reaching it.

XIII

THE ROUTES ACROSS THE ALPS
(1) POLYBIUS' MEASUREMENTS

WE left Hannibal poised near Grenoble for the final attack on the main range of the Alps, and the reader may wonder why I broke off there to recapitulate the route we had so far travelled instead of waiting until the journey was finished. The reason is that the whole nature of the problem changes at this point. Hitherto we have been trying to unravel a tangle of conflicting evidence—or so at least it seemed—and we have had to cut some knots and tidy up some loose ends in the process. But from now on there is no longer any problem of that sort. For the last stage of the march across the mountains into Italy Polybius and Livy tell substantially the same straightforward story: there are no serious discrepancies between them and no internal inconsistencies in either version to be ironed out. We need no longer, therefore, pore over the texts to extract the last ounce of implication from the evidence or pit one narrative against the other; nor need we traverse in detail the interpretations of the commentators, for henceforth there are no rival theories of vexed passages, only different geographical identifications of one and the same narrative—and, above all, different passes over the Alps.

The description of this part of the march in Polybius and Livy can be, and all too often has been, identified with any number of different routes, each proclaimed by its sponsor to be the one and only route that fits the description; but the truth is, as Kahrstedt remarked,[1] that 'white cliffs and deep gorges, river valleys and steep declivities are everywhere', and topographical features can be found to match the description in half a dozen different itineraries. Therefore I shall not try to trace the route in detail, and I shall not propound any one solution of the problem of Hannibal's pass over the Alps. I shall

[1] p. 181.

limit myself to setting the framework within which a choice has to be made, and offering some guide-lines for the selection.

If we revert once again to Polybius' figure of 250 kilometres for the distance from the Rhône-crossing 'as far as the climb of the Alps into Italy', we have consumed, say, 60 kilometres between the crossing-place and the 'Island' and about 150 kilometres from there to the point which we have taken as the end of the march 'along the river' somewhere short of the Bec de l'Échaillon (for this distance must have been near the upper limit of the range covered by Polybius' round figure of 800 stades), leaving a balance of about 40 kilometres. If we allow, say, 20 kilometres for the crossing of the Vercors between the point where the army left the river and the town near the modern Grenoble where it halted after the engagement on the pass, we are left with another 20 kilometres to reach what Polybius called 'the climb of the Alps into Italy', and a glance at a map will show that, whichever way Hannibal went, a march of about that distance beyond Grenoble would have brought him to a point at which the main massif of the Cottian Alps between France and Italy confronted him.

He might have continued from there all the way up the Isère to Bourg St. Maurice at the foot of the Little St. Bernard and crossed by that pass into Italy; but we have already seen that the Little St. Bernard is excluded as Hannibal's pass by the direct testimony of Livy, Varro, and Polybius himself.[2] It would in any case have been a very long way round, and the distance alone is enough to show that this cannot have been Polybius' view of the route, for it is over 300 kilometres to Bourg St. Maurice from Bourg St. Andéol (to take this as the nearest of all the places which have been proposed for the Rhône-crossing) and correspondingly further from any of the more probable locations—all well above Polybius' figure of 250 kilometres— while the distance from the supposed 'Island' in the confluence of the Rhône and the Isère, some 230 kilometres, is even less amenable to his figure of 143 kilometres for the march 'along the river'. I shall continue therefore to exclude the Little St. Bernard.

From the point to which we have brought Hannibal some 20 kilometres beyond Grenoble there are three other main

[2] p. 141 above.

routes into Italy, all converging on the plains of the Po near Turin. The first is a sharply angled route penetrating the northern part of the massif of the Cottian Alps up the Isère and then doubling back up its tributary, the Arc, to the Mont Cenis or the Col du Clapier; the second is an easier but longer route skirting the southern slopes of the massif, first up the valley of the Drac, then curving round over the Col Bayard to the upper valley of the Durance, which it either follows up to Briançon and the Col de Montgenèvre or crosses on a slightly shorter but more difficult route over the Col de la Traversette (or one of the other, smaller passes in the neighbourhood of Monte Viso); the third is a middle route cutting straight across the massif up the valley of the Romanche to the Col du Lautaret and dropping down from there to join the second route at Briançon and continue over the Montgenèvre. From a starting-point about 20 kilometres on from Grenoble to an end-point about 20 kilometres short of Turin, which we previously assumed to be the range of Polybius' last measurement of 214 kilometres for 'the crossing of the Alps',[3] the comparable distances by these routes are approximately: 215 kilometres by the Mont Cenis, 200 by the Col du Clapier, 265 by the long route over the Montgenèvre, 260 by the variant of the same route over the Traversette, and 190 by the short middle route over the Montgenèvre.

Obviously there is no sanctity about any of these figures. They depend on some rather arbitrary assumptions about the intervening section between the end of the march 'along the river' and the beginning of 'the climb of the Alps into Italy', and there is no fixed point at all at either end of the last section. However, though the figures are unreliable as absolute measurements, the relative differences between them and Polybius' figure of 214 kilometres do indicate degrees of probability between one route and another. The long route over the Col de Montgenèvre—the furthest removed from Polybius' figure—is the one favoured by De Sanctis,[4] and also apparently by Kahrstedt;[5] but since both these writers make the march of about 145 kilometres 'along the river' start from an 'Island' at the confluence of the Rhône and the Isère, which is less than 100 kilo-

---

[3] pp. 86–87 above, and Polybius III. 39. 10.
[4] pp. 22–3 and 69–72.   [5] pp. 187 and 381.

metres from Grenoble, their starting-point for the last section
of the march would be some 25 kilometres further on than mine,
and their distance for 'the crossing of the Alps' is therefore that
much closer than mine to Polybius' figure. On my itinerary the
discrepancy of about 50 kilometres by the long route over the
Montgenèvre is indeed a wide one, while that of the Traversette
route is not much less, and this certainly does cast a prima facie
doubt on either of those routes from a starting-point near
Grenoble.

De Beer makes the distance by the Traversette from his
starting-point at the Col de Grimone about 220 kilometres,
which is close enough to Polybius' 214, but he takes the end-
point at Saluzzo,[6] and Saluzzo, though certainly on 'the plains
of the Po', is too far from Turin to fit Polybius' account of the
storming of the chief town of the Taurini directly after the halt
in camp at the end of the march, which was one of my reasons
for assuming the end-point of his measurement to be somewhere about 20 kilometres short of Turin.[7] It is necessary to add
another 35 kilometres to de Beer's figure to bring the Col de la
Traversette within the same range of Turin, so that the comparable distance by his route becomes about 255 kilometres,
or nearly as far above Polybius' figure as the route over the
Traversette from a point near Grenoble.

On the other hand, those, like Perrin,[8] Macé,[9] Jullian,[10]
Walbank,[11] and Marquion,[12] who locate the 'Island' at the
confluence of the Rhône and the Isère and follow Napoleon in
tracing the march 'along the river' up the Isère above Grenoble
as far as its confluence with the Arc, fall equally far *short* of
Polybius' figure of 214 kilometres for the crossing of the Alps;
for they are left with only about 170 kilometres by the Mont
Cenis, and only 155 by the Col du Clapier, to a point at the
same distance from Turin, and this must be reckoned a further
objection to their location of the 'Island' if, as they think,
Hannibal crossed the Alps by one or other of those passes.

De Folard seems to have been the only writer who thought
that Hannibal took the short middle route over the Col du
Lautaret to Briançon and the Montgenèvre, which he believed

---

[6] p. 71.   [7] p. 85 above.   [8] pp. 79–81, 119–27, and 145.
[9] *Description du Dauphiné*, 1852, pp. 336–40.   [10] 478–85.
[11] *JRS* 1956, pp. 42–5.   [12] pp. 35–6 and 49.

was the route most frequented by the Gauls.[13] The objection to it is that the Col du Lautaret (a little over 2,000 metres above sea level) is as high as the Mont Cenis and appreciably higher than the Montgenèvre (about 1,850 metres), and there is no mention of any such intermediate pass in Polybius or Livy before the crossing of the final pass on the frontier. Walbank has argued that the same objection applies also to the longer route to the upper Durance valley by the Col Bayard;[14] but the objection is not so serious here, for the Col Bayard is only about 1,240 metres above sea level and it is approached by a relatively gentle slope on either side, as Colin pointed out;[15] and Holsten regarded this as one of the regular routes into Italy.[16]

The reader may be a little surprised that any route to the upper Durance valley and the Col de Montgenèvre should be entertained after I have relegated Livy's evidence for it as non-existent; and it is true, as Walbank has said,[17] that Livy's evidence (or rather, the conventional interpretation of it) is the only reason we have so far seen for bringing Hannibal back to the Durance from the Isère. But a caveat is necessary here: all we have demonstrated about Livy's evidence is that it does not *justify* a route to the upper valley of the Durance (and also that the approach to it could not have been by any of the short routes across the watershed between it and the Rhône valley). But we should beware of concluding that the same reasoning *excludes* such a route, for it does not; a route over the Col de Montgenèvre (or over a more southerly pass such as the Col de la Traversette) must still be regarded as one of the alternatives open for consideration on other grounds.

The other grounds for considering all these routes are to be found in the other ancient authors who left statements on the record about the Alpine passes, and we shall take our leave now, for a time at any rate, of Polybius and Livy and review this other body of more or less contemporary data. The problem is rather like one of those Happy Family brain-teasers in the Sunday supplements which our children solve with the aid of a Venn diagram, only here some Diophantine analysis seems to be

---

[13] *Observations*, in Dom V. Thuillier, *Histoire de Polybe nouvellement traduite du grec.*, 1728, Vol. 4, pp. 89–90.
[14] *JRS* 1956, p. 45.   [15] p. 17.   [16] p. 18.   [17] *JRS* 1956, p. 45.

needed too, for there is no one-to-one correspondence between the variables. It is also a little like the logical puzzle about the truthful and the untruthful sentries at the castle doors, for the earliest collateral testimony we have is that of Pompey the Great and Varro, who were both still alive when Livy was a boy; and since we know from Livy that the question of Hannibal's pass was already a subject of debate in his time,[18] we cannot be sure that either of them knew the facts either. We shall consider these references to the Alpine passes in other ancient authors in the next chapter.

[18] xxi. 38. 6–9.

XIV

THE ROUTES ACROSS THE ALPS
(2) THE ANCIENT AUTHORITIES

VARRO set the field for a review of the Alpine passes in a list preserved by Servius about A.D. 400 in the following note on a passage in the Aeneid:

Sane omnes *altitudines* montium licet a Gallis *Alpes* vocentur, proprie tamen *juga* montium Gallicorum sunt, quas quinque viis Varro dicit transiri posse: una, quae est juxta mare per Ligures; altera, qua Hannibal transiit; tertia, qua Pompeius ad Hispaniense bellum profectus est; quarta, qua Hasdrubal de Gallia in Italiam venit; quinta, quae quondam a Graecis possessa est, quae exinde Alpes Graiae appellantur.[1]

Although all the *heights* of the mountains are called by the Gauls *Alps*, yet they are properly the *chains* of the Gallic mountains, which Varro says can be crossed by five routes: one next to the sea through the Ligurians; a second by which Hannibal crossed; a third by which Pompey set out for the war in Spain; a fourth by which Hasdrubal came from Gaul into Italy; a fifth [in the Alps] which were once possessed by the Greeks and which since then have been called the Graian Alps.

It is worth while pausing at this point to consider what a learned Roman's ideas of the Alpine passes would have been at the time when Varro was writing in the second half of the first century B.C. Perhaps the first thing to notice is that the Romans used for the Alpine passes the names which to us mean groups of Alps. They were always more interested in the routes across the mountain barrier than in the mountains themselves; the phrase '*juga* montium' in the above extract, for which I have adopted the classical translation, '*chains* of mountains', came to mean 'passes' in later Latin. Indeed, I suspect that the word *alpes* itself meant first and foremost a pass to the Roman mind, and Varro's use of the expression *Alpes Graiae* here to

[1] Servius *ad Aeneidem* x. 13.

denote the Little St. Bernard (for this is the only available pass
in the Graian Alps) seems an example of this. The words which
I have had to insert in square brackets in the English translation
were evidently quite superfluous to him.

In Varro's time the Romans knew only two such names in the
western Alps—the Pennine and Graian Alps. The name
'Cottian Alps' dates from the reign of Augustus, when the local
king Cottius engineered the road over the Montgenèvre, the
principal pass across them; and the Montgenèvre itself only
acquired its Roman name *Matrona* much later.[2] This explains
why, apart from the road 'next to the sea through the Ligurians',
Varro gave only one proper name of a pass, the Graian Alps,
in his list, and had to identify the others by the people who had
used them. He would certainly have quoted the name 'Pennine
Alps' if he had had occasion to mention them. He omitted them
because his list was concerned with the passes across the *Gallic*
mountains, by which he evidently meant the westward passes
leading into the country which we still think of as ancient 'Gaul'
today. The pass in the Pennine Alps, the Great St. Bernard, is a
northward pass leading into a territory whose inhabitants Livy
called 'half-German', and this was one of his reasons for excluding it as Hannibal's pass.[3]

The Little St. Bernard, then, is the most northerly of Varro's
five routes and the coast road the most southerly, and since they
are put last and first respectively in his list, one cannot avoid
the impression that he meant the intermediate passes too to be
in geographical order from south to north. Varro was a meth-
odical man, and since the order was plainly not chronological
(Pompey's pass being sandwiched between those of Hannibal
and Hasdrubal), one feels it must have been geographical.
Polybius' list of four Alpine passes to which I have previously
referred—those through the Ligurians, the Taurini, the Salassi,
and the Rhaeti[4]—certainly *was* in geographical order from
south to north, which, as I have said before, was the natural
geographical direction to a Roman looking towards countries
north of the Mediterranean, and it seems only natural to read
Varro's list in the same way. In that case Varro must have
located Hannibal's, Pompey's, and Hasdrubal's passes in that

---

[2] Ammianus Marcellinus xv. 10. 2–6.   [3] xxi. 38. 6–8.
[4] Strabo iv. 6. 12 and Polybius xxxiv. 10. 18.

order from south to north between the coast road and the Little St. Bernard.

This sector of the Alps, comprising the groups known to us as the Maritime and Cottian Alps, was still virtually unexplored territory to Varro and his contemporaries. The Romans of his time knew of the Great and Little St. Bernard, as I have said, and half a dozen Roman expeditions had fought their way along the coast road through the Ligurians and the Salluvii to found and consolidate the new province of Gallia Narbonensis, culminating in Marius' defeat of the invading German hordes near Aix in 102 B.C.; but Marius, according to Heitland,[5] shipped his army by sea, and there is no evidence that any of these Roman armies took any other route than the coast road before Pompey crossed the western Alps on his way to fight Sertorius in Spain in 77 B.C. Before that it was a marvel to the Romans that an army could cross the Alps at all: 'In portento prope maiores habuere Alpes ab Hannibale exsuperatas et postea a Cimbris', wrote Pliny a century and a half later.[6]

It is as near certain as anything can be that Pompey's pass was the Montgenèvre. He himself in a letter to the Senate a few years afterwards claimed that he had 'opened a route across the Alps which was different from Hannibal's and more convenient for us',[7] and Appian two hundred years later described his pass in terms which can only be identified with the Montgenèvre, adding, as Varro and Pompey himself had said, that Hannibal's pass was a different one.* The Montgenèvre was

---

[5] *The Roman Republic*, 1923, Vol. 2, p. 372.   [6] *HN* xxxvi. 1. 2.

[7] Sallust, *ex Historiis*, Frag. 98. 4.

---

* Appian's description, that the pass straddled the sources of the Rhône and the Po which rose close together on either side (*Bella Civilia*, I. 109), is generally equated with Strabo's similar description of the sources of the Durance and the Dora (tributaries of the Rhône and the Po respectively) as rising close together at a place in the mountains which must have been the Montgenèvre (IV. 6. 5). Strabo seems to have confused the Dora Riparia (which rises close to the source of the Durance on the other side of the Montgenèvre) with the Dora Baltea when he went on to describe it as flowing through the territory of the Salassi (in the Valle d' Aosta); and from this Jullian has argued (p. 45) that he must have confused the Durance with the Drance and that the whole nexus should be transferred from the Mongenèvre to the Great St. Bernard. Jullian's argument is too far-fetched to need refutation: it is only necessary to point out here that, if the same nexus is to be equated with Appian's description of Pompey's pass, it entails the absurd conclusion that Pompey set out on a journey to Spain by crossing a difficult pass into Switzerland.

indeed 'more convenient' for the Romans than any of the routes previously known to them. The coast road was, as Hyde described it in almost the same words as Strabo had used 2,000 years before,[8] 'a mere ribbon of land between the mountains and an almost harborless sea',[9] and it was not until the reign of Augustus that a proper road was constructed, the *Via Julia Augusta*, to join up with the *Via Domitia* at the Rhône: before that a difficult transit had to be made through the hostile Ligurians and Salluvii. The routes across the Great or Little St. Bernard in the Pennine or Graian Alps entailed a long approach march up the narrow Valle d' Aosta through the lawless Salassi, which again was only made secure when Augustus constructed a new road and founded *Augusta Praetoria* at the head of the valley. All these routes, too, were longer than that by the Montgenèvre, which Strabo described as the shortest road between the Rhône valley and Italy,[10] and the Montgenèvre is the lowest and easiest of all the passes in the western Alps.

All this adds up to near certainty, as I have said, that Pompey's pass was the Montgenèvre, and most of the modern historians have accepted it as such without reservation.[11] But they raise an unsuspected difficulty when they go on to say (to quote, for example, R. Gardner in the *Cambridge Ancient History*)[11] that Pompey 'built a new road' there, for there is no record elsewhere of a road having been made by the Romans across the Montgenèvre before the local king Cottius constructed one in the reign of Augustus. The basis of the statement is, no doubt, Pompey's own claim to have 'opened' the route (*patefeci*), coupled with a rather strange remark of Appian's in the passage to which I have referred above, that he 'made a different cut' from Hannibal's—ἑτέραν ἐχάρασσεν.[12] But Ammianus Marcellinus, who, though he was writing over 400 years after the event, professed to be drawing for his description of Gaul on the Greek writer Timagenes of Alexandria,[13] who was not merely a contemporary of Pompey but is said to have been brought to Rome by him as a prisoner of war, gives a highly

---

[8] IV. 1. 9 and 6. 2.   [9] p. 48.   [10] IV. 1. 3 and 1. 12.

[11] e.g. Mommsen, Dickson's translation, Vol. 4, 1862–75, p. 27; Hyde, pp. 51–2; *CAH* Vol. 9, p. 321.

[12] *Bella Civilia*, I. 109.   [13] XV. 9. 2.

coloured description of the difficulty and dangers of the ascent on the steep Italian side of the Montgenèvre before it was made safe for travellers by Cottius, who, he says, 'constructed roads by great works'—*molibus magnis exstruxit*; and he says nothing of any earlier road having been made by Pompey;[14] so that, if Pompey did build a road across his pass, this evidence would suggest that it must have been some other pass than the Montgenèvre.

The difficulty, however, though it has seemed right to mention it since it has gone so largely unrecognized, is by no means fatal to the identification of Pompey's pass with the Montgenèvre. Whether or not he constructed some kind of road there, the Montgenèvre was certainly in use by the Romans soon afterwards, for Julius Caesar records that on his first expedition into Gaul in 58 B.C. he took 'the nearest route across the Alps to further Gaul' from Ocelum,[15] and this must have been the Montgenèvre—ἡ σύντομος, as Strabo called it,[16] or *compendiaria*, as Ammianus called it;[17] and Caesar himself provided a parallel for Pompey's claim to have 'opened' the route when he recorded on another occasion that he dispatched Sergius Galba against the tribes round the Lake of Geneva because he wished to 'open'—*patefieri volebat*—the route over the Great St. Bernard,[18] although no proper road was built across the Great St. Bernard until much later in Imperial times.

Pompey was naturally proud to have blazed a trail across the Alps when no Roman general had ever led an army across them before, and Appian may have glossed his boast with his own embroidery when he added the word ἐχάρασσεν two hundred years later. Caesar would not have gone out of his way to give his despised son-in-law the credit for opening the Montgenèvre route, and Timagenes (if he was indeed Ammianus' authority, and if the story about him is true) may have been glad to pay off an old score against his captor by suppressing it; but Varro, who fought on Pompey's side in the civil war, gave his old leader his due. However, this is all no more than a pleasant field for surmise, and I have finessed Pompey's pass enough among the ancient historians: let us simply conclude, with the modern ones, that it was indeed the Mont-

---

[14] xv. 10. 2–6.   [15] *BG* i. 10. 4–5.   [16] iv. 1. 12.
[17] xv. 10. 8.   [18] *BG* iii. 1. 1.

genèvre. In fact, it must have been, for no other pass recognized by the Romans was on the direct road to Spain.

This brings us, then, to a discrepancy between the references in ancient authors to Hannibal's route across the Alps; for Ammianus Marcellinus says that the Montgenèvre was a middle route between Hannibal's pass and one 'near the Maritime Alps',[19] whereas Varro, if his list is to be read in geographical order from south to north, placed Hannibal's pass between it and the coast road.

Ammianus says that the road 'near the Maritime Alps' was constructed, according to legend, by the Theban Hercules on his way to destroy the tyrants Geryon and Tauriscus in Spain and Gaul; but he ludicrously piles Pelion on Ossa by adding that these Alps received the name 'Graian' Alps therefrom and that later they were called the 'Pennine' Alps after Hannibal's Punic transit—thus making a compost heap of three separate groups of Alps. There does seem to have been some confusion about the Graian Alps among ancient writers, perhaps because the legend of Hercules' journey was distributed between a coastal route and a more northerly one. The traces of the former still persist in the name Monaco, which, as Ammianus mentioned in this same passage and as Strabo also noted,[20] was originally the temple of Heracles 'Monoecus'; but Pliny[21] and Cornelius Nepos[22] both quoted Hercules' journey as the derivation of the name of the Graian Alps, which the former correctly located athwart the head of the Valle d' Aosta much further to the north. Ptolemy *suo more* (to borrow Holsten's expression) named Embrun, Susa, and Briançon as places in the Graian Alps though all three are in the heart of the Cottian Alps;[23] but we have seen before how unreliable Ptolemy's geographical indications could be. Pliny, it may be added, recorded, like Ammianus, the attribution of the name 'Pennine' Alps to the Punic march, although Livy had already refuted this derivation worthy of Hesychius, and shown that the name had a Celtic root,[24] which is, in fact, akin to the 'Pens' and 'Bens' of our own Celtic fringe.

However, though Ammianus went absurdly astray in his references to the Graian and Pennine Alps, he clearly meant, as

[19] xv. 10. 8–9.   [20] iv. 6. 3.   [21] *HN* iii. 17.
[22] *Hannibal*, iii. 4.   [23] *Geographica*, iii. 1. 35–6.   [24] xxi. 38. 9.

indeed he said, that Hercules' journey was 'near the Maritime Alps'; and we are therefore left with a contradiction between his description of Hannibal's route as lying to the north of the Montgenèvre and Varro's apparent location of it between the Montgenèvre and the coast road. And since Varro lived four hundred years nearer the event and was certainly the sounder scholar, one is inclined to place more reliance on his version.

It remains to consider Hasdrubal's pass. After Hannibal had been marching and countermarching up and down Italy for eleven years, beating the Romans in every battle and capturing every city except Rome itself, his brother Hasdrubal, whom he had left behind with the garrison in Spain, marched across the Alps with reinforcements to join him. He never did join him, for his army was utterly defeated, and he himself was killed, at the battle of the Metaurus while he was still on the way; but his route across the Alps is another piece of the data to be processed, or another variable to be determined, in solving the equation of Hannibal's route. He came from Spain round the western, not, like Hannibal, the eastern, end of the Pyrenees for he came through Auvergne, so Livy tells us;[25] but this does not necessarily mean that his route across the Alps was different, for the roads from Auvergne converge on the Isère near Grenoble, and he would have had virtually the same choice of routes from there on.

We have no account of his march from Polybius, because the part of his *History* in which he dealt with it has been lost; but Livy says that Hasdrubal had a much easier passage across the Alps than his brother, because the local tribes had grown accustomed to foreigners passing through their territory in the eleven years since Hannibal's transit, and now that they realized that they themselves were not the objective, but that the two chief Mediterranean powers were wrestling with each other for dominion in Italy, they were quite content to let reinforcements go through.[26] Appian too says that Hasdrubal profited from the fact that his brother had blazed a trail over the mountains—τὰ Ἄλπεια ὄρη ὡδοποιημένα πρότερον ὑπὸ Ἀννίβου; and he purports to point the contrast between them by saying that Hasdrubal took only two months on a journey which had taken Hannibal six (this is Appian's figure),[27]

[25] XXVII. 39. 7.   [26] XXVII. 39. 4-7.   [27] Ἀννιβαϊκή, 52.

forgetting that Hannibal spent most of his time in Spain, coming from the south and fighting his way through the tribes north of the Ebro before he reached the Pyrenees, and that his time from there to the plains of the Po was exactly the same as Hasdrubal's—two months. Walbank says of these two passages: 'Livy and Appian both agree that Hasdrubal crossed by the same pass as his brother',[28] and de Beer says much the same.[29] But this is reading too much into them: neither Livy nor Appian says anything so precise, and there is nothing in either passage which contradicts the plain statement of Varro that Hasdrubal's pass was different from Hannibal's; and Varro placed it, if we continue to read his list in geographical order and adopt the conclusion we have reached about Pompey's pass, somewhere between the Montgenèvre and the Little St. Bernard.

We have, then, three passes, according to Varro, to allocate between Hannibal, Pompey, and Hasdrubal from among those in the western Alps between the coast road and the Little St. Bernard; and we start with a moral certainty that Pompey's pass was the Montgenèvre, which in that case Varro and Ammianus agreed to be the middle one, and a predisposition in favour of Varro's apparent location of Hannibal's pass to the south of it against Ammianus' to the north. It is tempting to equate Varro's three passes with the only three passes on east–west routes across the same sector of the western Alps which carry motor roads today—the Col de Larche, Montgenèvre, and Mont Cenis.* But this would be too facile, for armies in those days, with large numbers of horses and mules but probably no wheeled vehicles, were not necessarily restricted to the graded routes of a modern road (though Hannibal's elephants might have imposed some similar limitation), and two of the passes advocated today as Hannibal's pass, the Col de la Traversette and the Col du Clapier, have no roads across them. Spenser Wilkinson, writing early in this century, said that at that time there were more than thirty passes crossed by regular

---

[28] *JRS* 1956, pp. 44–5.   [29] p. 49.

* The Col de Tende and the minor Col de Lombarde in the Maritime Alps also carry motor roads (the former now in a tunnel under the pass), but they are local north-south links between Piedmont and the Riviera, not east-west routes between Italy and the rest of France.

mule-tracks or footpaths between Mont Blanc and the sea,[30] and it is clear that we must use a rather finer mesh than that of a Michelin road map.

Much the same applies to any correlation of Hannibal's route with the *Roman* roads across the Alps. It is sometimes argued that he could not, for instance, have taken the Mont Cenis route because there is no evidence that it was known to the Romans;[31] and against this it has been argued that it *was* known to the Romans even though there is no evidence for it, and that it could therefore have been used either by Hannibal or by Hasdrubal.[32] But both arguments are equally beside the point. One receives a distinct impression from the way in which the ancient authors speak of Hannibal's pass that it was *not* one of the passes with which the Romans themselves were familiar, or ever came to be familiar. Varro, Pompey, Strabo, Cornelius Nepos, Appian, and Ammianus Marcellinus, apart from Polybius and Livy themselves, all mentioned Hannibal's pass in one context or another, but not one of them gave it a name or referred to it in any other way than as Hannibal's pass, and one feels that one or other of them must have given some indication that it afterwards came into use by the Romans if this had been the case. It is surely among the other passes, not the ones authenticated as Roman by literary or archaeological evidence, that one should look for Hannibal's pass.

One feels that there must have been something wrong with Hannibal's pass and that this is why the Romans never adopted it themselves; and if one accepts the evidence of Varro that Hasdrubal's pass too was a different one—which, as I have said, is not contradicted by anything in Livy's or Appian's account —it seems that he likewise found some better way across the Alps than his brother had, since otherwise he would have followed in his footsteps. Livy says that Hannibal several times lost the way on the final stages of the climb.[33] Magilus and the Boian chieftains who came to meet him at the Rhône and promised to guide him across the Alps[34] drop completely out of sight thereafter: neither Polybius nor Livy ever mentions

---

[30] p. 46.   [31] e.g. Holsten, p. 24 or de Luc, pp. 280–3.
[32] e.g. Jullian, p. 479; D. W. Freshfield, *Hannibal Once More*, 1914, pp. 110–17; Walbank, *JRS*, 1956, p. 45.
[33] XXI. 35. 4.   [34] Polybius III. 44. 7 and Livy XXI. 29. 6.

them again.* Both of them relate, on the contrary, how Hannibal accepted with much suspicion an offer of guidance on the road from a tribe who lived near the pass and who subsequently proved treacherous;[35] and Livy says that as a result, or else as a result of guessing for itself rather than trust the guides, the army several times entered valleys which proved to have no egress; so it may well be that the pass at which it eventually arrived was not the one at which it was originally aiming. However this may be, it is certain that the crossing of the pass and, still more, the descent on the other side were attended by great difficulty, and in the next chapter we shall return to our original authors and review the evidence which emerges from their accounts about the nature of the pass.

[35] Polybius III. 52. 7 and Livy XXI. 34. 3–4.

---

* Polybius may have been referring to them, as I suggested on p. 158 above, when he spoke of 'some of the Gaulish guides'—τινας τῶν καθηγουμένων αὐτοῖς Γαλατῶν (III. 50. 6)—who gained information for Hannibal about the enemy's movements on the army's first entry into the mountains at the end of the march 'along the river'. But even there Polybius does not say that they were actually guiding the army on its way. It seems probable that the Boians did not know the northern route across the Alps which Hannibal took after he had marched up the Rhône to avoid Scipio.

XV

THE NATURE OF THE PASS

WE noticed in our discussion of the time of year marked
by the setting of the Pleiades in Part I that both
Polybius and Livy reported falls of snow while the
army was on the pass, as is common enough in autumn on any
of the passes. The significant feature in their narrative, however,
is not the falls of new snow, but the description of a deep drift
of frozen snow from the previous winter overlain by the fresh
snow, in which the army was trapped on the descent from the
pass on the Italian side. The substratum of old snow was strong
enough to bear the men, who skidded down the steep slope
quite out of control on its slippery surface; but it was deep
enough to engulf the pack-animals when the surface gave way
under their greater weight, and the wretched beasts sank in
deeper, packs and all, and got more firmly wedged the more
they plunged about to extricate themselves.*

This has an obvious bearing on the question which pass it
was, for the passes across the western Alps vary greatly in
altitude, and for such conditions to develop one would think
that it must have been one of the higher ones. The heights
above sea level of the main passes in geographical order from
south to north are:

	metres
Col de Larche	1,995
Col de la Traversette	2,914
Montgenèvre	1,864
Col du Clapier	2,482
Mont Cenis	2,091
Little St. Bernard	2,188
Great St. Bernard	2,472

The question of aspect is perhaps even more important, and on

* The elephants did not attempt the passage until Hannibal had spent 3 days
making a new path, the old one having been carried away by a landslide—Polybius III. 55. 4–8 and Livy XXI. 36. 6 to 37. 4.

this score the Traversette, Montgenèvre, and Little St. Bernard, which face north-east on the Italian side, must be accounted rather more probable than the Col de Larche and Col du Clapier, which face south-east, and certainly more than the Mont Cenis or Great St. Bernard, the descents from which run almost due south.

Whether the old snow in which the animals floundered was really the previous winter's snow, as Polybius said, may be doubted. He himself said later that the Alpine passes were under snow all the year round,[1] and it used to be accepted that this was the case in Roman times;[2] but the modern view is that there is no warrant for such an assumption.[3] All the passes today are below the level of perpetual snow, which de Beer puts at roughly 10,000 feet, or say 3,000 metres; and he has quoted scientific evidence to the effect that the climate in 218 B.C. was certainly no colder than it is now, so that the snow-line can have been no lower.[4] Freshfield has instanced from his own experience how the snow from an early snowfall, which is to be expected from the end of August onwards, can easily be mistaken a month or two later, after it has lain and consolidated, for the previous winter's snow.[5]

However, whether it was old snow from the previous winter or an accumulation from earlier snowfalls in the same season, it may well have lasted longer on a sunless eastern face than the snow on the pass itself, and the higher the altitude the thicker it will have been. De Beer is therefore abundantly justified in claiming that conditions such as Polybius and Livy described are most likely on the Traversette, which is the highest of all the passes and faces north-east on the Italian side, though he may be going too far when he argues that all the others are absolutely excluded by their lack of height.[6]

The evidence about vegetation also tells in favour of a high pass like the Traversette. Both Polybius and Livy say that the elephants and pack-animals were famished on the descent from the pass because there had been no grazing there;[7] and though this might have been the case anywhere after a fresh fall of snow,

---

[1] III. 55. 9.   [2] e.g. Arnold, *The Second Punic War*, 1886, p. 25.
[3] M. Cary, *Geographic Background of Greek and Roman History*, 1949, pp. 247–8.
[4] pp. 65 and 104–7.   [5] *Hannibal Once More*, 1914, pp. 43–4.
[6] p. 66.   [7] Polybius III. 55. 8–9 and Livy XXI. 37. 4.

Polybius goes out of his way to explain that all the ground abutting on the pass was completely treeless and bare because the snow stayed on it continually winter and summer. This may not have been strictly true, as I have said, but at least it points to a very high pass, not to one of the lower ones where there was normally plenty of herbage. It is extraordinary, in the face of this, that one or other of the lower passes should have been thought by some commentators to be recommended by its excellent pasture as a candidate for Hannibal's pass—e.g. the Montgenèvre by Westcott,[8] the Mont Cenis by Jullian,[9] and both of them by De Sanctis.[10]

The situation is reversed, however, when one considers the amount of space on the pass. Polybius[11] and Livy[12] both record that Hannibal camped for two nights on the pass to rest his men and give the stragglers a chance to catch up, and Livy uses the unfamiliar word *stativa* to mark the fact that the halt was something more than a one-night stand. The army at this stage consisted of some 30,000 men, about 6,000 horses, and a host of pack-animals,[13] so that it must have required a considerable area of level ground for an encampment. Not surprisingly, the Traversette, perched high in the mountains, yields no such area:[14] even de Beer, its chief defender, agrees that it is only 'a narrow ridge',[15] and he refrains from mentioning the two-day camp in his own exposition. The Col du Clapier, the next highest pass, does offer a camping-ground, not on the actual summit but a little way short of it, and this has generally been accepted as answering to the requirements, e.g. by Hyde[16] and Marquion,[17] though Jullian questioned whether it was good enough.[18] The Mont Cenis and the Montgenèvre, two of the lowest passes, are, as one would expect, the ones which offer indubitably good camping-sites,[19] and, being lower and more sheltered by the surrounding massifs, either of them would make it a little less surprising that Hannibal should have chosen to spend two nights in such an inhospitable place as the top of a mountain pass in wintry weather.

The last desideratum to be satisfied is that Polybius and

---

[8] *Titi Livi libri I, XXI, XXII*, 1892, notes on *XXI*. 35. 5 and 37. 2.
[9] pp. 486–7.   [10] 75–6.   [11] III. 53. 9.   [12] XXI. 35. 5.
[13] Polybius III. 56. 4 and 60. 5.   [14] Hyde, p. 208; Devos, p. 125.
[15] p. 67.   [16] p. 208.   [17] pp. 56 and 137.
[18] p. 486.   [19] De Sanctis, pp. 75–6; Jullian, p. 486; Devos, p. 125.

Livy both describe how Hannibal displayed to his dispirited troops from the pass, like the Promised Land from Pisgah, the rich plains of the Po spread out below. The question naturally arises, which are the passes that command a view of the plain? The only difference between the accounts of the two authors is that Polybius makes the episode occur during the halt on the pass itself,[20] whereas Livy says that Hannibal gave the word to halt soon after the army had moved off, at a certain promontory from which there was a wide and distant view.[21] Josias Simler, as I mentioned earlier,[22] claimed that the Montgenèvre and the Mont Cenis qualified as Hannibal's pass on this ground, but no-one since has agreed with him that the Montgenèvre commands a view of the plain, and it certainly does not. There is rather more to be said for the Mont Cenis, where Jullian has argued that a view is to be had from a neighbouring eminence on the way down from the pass;[23] but a considerable détour is needed to reach the place, and no one else has thought that the Mont Cenis answers to Livy's description, still less to that of Polybius. All agree that no such view is to be had from the Col de Larche or from the Great or Little St. Bernard. The only two passes in our list which answer to the requirement—Devos somehow finds it possible to deny the fact,[24] but there is no room for doubt about it—are the Traversette, which gives a view down into the plain from the pass itself,[25] and the Col du Clapier, where a still more extensive view is to be had from a near-by spur.[26]

Another feature in Polybius' and Livy's description has been claimed as evidence in favour of one of the higher passes—the difficulty of the steep descent on the Italian side compared with the gentler slope of the ascent.[27] Obviously this is more pronounced on, say, the Traversette or the Col du Clapier, as de Beer[28] and Marquion[29] respectively have argued, than on any of the lower passes; but the western Alps as a whole have a more sharply defined escarpment on the Italian side, with a complicated system of valleys and subsidiary ranges leading up to it from the west, and no strong argument can be built on this

---

[20] III. 54. 2–3.   [21] XXI. 35. 8.
[22] p. 137 above.   [23] p. 488.   [24] pp. 124–5.
[25] de Beer, pp. 66–7; Hyde, p. 208.
[26] Hyde, p. 208; de Beer, p. 67; Marquion, pp. 57–8.
[27] Polybius III. 54. 4–5 and Livy XXI. 35. 11.
[28] p. 66.   [29] pp. 54 and 57.

in favour of any particular pass. Ammianus, it may be remembered, stressed the difficulty and dangers of the ascent on the Italian side of the Montgenèvre, the lowest pass of all, and Jullian gives a similar description of the descent from the Mont Cenis,[30] the next lowest but one.

One other item must be mentioned before we conclude this résumé of the evidence about the nature of the pass. Polybius said that the tribesmen who came out to meet the army and offered to guide it up to the pass, and who subsequently proved treacherous, approached bearing branches—θαλλούς—which Polybius explained were the token of friendship among nearly all the barbarians just as the herald's staff was among the Greeks;[31] and the normal meaning of θαλλοί, which has persisted down the ages with the same connotation, was *olive*-branches, as the Loeb translator has quite properly translated it here. But the olive-line is as sharply defined horizontally as the snow-line vertically, and if this is what the word meant here, the episode puts a definite northern limit on the location of Hannibal's pass.

Today the olive-line in Provence, after jutting northward in a salient up the Durance valley as far as Sisteron, runs roughly eastward from a point near Draguignan to the *corniche* of the Riviera between the mountains and the sea—well to the south of any approach route to the frontier range of the Alps. The olive, however, has been in retreat for a long time now, and, according to Saint-Simon, there were olives at Barcelonette on the way up to the Col de Larche in the mid-eighteenth century, though not, he said, anywhere in the Pennine, Graian, or Cottian Alps, and this was one of his grounds for claiming the Col de Larche as Hannibal's pass.[32] It is just possible, since de Beer has shown that the climate in 218 B.C. was no colder, but may perhaps have been a little warmer, than it is now,[33] that the olive in those days spread still further to the north. But the olive is not indigenous in southern France: it is thought to have been introduced from Asia Minor by the Phocaeans who founded Marseilles about 600 B.C., and it seems unlikely that it would have been propagated far outside the Greek zone of influence along the coast in the intervening centuries. It was

[30] p. 488.   [31] III. 52. 3.
[32] *Histoire de la guerre des Alpes, 1744,* 1770, pp. xxxi–xxxiv.   [33] pp. 104–7.

certainly not cultivated far from the coast at the end of the first
century B.C., for Strabo described how the Ligurians in the
mountains brought their produce of timber, flocks, hides, and
honey down to Genoa to trade for olive-oil and wine.[34]

In any case, the olive cannot possibly have established itself
in countries as far from the Mediterranean as those of 'nearly
all the barbarians' known to Polybius and his contemporaries
from Scythia to Aquitaine; and Polybius, though he used the
word which normally meant olive-branches in his native
Arcadia, must have known very well that it stood for some
other tree in those regions. It seems probable that the tree in
question here was some form of willow—the tree whose grey-
green, feathery foliage makes it the olive of the north to the
seeing eye if not to the housewife or the husbandman. The
willow was credited with the same healing qualities by the
Teutonic peoples as the olive had been in pagan antiquity;
each of them is the first tree in its own region to bud in the spring,
and in Christendom outside the empire of the palm the sprout-
ing branches of either serve the same office in the liturgy of
Palm Sunday.[35] Even in the Bible lands themselves, the home
of the olive, the willow had its sacerdotal function,[36] and it
does not seem too fanciful to suggest, since Polybius disclaimed
the usage of the olive as a symbol of friendship among the
Greeks, its propagators in Europe, that Noah's dove has somehow usurped for the olive a place in folklore which properly
belongs to the willow. Be that as it may, one must conclude,
with all the commentators except Saint-Simon who have
noticed the point at all, that the tree in question here cannot
have been the olive and that the deceiving branches with which
Hannibal was greeted on his way up to the pass must have been
something different,[37] in which case this particular episode has
no significance for the geography of the march.

I have now displayed to the reader those references to Hannibal's pass in other ancient authors which have a bearing on the
question which pass it was, and I have picked out the significant
evidence in Polybius and Livy themselves about the nature of
the pass. In the next chapter we shall assemble the data in our
own Venn diagram and try to stake out an area of intersection.

---

[34] IV. 6. 2.   [35] *Encyclopaedia Britannica*, 11th edn., Vol. 20, p. 651.
[36] Leviticus 23: 40.   [37] e.g. Jullian, p. 483.

XVI

CONCLUSIONS

THE reader will probably agree that the preponderance of
the evidence we have been considering about the nature
of Hannibal's pass—the deep drift of old snow, the lack of
herbage, the view of the plain of Piedmont, the fact that the
army several times lost its way during the climb, and perhaps
the difficulties of the descent, everything, in fact, except the
question of the camping-site and that of the branches which we
have decided to ignore—is in favour of one of the higher, less
accessible passes; and we shall begin our review of the possible
candidates with at least an initial presumption against either of
the two lowest ones—the Montgenèvre and the Col de Larche.
We shall find, in fact, that there are decisive reasons against
both of them, quite apart from the internal evidence about the
nature of the pass.

The Col de Larche (or Col de l'Argentière or Col de la
Madeleine as it is also called) near the northern boundary of the
Maritime Alps is the most southerly of all the passes which
have been proposed at one time or another as Hannibal's pass,
and it is this which effectively rules it out as a serious candidate,
for it is too far from the scene of operations as described by
Polybius and Livy to answer to the facts of the narrative. One
would think from a glance at a map that it offers one of the
shortest, most direct, and easiest routes from France into Italy,
but it has never attained the status of a major route, nor did
it in antiquity. It was the pass by which François I crossed the
Alps with artillery in 1515, and it was the scene of the abortive
campaign of the Prince de Conti against the King of Sardinia in
1744 during the war of the Austrian Succession. Both the
Gauls and the Romans must have used it at some time, for
Celtic remains and Latin inscriptions have been found near the
summit;[1] but Strabo does not mention it in his account of the

[1] Hyde, p. 49.

roads from Narbonese Gaul into Italy,[2] and there is not a single reference to it in the surviving ancient literature.

Saint-Simon, the chronicler of the Prince de Conti's 'War in the Alps', seems to have been the first person to suggest that the Col de Larche might also have been Hannibal's pass, adducing, as I have mentioned, the evidence of the olive-branches in its favour;[3] but few have followed him since except Freshfield[4] and (somewhat half-heartedly) Torr.[5] Saint-Simon[6] and Freshfield[7] both adopted Cluver's identification of the 'Island' with the confluence of the Rhône and the Isère near Valence, and their route from there ran diagonally across the Dauphiné by way of the valley of the Drôme and the Col de Cabre to a crossing of the Durance near Tallard and then up the valley of its tributary the Ubaye to Barcelonette and the Col de Larche. This was certainly an ancient route,[8] and the distances by it from such a starting-point can be reconciled well enough with Polybius' measurements of 250 kilometres from the crossing of the Rhône 'as far as the climb of the Alps into Italy' and 214 kilometres for the crossing of the Alps, though the latter measurement is too short to fit a route by the Col de Larche from my starting-point near Grenoble.

The objection to it is that, like all the similar routes of the French writers of the eighteenth century, it bears no resemblance to Polybius' description of the march in the flat country 'along the river' through the territory of the Allobroges; and, since it cuts across the middle of the territory of the Vocontii and does not debouch into that of the Tricorii, it offends against Livy's indications too, except only his misplaced reference to a crossing of the Durance. But the objection which is fatal to the Col de Larche as Hannibal's pass is that, entering Italy from north-west to south-east and leading to Cuneo, not Turin, it would have brought him down into the territory of the Vagienni, not the Taurini, indeed not into the 'plains of the Po' at all, and as far to the south of Turin as the Little St. Bernard is to the north—quite out of range of the operations against the chief town of the Taurini which followed the descent from the

---

[2] iv. 1. 3 and 1. 12.　　　[3] *Histoire de la guerre des Alpes, 1744,* 1770, pp. xxxi–xxxiv.

[4] *Hannibal Once More,* 1914, p. 53.

[5] *Hannibal Crosses the Alps,* 1924, pp. 25 and 37.

[6] op. cit., pp. xiv–xv.　　　[7] op. cit., p. 31.

[8] de Manteyer, *La Voie fluviale du Rhône et ses chemins primitifs,* 1945, pp. 28–31.

pass. The Col de Larche must be rejected as Hannibal's pass for this reason, as Devos has pointed out;[9] and it may be mentioned in passing that substantially the same objections apply to the minor Col de Mary a little way to the north of it, which was de Manteyer's candidate as Hannibal's pass,[10] and which de Beer has admitted as a possible alternative to his own preferred route, the Col de la Traversette, in the revised edition of his book.[11]

The Montgenèvre, though it has had many adherents—perhaps, down the centuries, more than any other pass—is the lowest pass of all and therefore the least amenable to the evidence we have reviewed about the nature of Hannibal's pass, and it became one of the principal passes used by the Romans; the distance by it is the furthest removed after the Col de Larche from Polybius' measurement for the crossing of the Alps according to my analysis of the approach march; it was explicitly excluded as Hannibal's pass by Ammianus Marcellinus and almost as explicitly by Varro, Appian, and Pompey the Great when they identified it unmistakably as Pompey's pass and said that Hannibal's was a different one. The sole point in its favour is that it offers indubitably good camping-ground, but other passes too can claim the same advantage. It does not seem to require any further argument to conclude, despite the weight of opinion in support of it, that the Montgenèvre cannot have been Hannibal's pass.

Between the Col de Larche and the Montgenèvre is the little-used pass of the Traversette on the slopes of Monte Viso (so called because the Marquis de Saluzzo made a tunnel under the summit in 1478),[12] the most southerly of the passes in the Cottian Alps which are at about the right radius from Turin to fit the narrative of Hannibal's operations after the descent from the Alps, and the highest and most difficult of all the passes which have been proposed for his crossing. The route across it is still only a rough track: there is a minor approach road up the valley of the Guil, but it peters out some 6 kilometres short of the pass. This is the pass which Denina first suggested as Hannibal's pass in 1805, regarding it as a more likely candidate than the Montgenèvre,[13] and which Torr bracketed as an equal

[9] p. 100.   [10] *La Traversée des Alpes par Hannibal*, 1944, p. 24.
[11] p. 210 n. below.   [12] Hyde, p. 49.
[13] *Tableau historique, statistique et moral de la Haute Italie*, 1805, pp. 178–80.

possibility with the Col de Larche;[14] but its one unequivocal advocate is de Beer,[15] who has made out a most persuasive case in its favour.*

The Col de la Traversette, as the highest pass of all, has the best claim in sheer altitude to the arguments in favour of a high pass which we have discussed—the deep drift of old snow, the lack of herbage, and the view down into the plain; but it offers no camping-ground, and the distance by it from our starting-point near Grenoble is the furthest but one from Polybius' measurement for the crossing of the Alps.[16] All the same, the sheer difficulty and danger of the transit (before the tunnel was made) and the fact that the Traversette was never taken into use by the Romans suggest that it could have been the pass at which the army eventually arrived after being led astray by deceitful guides; it is in the right place between the coast road and the Montgenèvre to fill the position of Hannibal's pass in Varro's list, though not in that of Ammianus, and Varro, as I have said, must be regarded as the better authority. The case for it must be reckoned, on balance, the strongest of the passes we have so far considered.

There remain the two most northerly passes in the Cottian Alps at about the same radius from Turin as the Traversette—the Mont Cenis and the Col du Clapier. Either of them, according to Ammianus, might have been Hannibal's pass; either of them, according to Varro, Hasdrubal's; they are the two passes which come closest to Polybius' measurement for the last section of the march from our starting-point near Grenoble.[16] There is no evidence, literary or archaeological, that either of them was used by the Romans, and the Col du Clapier, a difficult, high pass akin in that respect to the Traversette, certainly would not have been. The earliest recorded transit of the Mont Cenis is Charlemagne's march across the Alps in

[14] op. cit., pp. 25 and 37.   [15] pp. 65–9.   [16] p. 187 above.

---

* In the revised edition of his book (*Hannibal's March*, 1967, pp. 94 and 107–9) de Beer admits de Manteyer's candidate, the Col de Mary, and its neighbour, the Col de Roure, as possible alternatives, though he himself still prefers the Col de la Traversette. Both these passes appear to me to be open to the same objection as the Col de Larche: that they are too far south to have been within range of 'the chief town of the Taurini' after the descent from the pass.

A.D. 773.[17]* It has been argued, as I have mentioned, that it must have been used by the Romans despite the lack of evidence; but it is not mentioned in Strabo's account of the roads from Gaul into Italy, and it had no place in the road-building programme of Augustus which gave new highways to the coast route and to those across the Montgenèvre, the Great St. Bernard, and the Little St. Bernard.[18]

The two passes are both variants of the same route up the valley of the Arc from its confluence with the Isère as far as the village of Bramans between Modane and Lanslebourg. From Bramans the present main road continues for another 23 kilometres to the relatively easy Col du Mont Cenis a little over 2,000 metres above sea level, but a minor road branches off to the right towards the considerably higher Col du Clapier for about 8 kilometres before petering out some 8 to 10 kilometres short of the pass. Both passes offer good camping-ground on or near the summit, as I have mentioned. The Col du Clapier, in addition to its general claims as the higher of the two passes, offers a view of the plain from a projecting spur early in the descent just as Livy described, whereas a considerable détour has to be made to gain a corresponding view on the descent from the Mont Cenis, as Jullian, one of its sponsors, admitted.[19]

[17] Cluver, p. 383.   [18] Hyde, pp. 40–60.   [19] p. 488.

---

*Gibbon (*Decline and Fall*, Vol. 2, edition of 1825, pp. 81–2) assigned to the Mont Cenis Constantine's route on his march across the Alps from Gaul into Italy in A.D. 312, but his reasons for doing so were strangely perverse. He said that 'Constantine preferred the road of the Cottian Alps, or, as it is now called, the mount Cenis', mentioning in support of this identification of the pass that Susa, to which Constantine descended, 'is situated at the foot of mount Cenis'; but the pass in the Cottian Alps which was much better known to the Romans in Imperial times was the Montgenèvre, and this also leads direct to Susa. Gibbon seems to imply, too, that Constantine availed himself of one of 'the stupendous highways which the Romans had carried over the Alps', and there is no record of any Roman highway having been constructed over the Mont Cenis. Constantine's pass must have been the Montgenèvre.

Gibbon, though he completely ignored the Mont Cenis in his own discussion of Hannibal's pass, seems to have had a curious obsession with it in other contexts. He mistakenly called it *Mons Matrona*, although Ammianus' description of the pass that was known by that name as one that lay between Susa and Briançon (xv. 10. 3–6) fixes it quite certainly as the Montgenèvre; and he attributed to the Mont Cenis not only the march of Constantine but also that of Pompey, contrary to the overwhelming evidence of the ancient authors that Pompey's pass too was the Montgenèvre (*Nomina Gentesque Antiquae Italiae*, Miscellaneous Works, Vol. 4, 1814, p. 172).

The Mont Cenis has been adopted as Hannibal's pass, since Napoleon brought it into currency, by Larauza,[20] Macé,[21] Maissiat,[22] Osiander,[23] and Jullian.[24] Walbank brackets it with the Col du Clapier without declaring a preference between them.[25] Of the two it would seem that on the evidence we have reviewed the Col du Clapier has decidedly the stronger claim, and this has been the view of Perrin,[26] Colin,[27] Spenser Wilkinson,[28] Dunbabin,[29] and Marquion.[30] If one or other of the two was Hannibal's route, one would think that he may well have been aiming for the easier Mont Cenis before he lost his way and then found himself on the Col du Clapier. In that case it would be reasonable to suppose that Hasdrubal, following eleven years afterwards, managed to keep to the right road and crossed by the Mont Cenis. The latter was Cluver's solution to the problem of Hasdrubal's pass,[31] and it would conform with Varro's evidence that Hasdrubal crossed by a different pass from Hannibal, while giving full value to the general indications of Livy and Appian that he profited from the fact that his brother had blazed a trail across the mountains.

One is inclined, therefore, to give first preference on the evidence we have reviewed to the Col du Clapier, with the Traversette as second choice. The only objection to the former is that it is not in the right position to fit Varro's location of Hannibal's pass if his list is to be read in geographical order from south to north, while the objection to the latter is the more serious one that the army could not possibly have camped there for two nights. Also, the distance by the Traversette is the furthest but one from Polybius' measurement for the crossing of the Alps according to my analysis of the approach-route. But there is another possible objection which must give us pause before we register a conclusion in favour of either of them—the difficulty of reconciling one of these little-known, dangerously high passes with Polybius' list of Alpine passes to which I have previously referred,[32] read in conjunction with his statement that he had crossed the Alps himself to visit the scenes of Hanni-

[20] *Histoire critique du passage des Alpes par Annibal*, 1826.
[21] *Description du Dauphiné*, 1852, p. 340.
[22] *Annibal en Gaule*, 1874, pp. 210–11.   [23] *Der Hannibalweg*, 1900, ch. III.
[24] p. 485.   [25] *JRS* 1956, p. 45.   [26] p. 145.   [27] pp. 317–18.
[28] pp. 9–11 and 32–6.   [29] p. 53.   [30] pp. 56–8.   [31] p. 383.
[32] pp. 85 and 141 above.

bal's march.[33] The point does not seem to have been noticed by any of the sponsors of the Col du Clapier or the Traversette—or, for that matter, by those who might have been expected to quote it as an argument in favour of the Montgenèvre—but it needs to be considered all the same.

According to a passage in Strabo which has also been preserved in a digest of one of the lost later books of Polybius himself, Polybius recognized only four routes across the Alps—the coast road through Liguria, one leading into the territory of the Taurini by which Hannibal crossed, one leading into that of the Salassi, and one in the Rhaetian Alps—[34] of which only the two middle ones are routes across the western Alps with which we are concerned. The words 'by which Hannibal crossed' are not in all the MSS., as I mentioned earlier, and there may be room for doubt whether they were written by Polybius or added by a later hand. But we have seen that there is *no* room for doubt that the pass by which Hannibal crossed did in fact lead into the territory of the Taurini, and this is the point of difficulty in the present context; for, if Polybius believed that Hannibal's pass was one of the difficult, little-known ones, as there is reason to think it was, this implies that he omitted the Montgenèvre and the Mont Cenis from his list, both of which also led into the territory of the Taurini, and it seems surprising that he should have failed to mention one or other of them. The omission of the Mont Cenis is not surprising, for no Roman writer ever did mention it, but that of the Montgenèvre, which later became a well-known pass, does seem to call for some explanation.

It lies in the state of knowledge about the western Alps at the time when Polybius was writing. The Romans of his time knew that Hannibal and Hasdrubal had crossed the Alps somewhere with their armies, and Polybius himself stresssed the fact that the Gauls had done so many times in large numbers.[35] He clearly knew of the Little St. Bernard (for this, not the Great St. Bernard, must have been the pass which he meant by the one that led 'into the territory of the Salassi'); but there is no sign that the Romans knew of the Montgenèvre before Pompey 'opened' it in 77 B.C. over forty years after Polybius died. Even

[33] III. 48. 12.   [34] Strabo, IV. 6. 12 and Polybius XXXIV. 10. 18.
[35] III. 48. 6.

15—H.M.I.H.

then, Varro could still only refer to it as the pass 'by which Pompey set out for the war in Spain', and the Little St. Bernard was the only pass for which he had a name, the 'Graian Alps', between the Great St. Bernard and the coast road. When Polybius was writing a hundred years earlier, when Latin Italy stopped at the Rubicon, the whole sector of the western Alps known to us as the Cottian and Maritime Alps was *terra incognita* to the Romans; and if Polybius did think that Hannibal crossed by one of the difficult, high passes that led into the territory of the Taurini, he can have had no idea that he was omitting an important pass from his list by not mentioning the Montgenèvre as well, for he was not aware of its existence as a separate route across the Alps. There is therefore no reason to draw any inference about Hannibal's pass one way or the other from Polybius' silence about the Montgenèvre.

We are still left, however, with the difficulty about his own journey. Clearly Polybius must have crossed the Alps either by the same pass as the one which brought Hannibal down into the territory of the Taurini or by the Little St. Bernard, these being the only two passes in the western Alps which he included in his list. It is commonly assumed that he did cross the Alps by the same pass as Hannibal in the reverse direction, and, if so, this is certainly a prima facie objection to a difficult high pass like the Traversette or the Col du Clapier as Hannibal's pass; for, though Polybius was an intrepid man and is likely to have been in the prime of life when he made the journey,* and though he is known to have been a keen sportsman who died from a fall from his horse at the ripe age of 82, it is inherently improbable that he would have tackled the forbidding ascent of either of those passes from the Italian side on his own journey. He is much more likely to have taken an easier pass, which, on the assumption that he crossed by the same pass as Hannibal, would mean that Hannibal's pass too, contrary to all the evidence we have considered, must have been one of the

---

* Polybius was about 37 when he was first brought to Rome from Arcadia in 167 B.C. Even if he did not make the journey specially to see the scenes of the march for himself, as his words at III. 48. 12 suggest, the last occasion when he could have crossed the Alps before writing his *History* was the journey which he almost certainly made with Scipio Aemilianus to Spain and Numidia in 151 B.C.

lower ones leading into the territory of the Taurini, in other words, either the Mont Cenis or the Montgenèvre.

We need not concern ourselves with the Mont Cenis, for, if Polybius himself had crossed by that pass, it would certainly not have dropped out of subsequent history in the way it did. But the Montgenèvre is another matter. If Polybius crossed by the Montgenèvre, and if the assumption that he crossed by the same pass as Hannibal has to be accepted, this would be the first good reason we have found for adopting it as Hannibal's pass. For, not only have we seen that practically everything about the Montgenèvre is in conflict with the evidence of the narrative in Polybius and Livy; we have found it a virtual certainty that Varro, Pompey, Appian, and Ammianus Marcellinus unanimously rejected it as Hannibal's pass—in fact, that this was the one thing on which they all agreed; and we have seen, too, that there is good reason to think that the existence of the Montgenèvre was not even known to the Romans in Polybius' time.

The only reason for sweeping aside all this evidence in deference to a syllogism based on Polybius' statements about the Alpine passes is the assumption that he did cross the Alps by the same pass as Hannibal, and, in point of fact, there is no sufficient justification for that assumption. He himself merely said that he crossed the Alps to see the country for himself:[36] he never said that he crossed by the same pass as Hannibal, and it has been much too readily assumed by some modern writers that he did.[37] Once this *idée fixe* is abandoned, there is no longer any need to ignore the evidence about Hannibal's pass in an attempt to identify it with one which Polybius could have taken. We can conclude that Hannibal's pass was one of the dangerously high ones, as all the other evidence about it has led us to think, and that Polybius took an easier one on his own journey.

In that case, since Hannibal's pass led into the territory of the Taurini, Polybius must have travelled by the only other pass across the western Alps included in his own list—the one that led into the territory of the Salassi. This can only have been the Little St. Bernard, for, though the Great St. Bernard also led into the territory of the Salassi on the Italian side, it led on the other side into country far removed from the scenes of Hannibal's march which Polybius wanted to explore. In point of fact,

---

[36] III. 48. 12.   [37] e.g. de Beer, p. 10 or Marquion, p. 66.

the Little St. Bernard must have been the only pass leading into Transalpine Gaul which was known to the Romans at the time when he made his journey. No Roman expedition had yet penetrated into the future province even along the coast road, and it was seventy to eighty years before Pompey 'opened' the Montgenèvre. The Little St. Bernard was the only route available at that time to a traveller who wanted to cross the mountains instead of taking the coast road, and Polybius' pass can have been no other.

We are free then, after all, to select Hannibal's pass from among those which we previously considered, without being deflected by considerations about the pass which Polybius himself took. I come back, therefore, to the Col du Clapier as the best attested of all the passes we have considered by sheer weight of evidence as Hannibal's pass, and I suggest that this must be our final conclusion. The one flaw in it is that the Col du Clapier is in the wrong position to fit what seemed to be Varro's location of Hannibal's pass. If the reader agrees with me that this is not sufficient to outweigh all the rest of the evidence, I must leave it to him to decide whether I have read too much into Varro's list in taking it to be in geographical order, or whether Ammianus Marcellinus four hundred years later somehow knew better than Varro, and Varro, for all his learning, was mistaken.

BIBLIOGRAPHY

The entries are arranged in chronological order within the following sections:

I: EDITIONS OF POLYBIUS AND LIVY

Polybius

Nicholas Perotto's Latin translation, 1473—bound up with the editions of Obsopoeus and Hervagius mentioned below.

Obsopoeus—*editio princeps*—1530.

Hervagius, 1549.

Casaubon, 1609—the first to introduce the reading Ἄραρος in the text.

Jacob Gronovius, 1670.

James Hampton's translation of the *General History of Polybius*, 1756.

J. A. Ernestius, 1764.

Schweighaeuser, 1789–95—the first to introduce the reading Ἰσάρας in the text.

Bekker, 1844.

Buettner-Wobst, 1882–1904 and 1905 (reprinted as the Teubner text).

Hultsch, 1888.

Paton, 1922 (Loeb).

Livy

Sweynheym & Pannartz—*editio princeps—c.* 1469.

Sigonio, 1555.

J. F. Gronovius, 1645.

Re-issue of J. F. Gronovius' edition by his son Jacob, with added notes of his own, 1678–9.

Drakenborch, 1738–46.

A. W. Ernesti, 1769.

Stroth, 1784.

A. W. Ernesti's recension of Drakenborch's edition, 1785.

Schaefer's re-issue of the Drakenborch/Ernesti edition, 1801–1804.

Kreyssig, 1823–7. Though this was based essentially on the edition of A. W. Ernesti of 1769, it was the first to introduce the reading *Isara* in the text.

Weissenborn, 1850–1.

Madvig and Ussing, 1861–2.

H. J. Mueller's recension of Weissenborn's edition, 1885, etc.

M. Mueller, 1900–08 (Teubner).

Conway and Walters, 1914 (Oxford).

Foster, 1929 (Loeb).

II. WORKS DEVOTED SPECIALLY TO THE MARCH OF HANNIBAL

PHILIP CLUVER, excursus in *Italia Antiqua*, 1624, Book I, pp. 365–84. He is generally referred to in Latin as 'Cluverius', though on the title-page of the book the name is spelt 'Cluverus'.

LUCAS HOLSTEN (in Latin 'Holstenius'), *Annotationes in Italiam Antiquam Cluverii*, 1666.

J-P. MANDAJORS, monographs in *Acta Academiae Parisinae*, 1725, Vol. 3, pp. 93 ff. and vol. 5, pp. 198 ff.—referred to as 'Examen de la route d'Hannibal entre le Rhône et les Alpes' and 'Mémoires sur la marche d'Annibal dans les Gaules'.

J. C. DE FOLARD, *Observations* in Vol. 4 of *Histoire de Polybe nouvellement traduite du grec* by Dom. V. Thuillier, 1728—described by Gibbon as 'the mixed offspring of a monk ignorant of tactics and a soldier ignorant of Greek'.

EDWARD GIBBON, excursus in his *Journal* for October 1763—*Miscellaneous Works*, Vol. 5, 1814, pp. 370–81—and *Nomina Gentesque Antiquae Italiae*—Miscellaneous Works, Vol. 4, pp. 172–173.

M. H. MARQUIS DE SAINT-SIMON, Introduction to his *Histoire de la guerre des Alpes, 1744, 1770*.

J. WHITAKER, *The Course of Hannibal over the Alps Ascertained*, 1794.

FORTIA D'URBAN, excursus in *Antiquités et monuments du département de Vaucluse*, 1808.

J. A. DE LUC, *Histoire du Passage des Alpes par Annibal*, 1818.

J. A. LARAUZA, *Histoire critique du passage des Alpes par Annibal*, 1826.

V. ROUSILLON, *Annibal et le Rhône*, 1865.

J. MAISSIAT, *Annibal en Gaule*, 1874.

J. B. PERRIN, *Marche d'Annibal des Pyrénées au Pô*, 1883.

W. OSIANDER, *Der Hannibalweg*, 1900.

J. L. A. COLIN, *Annibal en Gaule*, 1904.

H. SPENSER WILKINSON, *Hannibal's March through the Alps*, 1911.

D. W. FRESHFIELD, *Hannibal Once More*, 1914.

C. TORR, *Hannibal Crosses the Alps*, 1924.

R. L. DUNBABIN, *Classical Review*, 1931, pp. 52–7 and 121–5.

W. W. HYDE, excursus in *Roman Alpine Routes*, 1935, pp. 197–208 (Memoirs of the American Philosophical Society, Vol. 2.)

G. DE MANTEYER, *La Traversée des Alpes par Hannibal*, 1944.

Sir GAVIN DE BEER, *Alps and Elephants*, 1955.

F. W. WALBANK, *Journal of Roman Studies*, 1956, pp. 37–45.

J. HOYTE, *Trunk Road for Hannibal*, 1960.

P. MARQUION, *Sur les pas d'Annibal*, 1965.

G. DEVOS, *D'Espagne en Italie avec Hannibal*, 1966.

Sir GAVIN DE BEER, *Hannibal's March*, 1967.

Sir GAVIN DE BEER, *Hannibal*, 1969, pp. 120–82.

III OTHER WORKS CONTAINING DISCUSSIONS OF THE MARCH OF HANNIBAL

(1) *Miscellaneous*

DOMINICO MACCANEO, commentary on the *Lives* of Aurelius Victor falsely attributed to Cornelius Nepos, c. 1525.

PAOLO GIOVIO, *P. Jovii historiarum sui temporis libri*, 1553.

JOSIAS SIMLER, *De Alpibus Commentarius*, 1574—reproduced in *Josias Simler et les origines de l'Alpinisme jusqu'en 1600* by W. A. B. Coolidge, 1904.

J. B. BOURGUIGNON D'ANVILLE, *Notice de l'ancienne Gaule tirée des monuments Romains*, 1760.

P. J. GROSLEY, *Nouveaux mémoires ou observations sur l'Italie par deux gentilshommes suédois*, 1764.

C. G. M. DENINA, *Tableau historique, statistique et moral de la Haute Italie*, 1805.

C. J. F. T. DE MONTHOLON, *Mémoires . . . à Sainte-Hélène*, 1823—Vol. 4, edition of 1905, pp. 277–81.

A. MACÉ, *Description du Dauphiné*, 1852.

(2) *General Histories*

Th. Mommsen, *History of Rome* 1854–6. W. P. Dickson's translation, 1913.

T. Arnold, *The Second Punic War*, 1886.

C. Jullian, *Histoire de la Gaule*, Vol. 1, 1908.

U. Kahrstedt, *Geschichte der Karthager*, Vol. 3, 1913.

G. De Sanctis, *Storia dei Romani*, Vol. 3, ii, 1917.

W. E. Heitland, *The Roman Republic*, 1923.

B. L. Hallward, *Cambridge Ancient History*, Vol. 8, 1930.

F. W. Walbank, *Historical Commentary on Polybius*, Vol. 1, 1957.

IV: GEOGRAPHICAL DESCRIPTIONS OF SOUTHERN GAUL
AND/OR THE WESTERN ALPS

Polybius iii. 37. 7 to 39. 12, 47. 1–5 and 48. 5–12.

Strabo Book iv.

Pomponius Mela, *Chorographia*, ii. 5.

Pliny, *Historia Naturalis*, iii. 4.

Ptolemy, *Geographia*, ii. 10 and iii. 1.

Appian, *Bella Civilia*, i. 109.

Ammianus Marcellinus xv. 9–12.

Servius *ad Aeneidem* x. 13.

Josias Simler, *De Alpibus Commentarius*, 1574—reproduced in *Josias Simler et les origines de l'Alpinisme jusqu'en 1600* by W. A. B. Coolidge, 1904.

Cluverius, *Italia Antiqua*, Vol. 1, 1624, pp. 365–84.

Holstenius, *Annotationes in Italiam Antiquam Cluverii*, 1666, pp. 12–24.

J. B. Bourguignon D'Anville, *Notice de l'ancienne Gaule tirée des monuments Romains*, 1760.

C. G. M. Denina, *Tableau historique, statistique et moral de la haute Italie*, 1805.

A. Macé, *Description du Dauphiné*, 1852.

Camille Jullian, *Histoire de la Gaule*, Vol. 1, 1908.

G. de Manteyer, *Voies fluviales primitives et leurs cols dans les Alpes*, 1928.

J. H. Rose, *The Mediterranean in the Ancient World*, 1933.

H. F. Tozer, *Ancient Geography*, 1935.

W. W. Hyde, *Roman Alpine Routes*, 1935—Memoirs of the American Philosophical Society, Vol. 2—far the best work on the subject.

G. de Manteyer, *La Voie fluviale du Rhône*, 1945.

M. Cary, *Geographic Background of Greek and Roman History*, 1949.

V: THE SETTING OF THE PLEIADES

HESIOD, *Works and Days*, lines 383–7 and 615–17.
AUTOLYCUS, Περὶ ἀνατολῶν καὶ δύσεων, I. I.
ARATUS, *Phaenomena*, lines 264 ff.—*Aratus cum scholiis*, Bekker, 1828.
GEMINUS, 'Εἰσαγωγὴ εἰς τὰ φαινόμενα, under the month Σκόρπιον.
VARRO, *De Re Rustica*, I. 28.
PLINY, *Historia Naturalis*, II. 47 and XVIII. 25.
J. L. STRACHAN-DAVIDSON, *Selections from Polybius*, 1888, pp. 15–21.
A. W. MAIR, *Hesiod Translated*, 1908, pp. 106–47.
Sir GAVIN DE BEER, *Alps and Elephants*, 1955, pp. 100–3.
BOLL, *Fixsterne*, Pauly-Wissowa, Vol. 6. cols. 2423 ff.

VI: MARCHES OF ANCIENT ARMIES

HERODOTUS, V. 53 and VIII. 51.
XENOPHON, *Anabasis*, Book I.
VEGETIUS, *Epitoma Rei Militaris*, I. 9.
T. R. HOLMES, *Caesar's Conquest of Gaul*, 1911, p. 635.
G. VEITH, *Heerwesen und Kriegsfuehrung*, 1928, in Mueller's *Handbuch*,
   Abt. 4, Tl. 3, Bd. 2, pp. 354 and 422.
Sir FRANK ADCOCK, *The Roman Art of War under the Republic*, 1940,
   Martin Classical Lectures, Vol. 8, pp. 13–14.

VII: SHIPS AND SEA TRANSPORT

POLYBIUS I. 26. 7.
JULIUS CAESAR, *De Bello Gallico*, IV. 22. 3–4 and V. 8. 2–6.
LIVY, XXIV. 40. 5 and XLIII. 9. 5–6.
VEGETIUS, *Epitoma Rei Militaris*, IV. 39.
C. TORR, *Ancient Ships*, 1894 (mainly concerned with naval vessels,
   not transports).
A. KOESTER, *Das Antike Seewesen*, 1923, pp. 179–81.
W. KROLL, *Schiffahrt* in Pauly-Wissowa, Col. 410.
A. KOESTER and E. VON NISCHER, *Das Seekriegswesen bei der Roemern*,
   in Mueller's *Handbuch*, Abt. 4. Tl. 3, Bd. 2, p. 620.
Oxford Classical Dictionary, 2nd edn., 1970, pp. 725 and 984.

15*

INDEX